KRUG...
NATIONAL PARK

QUESTIONS
AND
ANSWERS

Margie Snively 1992

Struik Publishers
(a member of The Struik Group (Pty) Ltd)
Cornelis Struik House
80 McKenzie Street
Cape Town 8001

Reg. No.: 63/00203/07

First published by SA Country Life 1978
Fifth edition 1989
First published by Struik Publishers 1992

Copyright © Text: P F Fourie and G de Graaff 1992
Copyright © Illustrations: David Thorpe 1992
Copyright © Maps: Euan Waugh 1992
Copyright © Cover photographs: Gerald Cubitt, with the exception of top right © Chris and Tilde Stuart

Editor: Leni Martin
Editorial assistant: Geoff Payne
Designer: Neville Poulter
Illustrator: David Thorpe
Maps: Euan Waugh

Typesetting by Suzanne Fortescue, Struik DTP
Reproduction by Bellset, Cape Town
Printing and binding by National Book Printers, Goodwood

ISBN 1 86825 191 8

ACKNOWLEDGEMENTS

No author can pretend that a general information book such as this is written in a vacuum. Since the first edition of *PF Fourie's Questions and Answers* appeared in 1978, many people have given us the benefit of their insight, especially the Nature Conservation Section of the National Parks Board in Skukuza. I thank them for their contributions. I would also like to thank the Reservations Office, National Parks Board, Pretoria (especially Mrs S Greyling) for reviewing the data given on tourism. My thanks are also extended to Struik Publishers and personnel who have been instrumental in the publication of this edition – Peter Borchert, Eve Gracie and Marje Hemp, and the other members of the publishing team who always play a major rôle in the eventual result. Finally, I extend my gratitude to the senior author's widow, Mrs Chrissie Fourie, and her son Dr D Fourie, for trusting me with the task of updating their late husband and father's book.

G DE GRAAF

KRUGER NATIONAL PARK

QUESTIONS AND ANSWERS

P F FOURIE
M.Sc. (P.U. for C.H.E.), HED (Unisa)
Late Chief Information Officer, National Parks Board of South Africa

This edition revised and edited by
G DE GRAAFF
M.Sc. (WITS), D.Sc. (PRET), Sci Nat
Research Associate, Centre for Wildlife Research,
University of Pretoria

STRUIK

ABOUT THE AUTHOR

Pieter Hendrik Fourie was born in the Eastern Transvaal, attended primary school in Louis Trichardt and matriculated in Christiana in the Western Transvaal.

During his employment as an official in the gold mining industry he obtained a B.Sc. degree through the University of South Africa, followed by both an honours and a master's degree in science from Potchefstroom University, all part time.

Between 1969 and 1977 he was employed as Chief Information Officer (Educational and Interpretive Services) in the Kruger National Park.

It was during those years that Fritz, as he was known to his friends, met literally thousands of people from all walks of life and from all over the world. Sharing his knowledge with visitors was to him a most pleasant part of his work.

He was the author of more than 60 articles which appeared in *Custos*, the official monthly magazine of the National Parks Board, *Huisgenoot* and other periodicals.

Fritz was later employed as a senior agricultural researcher at the Institute for Tropical and Sub-tropical Crops, doing research on the Lowveld citrus mite for his doctorate. He passed away in April 1989 at the age of 53.

CONTENTS

Foreword to the sixth edition . . . 6

Preface to the sixth edition 7

History 8

Ecological aspects of the
Kruger National Park 11

General code of conduct 14

Tourism 23

Nature conservation 36

Culling 45

The role of fire in ecology
and nature management . . . 50

Poaching 53

Chacma baboon 56

Vervet monkey 61

Bushbabies 63

Bushpig 65

Warthog 67

Antelopes 70

African buffalo 104

Giraffe 107

Hippopotamus 117

Burchell's zebra 122

Rhinoceros 126

Elephant 135

Lion 145

Leopard 157

Cheetah 161

Serval 167

Caracal 169

African wild cat 171

Hyena 172

Wild dog 179

Aardwolf 184

Jackal 185

Bat-eared fox 188

African civet 190

Genets 192

Mongoose 194

Striped Polecat 197

Cape clawless otter 198

Ratel or honey badger 199

Pangolin or scaly anteater . . . 201

Aardvark 203

South African hedgehog . . . 205

Dassies 206

Cape porcupine 209

Tree squirrel 211

Springhare 213

Snakes 214

Lizards 226

Leguaans 227

Crocodile 229

Literature 236

Index 238

FOREWORD TO THE SIXTH EDITION

Essentially, the mission of the National Parks Board of South Africa is two-fold: the preservation of ecosystems representing the total eco-diversity of South Africa in their most pristine state and, secondly, the promotion of a conservation and environmental ethic. To preserve the integrity of the ecosystems, together with their total species diversity and dynamic ecological processes, requires an intimate knowledge of the intricacies of nature. To promote a conservational and environmental ethic requires that knowledge is disseminated to serve as cornerstones of that ethic – respect and appreciation.

The late PF (Fritz) Fourie served for many years as Environmental Education Officer in the Kruger National Park. In this time he built up an intimate knowledge of the Park, including its history, natural attributes and its fascinating ecology – and nothing gave him greater satisfaction than to share this knowledge with others. To Fritz, achievement meant the twinkle in a visitor's eye when he suddenly grasped the wonder of the harmonious, interactive workings of the compenents of an ecosystem. Through his experience and dedication, Fritz also formulated his own style of communication with the public; a style which was to the point, simple and effective. That style is clearly reflected in the wide range of the questions and answers presented in this book. In its sixth edition, this book contains the questions most commonly asked by both the uninitiated and by more informed visitor to the Kruger National Park, and provides accurate answers in an easy-to-read, unpretentious style.

While *The Kruger National Park – Questions and Answers* will continue to serve as a tribute to the late PF Fourie, the contents of this latest edition have been extended and elaborated on by the equally well-known conservationist Dr Gerrie de Graaff. This latest edition is in all respects an improvement on previous editions – this book should be on the shelf of all nature enthusiasts.

The original objective of this book was to to provide a concise source of vital information to visitors to the Kruger National Park. To maintain its value, and to serve its original purpose, colour photographs have been replaced by more than 50 excellent black-and-white line drawings by the well-known wildlife illustrator, David Thorpe. While the illustrations remain of an excellent quality, the deletion of colour photographs has – in line with the original intent of the book – enabled the publisher to keep the price within easy reach of the bulk of the visitors to the Park. This is in itself a commendable approach and all the more reason why this excellent and highly informative book should be the constant companion of all visitors to the Kruger National Park.

I would like to wish this new edition all the success it deserves. I personally take pride in being associated with such a worthy contribution towards a better understanding of our natural heritage.

Dr S C J Joubert
Executive Director:
Kruger National Park
July 1992

PREFACE TO THE SIXTH EDITION

This edition of *Kruger National Park – Questions and Answers* by the late P.F. Fourie introduces a new editor. It does not introduce any change in policy or intent. When Fritz Fourie asked me to take over this revision some months before his death I felt honoured because I have known and liked the book since the first edition appeared in 1978.

In the present edition I have made many small changes, correcting points where new information made this necessary. This has probably increased the length of the book to some extent. As is well known, it is usually easier to think of additions than to delete. The references have been brought up to date, and this has meant extending the bibliography, a useful place to start a search for more detailed information. The facts and figures given in answer to tourism-orientated questions may vary from year to year. Tariffs and other economic parameters are especially prone to change and whatever figures are given in this edition are correct, applicable as from 1 April 1992. They are presented to the reader only to give him or her some indication of the financial implications of a visit to the Kruger National Park. The latest tariff lists are always included with the relevant accommodation/entrance voucher.

The scope of this book is wide and the information concise. Fritz Fourie was Chief Information Officer in the Kruger National Park from 1969 to 1977, and it was during those years that he met literally thousands of people from all walks of life and from all over the world, putting questions to him, some of which form the contents of this book. Mr Fourie passed away on 28 April 1989 at the age of 53 years.

It is with a sense of personal loss that I have undertaken this revision. Fritz Fourie was a friend to me, and beloved husband and father to his wife and three children. This book was his dream and into its various editions he put many years of labour. In the fabric of these pages are reflected his love and respect for nature. For me it was a joy and a privilege to help him with the earlier editions and now finally to have taken an active part in this edition. We grieve that he is not here to see the publication of the sixth edition, but his spirit lives on in the pages of the book.

G de Graaff
Pretoria 1992

HISTORY

The Kruger National Park is the largest wildlife sanctuary in the Republic of South Africa, and one of the largest controlled nature reserves in the world. It is situated in the farthest north-eastern corner of the Republic, between the Crocodile River in the south (25°32'S) and the Limpopo River in the north (22°25'S). The international border with Mozambique (32°2'E), which follows the line of the Lebombo Mountains in the south and continues beyond them in the north, forms the Park's eastern boundary. The western boundary is very irregular. The Park as a whole forms a reversed 'L', and covers an area of 1 948 528 ha or nearly 20 000 km^2.

The first Europeans to set foot in the Eastern Transvaal Lowveld were 31 men led by Francois de Kuiper. Delagoa Bay was a Dutch possession at the time and in 1725 the Dutch East India Company ordered an expedition to proceed from Delagoa Bay, later Lourenço Marques and now Maputo, to investigate the possibility of trade with the hinterland and also to check existing trade routes to the interior. At Gomondwane, north of the present Crocodile Bridge Rest Camp, they met a party of hostile natives and after a skirmish beat a hasty retreat.

The next Europeans to pass through the territory were two parties of Voortrekkers who travelled through the central part of the Park and crossed into Mozambique via the Shilowa and Mbhatsi gorges through the Lebombo Mountains. In 1844 Chief Commandant A H Potgieter came to an agreement with the Portuguese and defined the boundary between the South African and Mozambiquan territories more or less as we know it today. Two years later Potgieter bartered with the Swazis to acquire territory between the Crocodile and Olifants rivers.

In 1869 gold was discovered in the Lydenburg district, and people soon flocked to the area. The Lowveld had been practically unknown before but soon became a popular hunting ground. Highveld farmers came down the escarpment to find winter-grazing for their herds and, finding themselves in a game-rich area, proceeded to hunt. Professional hunters came too, seeking ivory, horns and skins. Game numbers declined rapidly and in 1884 President S J P Kruger proposed in the Volksraad that a game sanctuary be established to preserve the fast-disappearing fauna of the Transvaal. At that stage his was a lone voice crying in the wilderness. Public opinion was not favourable. It was some 14 years later that the area between the Crocodile and Sabie rivers was proclaimed a wildlife sanctuary in which any person found guilty of destroying, hunting or wounding game animals would be prosecuted and penalized. The proclamation was signed on 26 March 1898. The small Sabie Game Reserve and the Shingwedzi Reserve were the beginnings of what has grown into the world-renowned Kruger National Park. The area of the Sabie Game Reserve was only about 4 600 km.

One of the reserve's first two game rangers was Paul Machiel Bester (1872-1952) of the ZAR Police at Komatipoort. Having erected the first rondavel where the present Skukuza camp is now situated, he covered the doorway with a wildebeest hide. Occasionally hyenas tore off this hide and he then had to frighten them off to retrieve it. The other ranger appointed was Izak Cornelis Holtzhausen from the ZAR Police at Nelspruit (Pienaar, 1990).

The Anglo-Boer War broke out in 1899 and the Sabie Game Reserve was all but forgotten. After the Peace of Vereeniging in 1902 the interim government under Lord Milner decided to reproclaim the Reserve and appointed Major (later Colonel) James Stevenson-Hamilton as warden. This Scottish professional soldier obtained a two-year leave of absence from his regiment to begin the great task of saving what remained of the once-great herds of game which had been decimated by hunters and by both Boer and British soldiers. He became involved in the welfare of his animal charges to such an extent that he stayed for more than 40 years, until his retirement in 1946. The continued existence and development of the Kruger National Park is largely due to his dedication and sound administration.

When Stevenson-Hamilton settled on the banks of the Sabie River the balance of nature was seriously impaired, especially with regard to the larger mammals, and game laws existed virtually on paper only. Giraffe, hippo, buffalo and rhino were extremely rare, elephants occasionally wandered in from Mozambique but did not stay at first, and other species were numerically few.

The new warden's instructions were very vague. The only one he remembered clearly was 'to make himself as unpopular as possible' amongst the hunters and poachers. He set to it with fervour, earning for himself the nickname 'Skukuza' – the man who changes everything. In 1904 he succeeded in obtaining control, and thus game protection, over approximately 10 000 km of land north of the Sabie River which had belonged to land-owning and mining companies and private individuals. To centralize control of the area under his jurisdiction, he became Native Commissioner, Customs Official and Justice of the Peace for the territory, appointing rangers to help him in his task.

In 1922, in the aftermath of the First World War, a demand for more agricultural land to be made available by the government and for industries to be developed, coupled to the largely unsympathetic attitude of most Lowvelders of the time, seriously jeopardized the continued existence of the Sabie Game Reserve. By this time Stevenson-Hamilton had realized the Reserve should become a national park under central governmental control if its future was to be safeguarded. Fortunately he had influential friends. After a change of government which for a time seemed to cancel all his efforts, he finally won the confidence and support of the new Minister of Lands, P J Grobler, a grand-nephew of President Kruger.

His efforts were crowned with success when, on 31 May 1926, the National Parks Act was adopted unanimously, adding many hectares of land north of the Sabie River to the old Sabie Game Reserve, which was henceforth known as the Kruger National Park in honour of President S J P Kruger who had done much for wildlife conservation in South Africa.

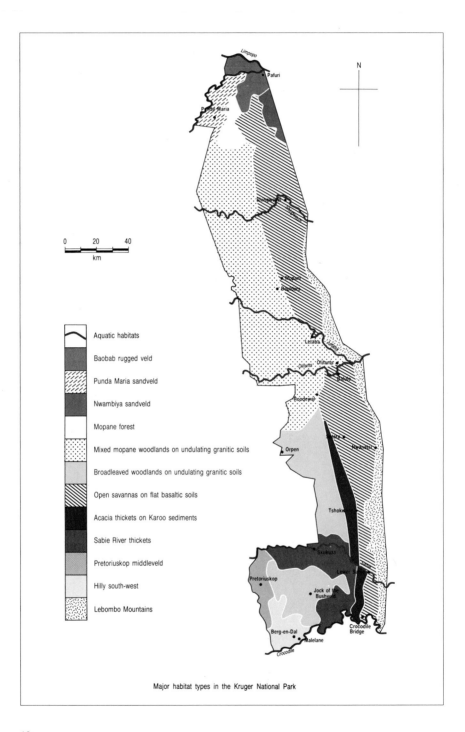

Major habitat types in the Kruger National Park

ECOLOGICAL ASPECTS OF THE KRUGER NATIONAL PARK

Topography

The greater part of the Park is a more or less flat area of bush and parkland savanna, with occasional rocky inselbergs of granite. The altitude varies from 442 m above sea level at Punda Maria in the north to 839 m at Khandizwe near Malelane, with the central part approximately 260 m. The lowest point is the gorge of the Sabie River, some 122 m above sea level, and the altitudes of the other river gorges are Shingwedzi 244 m, Olifants 152 m, Nwanetsi 152 metres and Nwaswitsontso 183 metres.

Geologically the park is divided into two almost equal sections from south to north by a narrow belt of shale and sandstone with predominantly granitic formations in the west and basalts in the east. The granites give rise to soils which are mainly sandy and light in colour while the basalts give rise to dark soils with a high clay content (Joubert, 1986). Two sandveld areas occur in the north, one at Punda Maria and the other on the northern part of the eastern boundary. The latter, called the Nyandu Sandveld, has a vegetation community that is very different from the rest of the Park.

Rivers

The major rivers are the Crocodile which forms the Park's southern boundary, and the Limpopo which forms the northern boundary. Other perennial rivers, flowing from west to east, include the Sabie, Olifants, Letaba and the Luvuvhu. Of the seasonal rivers the Shisa, Mphongolo, Shingwedzi, Tsende, Timbavati, Nwaswitsontso, Nwatindlopfu and Mbyamiti are the most important. All these rivers drain into the Indian Ocean.

Rainfall

The rainy season starts in September or October and lasts until March or April, and is followed by a period of very little or no rainfall. About 80% of the precipitation occurs in the form of quick thunder showers and is very erratic. Around Pretoriuskop in the south the annual rainfall is about 760 mm. The amount decreases noticeably further north, and in the central area the rainfall is about 540 mm per year. It rises again to about 640 mm per annum at Punda Maria in the north-west, while at Pafuri in the north-east it can be as low as 210 mm.

Temperatures

The average daily maximum in January is 30 °C and in July 23 °C. The extreme maximum can be 47 °C for January and 35 °C for July. The average daily minimum (night temperature) in January is 18 °C and in July 8 °C. The extreme minimum can fall to 7 °C in January and -4,2 °C in July. Light frost occurs occasionally, mostly in low-lying areas.

Vegetation

The plantlife varies from subtropical to tropical, as approximately one third of the Park lies within the tropic belt to the north of the Tropic of Capricorn. Its vegetation can be divided into eight major categories, which are shown on the map on page 10. On a finer scale a total of 35 landscape types have been identified.

A total of 1 986 plant species, including 457 tree and shrub species, as well as 235 species of grass, have been recorded in the Park. Succulents, xerophytes and epiphytes, including orchids, are also fairly well represented.

Animals

Few, if any, of the other national parks in the world can boast a diversity of animal and plantlife comparable to that of the Kruger National Park. Of the true cat species alone, six of the seven found in Africa occur in the Park.

The 1990 census produced the following estimated numbers for the more conspicuous animal species in the Park:

Predators

Lion (*Panthera leo*)	1 500
Leopard (*Panthera pardus*)	600-900
Cheetah (*Acinonyx jubatus*)	250-300
Spotted hyena (*Crocuta crocuta*)	2 000
Wild dog (*Lycaon pictus*)	350

Herbivores

Impala (*Aepyceros melampus*)	116 223
Cape buffalo (*Syncerus caffer*)	27 857
Burchell's zebra (*Equus burchellii*)	31 910
Blue wildebeest (*Connochaetes taurinus*)	14 293
Kudu (*Tragelaphus strepsiceros*)	7 035
African elephant (*Loxodonta africana*)	7 278
Giraffe (*Giraffa camelopardalis*)	4 719
Waterbuck (*Kobus ellipsiprymnus*)	3 203
Warthog (*Phacochoerus aethiopicus*)	2 715
Hippopotamus (*Hippopotamus amphibius*)	2 575
Sable antelope (*Hippotragus niger*)	1 877
Bushbuck (*Tragelaphus scriptus*)	1 500
Reedbuck (*Redunca arundinum*)	1 500
White rhino (*Ceratotherium simum*)	1 284
Nyala (*Tragelaphus angasii*)	800
Eland (*Taurotragus oryx*)	744
Tsessebe (*Damaliscus lunatus*)	711
Roan antelope (*Hippotragus equinus*)	294
Black rhino (*Diceros bicornis*).	200
Mountain reedbuck (*Redunca fulvorufula*)	150
Oribi (*Ourebia ourebi*)	100

The mammals of the Kruger National Park are fairly well known, with 147 species recorded; the birdlife has been well documented (507 species), as well as the reptiles (114 species) and the amphibians (33 species).

The gently flowing waters of the rivers and streams afford sanctuary to 50 species of fish (including four vagrant marine species) which are not often seen by tourists. A bull shark (*Carcharhinus leucas*) was found at the confluence of the Luvuvhu and Limpopo rivers in 1950, but these cartilaginous fish are not normally represented in the rivers of the Kruger National Park.

Two species of the rare and unusual seasonal fish, *Nothobranchius rachovii* and *Nothobranchius orthonotus*, were restricted to a few seasonal pans on the eastern boundary of the Park, but have now been re-introduced into other suitable pans. The most extraordinary feature of this approximately 50-mm fish is that it lives for only one season. Eggs are laid in the mud of the pans where they lie dormant. After the pans have dried up they are often covered with grass-like vegetation which becomes dry at the end of winter and is sometimes destroyed by fire. The eggs, however, can survive this harsh treatment, because of the protective mud cover. Only after sufficient rain, when the water in the pan attains the correct osmotic pressure, will the eggs hatch. This mechanism of nature ensures that hatching will only occur when there is sufficient water for survival, and for propagation by the adults. The male *Nothobranchius* displays a splendid array of colours.

One of the most sought-after sporting fish, the tiger fish (*Hydrocynus vittatus*), is also found in the perennial rivers of the Park.

GENERAL CODE OF CONDUCT

'To ensure a pleasant and successful trip through the Park it is essential that you adhere strictly to the regulations which are intended for your protection and enjoyment. The feeding of animals is especially considered a very serious offence.'
National Parks Board.

The National Parks Board Act No. 47 of 1976 as amended and regulations made thereunder provide *inter alia* that:

1. It shall be an offence to alight from a motor vehicle elsewhere than in a rest camp or at a picnic spot or any other unauthorized place, even if you are only partly out of your car.

In some national parks in other countries visitors are permitted to alight from their vehicles, so why is this regulation applied in the Kruger National Park?
Wild animals harbour a natural fear of man. When you are inside your vehicle they do not recognize you as a human being and you can therefore observe them at close quarters. Should you leave your vehicle – even partly – they will immediately recognize you. They may run away, depriving you and other visitors of the pleasure of observing them, or they may even attack you.

Is there proof that it could be dangerous to alight from your vehicle?
On occasions tourists who left their cars have been charged by lions and have narrowly escaped serious injury, or even death. There have been cases of people being killed by wild animals in reserves where visitors were allowed to leave their vehicles. Long grass often conceals dangerous snakes and scorpions, and these pose additional danger.

What do I do in an emergency?
You may leave your vehicle to repair a breakdown, but you do so entirely at your own risk. Therefore, make sure that there are no dangerous animals around. A tourist passing by could also be requested to report your predicament to the nearest camp. The rest-camp manager would then send a message to the breakdown service operating in the Park to come to your assistance.

2. It is an offence to drive elsewhere than on an authorized road.

Why are we not allowed to drive off the road?
Driving off the road to follow animals disturbs them. Stones, stumps and potholes concealed by grass, or just unobserved, have caused many a tourist serious problems. Roads with signs forbidding entry are constructed to act as fire-breaks and are also used by rangers on patrol, as well as by research staff concerned with nature management activities. These roads often cannot be negotiated by ordinary

vehicles and are not patrolled regularly. Should you have any mishap on one of them, it could take days to locate you. Certain by-roads are not signposted and you could get lost as a result.

Such incidents have occurred, and in one instance an elderly couple were stranded on a fire-break and located only after a three-day search. They suffered severe shock and almost died of thirst.

3. It is an offence to exceed the indicated speed limit.

Why is the speed limit so low?
High speeds could be dangerous because wild animals frequently run across the road. People exceeding the speed limit have often been involved in serious accidents with game and other vehicles. Another mistake that visitors often make is to follow the vehicle in front too closely – a practice which also leads to accidents from time to time.

Just as important is the fact that by driving slowly and observing carefully, the chances of spotting game are greatly enhanced. A speed of 20 to 30 km/h is recommended.

Some Parks Board officials seem to travel fast at times. Why?
National Parks Board officials are normally restricted to a speed limit of 65 km/h, some 10 to 20 km/h faster than the public, depending on the limit of the particular road. If employees were bound to the same speed limits as the public many man hours of labour would be lost. In an emergency they may exceed the 65 km/h speed limit, but if they do so without a valid reason, they could be prosecuted.

It is said that high speed is dangerous with wild animals around. Does this not also apply to employees?
The visitor does not devote all his attention to the road – his main objective is to see as much game as possible. The official on the other hand has a job to do and he therefore concentrates on the road with eyes which are better trained than those of the visitor.

Large Park vehicles seem to travel too fast. Is this necessary?
The size of these vehicles and the noise they make creates the impression that they are travelling faster than they actually do. The senior author timed them from time to time and found that they kept mostly within their limit. They have strict orders not to exceed the speed limit and those caught in a speed trap could be heavily fined. These vehicles are also equipped with tachometers.

4. It is an offence to injure, feed or disturb any form of wildlife.

Why may I not feed the animals?
Feeding animals, especially baboons, monkeys and even hyenas, makes them lose their natural fear of human beings and they may become aggressive towards the

feeder. A number of people have been bitten as a result of feeding. Injuries sustained in this manner can be serious and the wounds tend to turn septic, often resulting in blood poisoning. Once an animal has become a danger or a nuisance to human beings it has to be destroyed. Such an action could be avoided by not feeding it.

Is it true that monkeys and baboons become so dependent on feeding that they can starve if the practice is discontinued?
No, they do not become domesticated. They will look for their natural food as soon as they feel hungry. Howwever, feeding can lead to deficiency diseases.

The fine for feeding animals appears to be very high – is it justified?
When one considers the fact that innocent people could be bitten or mauled as a result of this practice, one is inclined to regard the fine as too lenient.

It is understood that one should not injure an animal, but is one prohibited from helping an injured animal?
Firstly, alighting from your vehicle is against the regulations; secondly, very few injured animals recover; and thirdly, it could be dangerous.

The senior author once came across an injured lion cub. While he watching over it a tourist in a car parked at the side of the road put his head out of the window and asked whether he should take the cub to the veterinary surgeon at Skukuza. Although no other lions were visible, the reply was that such an act could be dangerous. The author then drove a little closer to the cub and a growling, tail-swishing lioness appeared from the long grass! The visitor got the point!

Am I allowed to make tape recordings of lion roars to play back in the hope of luring them closer to my vehicle?
Nothing prevents you from making the recordings. Playing them back, however, could disturb the animals and this is against the regulations. It could also be dangerous as lions may become aggressive and try to find the origin of the sounds. It is, therefore, advisable to rather use your recordings at home.

5. It is an offence to uproot, pick, cut or damage any plant or be in possession of any part of a plant indigenous to the Park.

May I collect seeds of plants in rest camps?
According to regulations, this is not permitted. Plants indigenous to the Park are sold in rest camps and at entrance gates. It is therefore not necessary for you to collect seed. There is also a well-run nursery at Skukuza where plants can be bought.

6. It is an offence to place any name, letter or figure, symbol, mark, sticker or picture on any object.
7. You may not discard a burning object in such a manner or place where

a fire could develop within the respective camps and the veld.

Have any fires been caused through the negligence of visitors?
A number of veld fires have been traced back to visitors. In most cases a burning cigarette butt was the cause. To throwing anything away, even an extinguished cigarette butt, is against regulations and is a form of pollution.

8. It is an offence to be in possession of any explosives or of an unsealed or loaded firearm.

Have there been any incidents regarding the above regulation?
Cases of poaching have occurred, and the offenders arrested have had to pay heavy fines. Their firearms and vehicles were also confiscated.

9. It is an offence to introduce into the Park any pets, whether domestic or otherwise.

What is the purpose of this regulation?
Pets tend to get lost. Even if they were tame wild pets rather than domestic ones, they could still be alien to the Park and would therefore be unwanted. Diseases can be brought in by pets alien to the indigenous fauna of the Park; they could also transmit wildlife diseases when they leave the Park.

What would happen if you should be caught smuggling in a pet?
Either an admission of guilt fine would have to be paid or you would have to appear in court. The animal concerned would be destroyed.

Do rangers keep dogs?
They are allowed to do so for safety reasons. The dogs are kept in a healthy condition and are prevented from interbreeding with any canids in the Park. If a ranger terminates his services and leaves the Park, his dog or dogs may not leave the Park because of veterinary restrictions.

Are staff members in the Park allowed to keep pets?
No. Pets attract predators to the staff village. Domestic cats interbreed with wild cats, especially the African wild cat (*Felis lybica*). The barking of dogs also disturbs the atmosphere in the rest camps.

What about stray animals found and reared by rangers?
Some attempts have been successful, but there have also been many failures. A wild animal is seldom reared successfully and one wonders whether the animal concerned really gains from the attempt. Probably the best approach would be to discourage this activity. Very few semi-tame animals have been successfully released in the wild; not only do they have no place in their species' social hierarchy, but they have not learned to fend for themselves and can seldom do so.

The animals are likely to be beyond the point at which they could re-adapt to living in the wild.

10. It is an offence to discard any article or any refuse otherwise than by placing it in a receptacle or place intended therefore.

Does the Parks Board experience problems in this respect?
Yes, indeed. Many man hours are spent cleaning up along the roads and in rest camps, as well as at picnic spots.

One should not litter anywhere. Littering is considered a serious offence by the Park authorities.

Apart from the aesthetic point of view, have there been cases when littering actually harmed wildlife?
A number of incidents have been recorded in which tins with sharp edges have become wedged over the muzzles of animals, causing severe injury and even, in extreme cases, death.

A plastic bag swallowed by an animal can cause fatal blockage of the alimentary canal. Broken glass can obviously cut an animal's hoof or paw.

11. It is an offence to drive or park in such a manner that it is a nuisance, disturbance, or an inconvenience to other persons.

Are the usual traffic laws also applicable in the Park?
Yes.

Have any problems been encountered in this respect?
A traffic jam often occurs when people see lion or other animals, and there may be a delay of an hour or more. Small children or sick passengers may suffer great discomfort while stuck in such a jam. One should always consider other visitors.

What precautions should one take?
Travel on the left-hand side of the road and do not park at a bend or in any other place that could be dangerous to yourself or other road users.

If it is necessary to park on the right-hand side, pull slightly off the road, but do not park in the veld. Adhere to normal traffic rules for safety's sake and be courteous to fellow visitors.

12. It is an offence to make a noise after 21:30 and before 06:00, which may disturb another person.

Why must visitors be quiet during this period?
Some people simply want to rest, while others would like to listen to the sounds made by nocturnal animals.

13. It is an offence to advertise or offer any goods for sale.

Why may no goods be offered for sale in the Park?
The National Parks Board has the sole right to sell any goods in the Park. The Board can, however, grant permission to suppliers to sell produce such as fruit, vegetables or meat directly to members of staff. Until the mid-1950s private individuals had concessions to trade in the Park, but subsequently the Board decided to take over all trading in national parks.

14. It is an offence to collect any money from the public or give public entertainment for reward.

May visitors supply free entertainment in the Park?
If the programme fits in with nature conservation, permission may be granted. Educational programmes such as slide and film shows on nature conservation would be considered. Permission may, on the other hand, be refused without explanation.

Young people would sometimes like to have some sort of entertainment. Is this possible?
The Kruger National Park was never meant to be a pleasure resort. The atmosphere experienced in this sanctuary is unique and should be kept that way. One could well imagine what the effect would be if dancing and discotheques were allowed. The very peace and quiet, which are among the main attractions of the Park, would be destroyed.

Is it not possible for young people to come together and have some fun without disturbing other visitors?
A request like this should be made to the camp manager. It depends on what they have in mind; if it is just chatting around a camp fire, it might be perfectly in order. However, there is always the possibility of a large group of people tending to be noisy.

Considering that one can enjoy social life all year round except for the few days or perhaps a week spent in the Park, one can surely do without socializing for a short while.

Some private game reserves do have certain social activities for those few who insist on carrying their everyday life into the bush. Those people who complain that the Park is 'too quiet' amount to only a fraction of 1%; the vast majority prefer it the way it is.

15. It is an offence to spend the night in any rest camp without the knowledge of the camp manager.'

If you sleep in your vehicle, is it really necessary to report to the camp manager?
Any person staying overnight must at least pay camping fees because he uses the ablution facilities and other amenities whether he sleeps in a vehicle or in a tent. If visitors fail to comply with this regulation, camping fees will be collected for every

night not paid for when their papers are checked as they leave the Park. A fine may also be imposed.

16. It is an offence to travel in the Kruger National Park during times other than those approved.

Why are visitors not allowed to drive out at night?
One's view at night is restricted to the beams of the vehicle's headlights and very few animals can be seen. Animals blinded by the light may dash across the road and cause accidents. Hippos are dangerous in this respect, especially near rivers.

Are certain people taken out at night?
This is rarely done, and such trips are restricted to scientists and radio or television teams if they are able to convince the authorities of their bona fides. If such a service were offered to the public, everyone would want to go out, causing considerable disturbance to game.

What are the normal travelling hours?
The times during which visitors may travel in the Park are subject to alteration without notice, and it is recommended that visitors check the times indicated on the entrance permit. Present travelling hours are:

Month	Camps open	Entrance gates open	Camps and gates close
January	05:30	05:30	18:30
February	05:30	05:30	18:30
March	05:30	05:30	18:00
April	06:00	06:00	17:30
May-August	06:30	06:30	17:30
September	06:00	06:00	18:00
October	05:30	05:30	18:00
November-December	05:30	05:30	18:30

Can visitors be prosecuted if they turn up late at a camp gate or an exit gate?
Avoidable travelling after the gates have closed is subject to a fine for the first half hour, and prosecution will follow for longer periods.

What happens if you are late due to unavoidable circumstances?
Each situation is judged on merit. However, some tourists make most unusual excuses when they could in fact have been on time. The officials know most of these excuses and can therefore usually determine whether they are genuine. A tourist who thought of a 'good' excuse deflated the spare wheel of his car when he

realized he would be late at the camp gate. He tendered the 'evidence' of a flat tyre when he arrived and was lucky to get away with it. The next day, while he was watching game at a waterhole, a fellow tourist drew his attention to a flat tyre on his vehicle. He got out to change it and found the spare deflated. When he complained loudly about his misfortune a young voice was heard from his car: 'But Daddy, don't you remember you let the air out of the tyre yesterday?'

17. It is an offence to spend the night in a place other than a rest camp.

Is it dangerous to sleep in a vehicle in the bush?
Not necessarily. If you stay inside your vehicle you are pretty safe, but when you have to get out for some reason it could be dangerous. If people are allowed to sleep in the bush it would be difficult to control law-breakers. It is a serious offence to spend the night outside a rest camp.

18. It is an offence to drive a vehicle in the Park without a driver's licence.

Is it a serious offence to drive a vehicle in the Park without a driver's licence?
It is regarded as a serious offence. The driver of a vehicle must have a licence valid for the type of vehicle he drives.
   It is also an offence to allow a child to sit on your lap while you are driving. Not only could the child be seriously or even fatally injured if an accident occurred, but also the driver does not have full control of the vehicle.

What is the maximum fine imposed in the Park?
Poaching of game leads to problems, as do infringements of the regulations. The illegal shooting (poaching) of rhino and elephant – R30 000 to R100 000; the poaching of small game – R4 000 to R8 000; arson – R1 000 to R6 000 and/or 18 months' imprisonment; the feeding of animals – R1 000 (maximum); and disturbing animals – R1 000 (maximum).

Why such high fines?
Teasing or disturbing potentially dangerous animals such as lion, elephant or rhino – to mention but a few – can be dangerous not only to the culprit, but also, and more importantly, to innocent people.
   Arson is another grave offence which could have severe consequences, and a heavy fine may be imposed for this crime.

Is it necessary to have one's entrance and accommodation documents in the car?
It is important to have your entrance documents and all relevant receipts readily accessible for inspection on demand while you are in the Park.
   Last, but not least, the above regulations are there for the protection of the public and to enable visitors to enjoy their stay in this wildlife sanctuary.

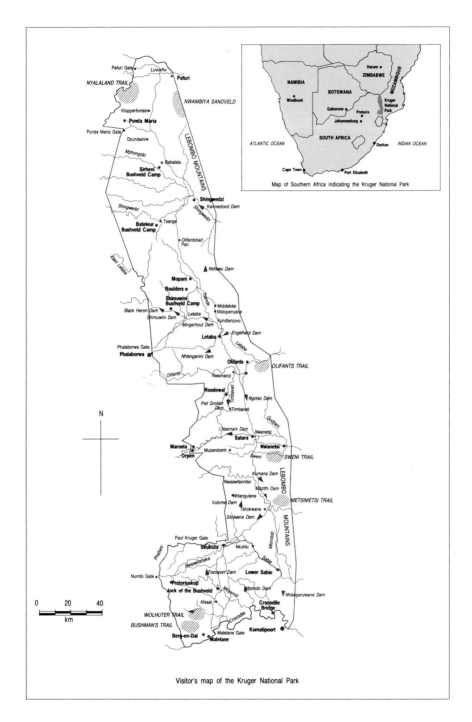

Visitor's map of the Kruger National Park

Map of Southern Africa indicating the Kruger National Park

TOURISM

How much accommodation is available in the Kruger National Park?
Accommodation is restricted in order to prevent overcrowding which would disturb the peaceful atmosphere. It is limited to 3 250 beds and 1 500 day visitors. However, the current demand for more accommodation throughout the year has led to Berg-en-dal rest camp having been completed, and the National Parks Board has decided to build another four medium and five small rest camps over the next 10 years. This will increase the available accommodation by 25%, and to compensate for the increase in traffic more roads will also be made available to the paying public.

Where does one reserve accommodation?
Accommodation, camping and caravan sites, and wilderness trails may be booked 12 months in advance. The number of persons (maximum 15 per party or eight for a trail), the rest camps preferred and the applicable dates must be stated. It is also advisable to indicate alternative camps and dates. All applications and enquiries should be sent to the Chief Executive Director, National Parks Board at either of the following addresses:

Pretoria	*Cape Town*
PO Box 787	PO Box 7400
Pretoria	Roggebaai
0001	8012
Fax: (012) 343-0905	(021) 24-6212
Telephone: (012) 343-1991	(021) 22-2816
Office hours:	
Monday to Friday	08:00 – 12:30
	13:00 – 15:50
Closed on Saturdays,	
Sundays and public holidays.	

Reservation vouchers must be produced on arrival at the Park.

Do day visitors have to book in advance?
Normally day visitors do not need to reserve admission in advance. However, as the numbers of vehicles entering the Park is restricted, even day visitors have to book in advance to travel through the Park during long weekends, public holidays and school holidays. Day visitors pay admission fees only.

Groups must obtain permits in advance. No groups are allowed during long weekends, public holidays or school holidays. Admission for day visitors is subject to a 10% surcharge during provincial school holidays, long weekends and public holidays.

How much are the admission fees?
The admission fees are revised annually on 1 April and subject to alteration
without advance notice. The following are effective as from 1 April 1992:

Visitor

Adult (16 years and older)	R17,00
Child (2 to under 16 years)	R9,00
Child (under 2 years)	Gratis

Plus vehicle

Motor vehicle	R15,00
Minibus (10 seats or fewer)	R17,00
Bus (11 – 25 seats)	R60,00
Bus (26 – 50 seats)	R75,00
Bus (51 and more seats)	R150,00
Autovilla	R25,00
Motorized caravan (larger than autovilla)	R36,00
Caravan	R15,00
Trailer	R6,00

(Vehicles with an axle load of more than 8 000 kg are not admitted.)

What type of accommodation is available?
Accommodation varies from two-bed huts to luxury guest houses. Generally it
consists of a two-bed or a three-bed hut with washbasin, shower and toilet.
Bedding and towels are supplied. Larger camps also have a number of family
cottages with a stove, fridge, cooking utensils and cutlery.

Can a group of people reserve a private camp en bloc?
The following camps must be reserved en bloc:
• Nwanetsi: 12 persons or fewer, with a maximum of 16 persons per night.
• Malelane: 12 persons or fewer, with a maximum of 18 persons per night.

Can a visitor reserve accommodation in a private camp?
Yes. This accommodation is available at:
• Jock of the Bushveld: 12 persons or fewer per night. (The nearest
  camp is Berg-en-dal.)
• Roodewal: 12 persons or fewer, with a maximum of 19 persons per night.
  (The nearest camp is Olifants.)
• Boulders: 12 persons or fewer. (The nearest camp is Letaba.)

Can a visitor also book donor-built accommodation?
Yes, visitors may book donor-built accommodation. These guest houses, cottages
or huts are held in reserve for the donors until three months or 11 months before
the date of the prospective visit. If they have not been reserved by then application
from other interested parties may be considered. Accommodation which is only

reserved for a Friday or Saturday, or for Friday and Saturday (weekend) is subject to a 10% surcharge. Bedding is included.

Donor-built accommodation falls into two categories. In the first, the accommodation is held in reserve for the donors until 3 months before the date of the prospective visit. If it has not been reserved, written application from other visitors is accepted four months in advance and confirmed 2 to three months in advance. Telephonic reservations are considered 2 months in advance. Donor houses, family cottages and huts in this category are at:

Lower Sabie
Moffett family cottage
(maximum 4 persons)

Berg-en-dal
J le Roux house
(maximum 6 persons)
2-bedroomed family cottages
(for 4 persons or fewer, maximum 6)

Pretoriuskop
Pierre Joubert house
(maximum 8 persons)
Doherty Bryant boma
(for 6 persons or fewer, maximum 9)

Skukuza
Volkskas house
(maximum 8 persons)
Moni house
(for 6 persons or fewer, maximum 9)
Struben family cottage
(for 4 persons or fewer, maximum 6)
Lion hut (maximum 2 persons)

Orpen
2-bedroomed family cottage – number 15 (for 4 persons or fewer, maximum 6)

Satara
Rudy Frankel house
(maximum 8 persons)
Stanley house
(for 6 persons or fewer, maximum 9)
Wells house (maximum 6 persons)
2-bedroomed family cottages
(for 4 persons, maximum 6)
Albert Froneman hut
(maximum 2 persons; there is no kitchen)

Olifants
C D Ellis house ((maximum 8 persons)

Letaba
Fish Eagle house (maximum 8 persons)
Melville house
(for 6 persons, maximum 9)
Certain 2-bedroomed family cottages
(for 4 persons, maximum 6)

In the second category the accommodation is held in reserve for the donors until 11 months before the date of the prospective visit. If it has not been booked written applications from other parties are accepted 13 months in advance and confirmed 10 to 11 months in advance. Reservations by telephone are considered from 10 months in advance. Donor houses, family cottages and huts in this category are at:

Lower Sabie
Keartland house
(for 6 persons, maximum 7)
Steenbok family cottage
(maximum 4 persons)

Skukuza
Nyathi house (maximum 8 persons)
Waterkant 1 house (8 persons)
Waterkant 2 family cottage
(maximum 4 persons)

Berg-en-dal
Rhino house (8 persons)

Shingwedzi
Rentmeerster house (6 persons)

Orpen
2-bedroomed family cottages
(for 4 persons, maximum 6)

Mopani
Mopani house (maximum 8 persons)
3-bedroomed family cottages
(for 4 persons, maximum 6)

Letaba
Certain 2-bedroomed family cottages
(for 4 persons, maximum 6)

Luxury Mopani huts
(for 2 persons, maximum 4)
Mopani huts (2 persons, maximum 4)

Bushveld camps that can be booked on the same basis are:

Mbyamiti
2-bedroomed family cottages
(for 4 persons, maximum 5)
1-bedroomed family cottages
(for 2 persons, maximum 4)

2-bedroomed family cottages
(for 4 persons, maximum 5)
1-bedroomed family cottages
(for 2 persons, maximum 4)

Talamati
2-bedroomed family cottages
(for 4 persons, maximum 6)
1-bedroomed family cottages
(for 2 persons, maximum 4)

'Bateleur
3-bedroomed family cottages
(for 4 persons, maximum 6)
2-bedroomed family cottages (4 persons)

Shimuwini
3-bedroomed family cottages
(for 4 persons, maximum 6)

Sirheni
2-bedroomed family cottages
(for 4 persons, maximum 6)
1-bedroomed family cottages
(for 2 persons, maximum 4)

Is a deposit required when reserving accommodation?
Deposits should not accompany applications, but will be requested after a reservation. Reservation receipts must be produced upon arrival at the Park.

In the event of a cancellation, will the deposit be refunded?
If you cancel 41 days or more before the first night reserved, 15% of the deposit will be forfeited. Cancelling between 14 and 40 days before the first night means you lose 25%, and cancelling between 1 and 14 days before the first night means you lose 50% of your deposit. If you cancel on the day that you were due to begin your visit to the Park the whole deposit is forfeited. The minimum cancellation fee is R10,00. Application for a refund must be received by the National Parks Board within 30 days after cancellation.

Is accommodation limited at certain times of the year?
During the March/April and June/July school holidays accommodation is limited to a maximum of 10 nights in the Park and a maximum of 5 nights per camp.

Why are day visitors restricted over long weekends and during school holidays?
To limit the amount of traffic and the overcrowding of restaurants, ablution blocks
and other facilities. Overcrowding makes the visit unpleasant.

Are all the camps open throughout the year?
In the past only certain camps were open during the summer months because the
number of visitors to the Park did not justify the cost of keeping more camps open.
With the increasing number of visitors, however, all camps are now open
throughout the year.

What can I buy in the rest-camp shops?
A large variety of groceries, including bread, butter, eggs, sterilized milk, fresh
meat and vegetables is available. You can also buy crockery, cooking utensils,
cigarettes, sweets, reading matter, camera film, curios, liquor and gas.

   Liquor is sold from 09:00, except on religious holidays (including Good Friday,
Ascension Day, the Day of the Vow and Christmas Day) and Sundays. Please note
that only essential commodities are sold on Sundays and religious holidays.

Do all shops in the Park have the same merchandise?
Skukuza, being the main camp, has the widest variety. Shops in the other big
camps have a fair selection of curios and groceries available, but stocks are limited
at the Numbi, Kruger, Crocodile Bridge, Punda and Phalaborwa gates.

What are the shopping hours?
At all the rest camps the shopping hours are as follows: 09:00 – 14:30 and
16:00 – 20:00 daily, including Sundays and public holidays.

Are game trophies sold in the Park?
Veterinary restrictions prevent the exportation of trophies. Treated skins,
however, are sold in the shops.

What hours do rest-camp offices keep?
The offices are open daily from 08:00 to half-an-hour after the closing of the gates.

Are road maps of the Park available?
Maps are obtainable from the National Parks Board and are also on sale at all
entrance gates and rest camps in the Park.

Does the National Parks Board provide transport for visitors?
No, but vehicles can be hired at the Avis car-hire agency at Skukuza.

Are there film shows in all the rest camps?
At times evening films are shown from Monday to Saturday in Skukuza, while
some of the other camps also provide shows for visitors. Enquire at the camp's
reception desk.

What kind of films are shown?
The films are all documentary, while slides on wildlife in general and nature conservation in particular are also screened.

Could one sue the National Parks Board for damage to one's vehicle caused by an animal?
No. You enter the Park entirely at your own risk. If you observe the speed limit and traffic rules, damage to your vehicle by an animal is minimal.

Are there restaurants and shops in all the rest camps?

Camp or Gate	Restaurant	Shop	Petrol	Diesel	Telephone
Skukuza	•	•	•	•	•
Kruger Gate	–	–	–	–	•
Numbi Gate	–	–	–	–	•
Pretoriuskop	•	•	•	•	•
Malelane	–	–	–	–	•
Berg-en-dal	•	•	•	•	–
Lower Sabie	•	•	•	•	–
Crocodile Bridge	–	•	•	–	•
Satara	•	•	•	•	–
Orpen	–	•	•	•	–
Maroela	–	–	–	–	–
Nwanetsi	–	–	–	–	–
Balule	–	–	–	–	–
Olifants Camp	•	•	•	•	–
Letaba	•	•	•	•	–
Phalaborwa Gate	–	–	–	–	•
Shingwedzi	•	•	•	•	–
Punda Maria	•	•	•	•	–
Mopani	•	•	•	•	–
Mbyamiti	–	–	–	–	–
Shimuwini	–	–	–	–	–
Talamati	–	–	–	–	–
Sirheni	–	–	–	–	–
Bateleur	–	–	–	–	–

Can visitors fly to the Park?
The commercial airline company, COMAIR, operates daily flights between Jan Smuts Airport, Skukuza and Phalaborwa and also conducts tours by mini-buses in the Kruger National Park.

May I bring a firearm to the Park?
Yes, but any firearm must be handed over to be sealed at the entrance gate. It will be unsealed at the gate upon departure.

Are there garages and workshops in the Park?
There is a workshop at Skukuza, and minor repairs may also be done at the Satara and Letaba rest camps. Breakdown assistance is provided by the Automobile Association of South Africa.

Are there any post offices and banks in the Park?
There is a post office at Skukuza, as well as a branch of Volkskas Bank.

Are couriers available?
Couriers may be hired. Reservations must be made in the Park.

Is electricity provided in all rest camps?
All the rest camps have electricity, with the exception of a few small ones. Where electricity is not available, solar power and/or gas or lanterns is provided. There are no floodlights outside and a torch is therefore essential.

No electricity is available at the bushveld camps, but solar power and gas are provided. With the exception of Malelane, electricity is not available in private camps. At Balule and at Orpen (excepting the cottages) lanterns only are in use, while at Nwanetsi gas stoves and lanterns are provided. Solar power and gas are available at Roodewal, Jock of the Bushveld and Boulders camps.

Are there laundry facilities in the rest camps?
Laundromats are available at Pretoriuskop, Lower Sabie, Olifants, Berg-en-dal, Mopani, Letaba, Satara, Skukuza and Shingwedzi. At all the other camps visitors should consult the tourist officer for information about washing and ironing facilities.

Can visitors prepare their own meals?
Visitors who have reserved accommodation without kitchens and wish to prepare their own meals must supply their own cooking and eating utensils. Outdoor cooking facilities are available in all the rest camps. Boiling water is supplied throughout the day.

What kind of payment is accepted in the Park?
Payment for entrance, accommodation, meals and merchandise must be paid for in cash or by travellers' cheques and/or bank guaranteed cheques. Visa, Mastercard, Diners Club, American Express, First National Bank and Volkskas cards are accepted for amounts of R5,00 or more. If in doubt about other credit cards, visitors should enquire at the National Parks Board or at the rest camps in the Park. Fuel can only be bought for cash, by means of bank guaranteed cheques or a petrocard.

What should I do in case of theft from my car or hut?
In Skukuza the case should be reported to the South African Police, but in other camps it should be reported to the ranger or camp manager, who will take the

necessary steps. You cannot claim from the National Parks Board. Fortunately, cases of theft are very rare. It is, however, advisable not to leave valuables, documents or money in your hut or an unlocked vehicle.

One occasionally sees some apparently unarmed men working on the roads. Is this not dangerous?
These people have a practical knowledge of wild animals; they take care not to disturb the animals and can usually spot potential danger, and take steps to avoid it. Moreover, the activities of a number of people working together usually deter wild animals from attacking.

Has any road worker been killed by a wild animal?
A few have been killed, but in every case they were not with the team but in places where they should not have been officially. Their own negligence led to their fate.

Have there been any tourist fatalities in the Park?
No fatalities to tourists have been caused by animals in the Park, although some people court danger by alighting from their vehicles in the presence of dangerous animals, especially lion and elephant. A number of people have, however, died in motor car accidents.

Have any visitors been injured by animals in the Park?
Many years ago three people in two different rest camps were injured by hyenas. Two slept on open verandas and one in a tent with the flaps open. Fences around the camps in those days were not as effective as those used at present and the victims, by sleeping in the open, were negligent. From time to time people who attempt to feed monkeys and baboons are bitten by these animals. It is advisable to close your windows when stopping to observe them.

If I run over an animal, what should I do?
Report the accident at the nearest camp. Do not get out of your vehicle to try to help the animal – it could be dangerous and you are unlikely to be successful.

What is the procedure when two or more vehicles are involved in a collision?
In the case of serious accident, send a report to the nearest traffic officer, a ranger or the police at Skukuza, or to the nearest rest camp. Wait for the officer to take measurements. Minor accidents can be settled between the owners of the vehicles or subsequently between their respective insurance companies.

May a tourist report law-breakers?
You are at liberty to do so, but you must also be prepared to testify against them in court if you wish to lay a charge.

How many kilometres of tourist roads are there in the Park?
At present there are 930 km of tarred roads and 1 476 km of gravel roads.

How many kilometres of fire-breaks are there?
About 4 266 km, 617 km of which are along the fences.

Will all the roads be tarred in the future?
It is most unlikely.

Have the tarred roads had any effect on the distribution and movements of game?
Vegetation along the tarred roads is relatively free of dust and therefore more palatable than that along untarred roads. Run-off water produces slightly more lush vegetation on the shoulders of tarred roads, and this attracts mainly small game. However, in certain areas in summer the growth is so lush that it impairs to some extent the visitor's view.

Lions tend to lie on tarred roads during winter, especially early in the morning and late afternoon, because the tarred surface gets warm quickly and retains heat for a longer period.

Generally speaking, it appears that tarred roads definitely have more advantages than disadvantages.

Are visitors inclined to speed on tarred roads?
Apparently not. The smooth, tarred, dust-free roads eliminate the desire to travel faster to avoid being covered in someone else's dust, or to eliminate the bumpiness and corrugations often encountered on dirt roads.

Why are staff at the huts often reluctant to help visitors with the washing of dishes or grilling of meat?
It is not part of their official duties. However, they can perform these tasks in their spare time if it does not interfere with their official duties.

What should be done in an after-hours emergency, such as serious illness?
Drive to the camp gate and blow the hooter several times. The camp manager will come to your assistance. If he knows of a medical doctor visiting the camp, he will refer you to him.

In Skukuza you can consult the resident doctor. If you do not know where to find his consulting rooms, ask the night watchman at the gate.

Are people taken out in cross-country vehicles off the beaten track?
Visiting scientists, important visitors, and media groups are taken out by National Parks Board staff. Occasionally private individuals are also taken out if staff is available. A fixed tariff is charged.

Will more areas be created where people can leave their cars to sit and watch game, in the open and at their leisure?
The National Parks Board is considering the creation of more places like Mlondozi Dam near Lower Sabie, the Eileen Orpen Dam near Tshokwane and the lookout at Nwanetsi. Lookouts have been established at Kanniedood Dam and Tshange.

Are there swimming pools in all the camps?

For many years the National Parks Board hesitated to provide this amenity but it was eventually decided to build natural-looking swimming pools in the larger camps. Swimming pools, fitted with filtering and purifying devices, have been built at Pretoriuskop, Berg-en-dal, Mopani and Shingwedzi camps.

Are wilderness trails conducted by the National Parks Board?

Wilderness trails, guided by experienced rangers, allow nature-lovers to make direct contact with nature in its unspoilt state. The seven trails now in existence are the Wolhuter and Bushman trails near Pretoriuskop (starting at Berg-en-dal), Metsi Metsi near Tshokwane (starting at Skukuza), the Olifants trail (starting at Letaba), the Nyalaland trail near Punda Maria, the Sweni near Satara, and the Napi. The last-mentioned is a new trail between Skukuza and Pretoriuskop.

Hikers need to be reasonably fit and the trails are therefore restricted to persons between the ages of 12 and 60 years. Children between the ages of 12 and 16 must be accompanied by a responsible adult. Those participating undertake the trail at their own risk and before setting out they are required to sign a form indemnifying the National Parks Board from all responsibility.

Further information about the trails may be obtained from the Chief Executive Director, National Parks Board, P O Box 787, Pretoria 0001.

What is a wilderness trail?

A wilderness trail is essentially a spiritual encounter with nature, whereby people are taken out of their everyday environment and exposed to the intricate elements that compromise the web of life. This is achieved, in part, by traversing large areas of unspoiled wilderness on foot and under the guidance of a trail ranger, whose role is an interpretive, protective and disciplinary one. It is not unusual to walk as much as 15 km per day and although the accent is not on endurance, a reasonable level of fitness is required.

The number of participants is limited to eight, and to derive the maximum benefit from the trail adventure it is recommended that persons of similar age, interest and level of fitness make their bookings together.

Trailists meet at the designated rest camps not later then 15:30 on Mondays and Fridays and from there, after a short briefing, they leave for their wilderness trail camp by vehicle. The accommodation for the wilderness trails comprises four small, 2-bedded units. Three nights and two days are spent in the bush, the group returning to the main rest camp after breakfast on the final morning.

What clothing, footwear and food should one take along?

This depends on the person, but clothing should be comfortable, allowing freedom of movement. It should be hard-wearing and preferably neutral in colour, e.g. khaki. Light-coloured (white or cream) garments should be avoided. T-shirts are not recommended as they don't protect the neck against the sun.

Although rucksacks, eating utensils, water bottles, beds and bedding are provided, it is suggested that the following items be taken along by the trailist:

3 shirts/blouses
3 pairs shorts
1 pair slacks/jeans
1 tracksuit
Underwear and socks
1 pair sandals/tackies (for use in camp)
1 jersey
1 all-weather jacket or rain coat
1 hat/cap (to protect head and neck)
1 torch and batteries

Footwear
This is probably the most important item of a trailist's equipment and should provide ankle support, have reasonably thick soles, and be durable and comfortable.

New shoes or boots should be broken in before the trail.

Food
All other equipment, including food, is included in the tariff, although liquor and soft drinks are not provided. The food is adequate and of a type that can be expected at a rustic bush camp. Special tastes are not catered for and special items should be provided by the trailists themselves.

Each base camp is equipped with a paraffin refrigerator, the use of which is primarily intended for perishable foodstuffs. Space permitting, it can be arranged for mixers and soft drinks to be kept cool.

Note:
To appreciate the wilderness experience a harmonious and co-operative approach is required. With this in mind, alcohol may be consumed only at the base camp. Inordinate consumption of liquor is likely to jeopardize the success of the entire trail.

Binoculars, camera and film
Suntan lotion
Mosquito repellant
Personal toiletries
Towel
Beverages (personal preferences)
Reference books (e.g. *Newman's Birds of the Kruger Park*, Sinclair and Whyte's *Field Guide to the Birds of the Kruger National Park*)

Malaria
As the Lowveld is an endemic malaria area, visitors should take a course of anti-malaria tablets before, during and after their stay, as prescribed. A mosquito repellant is also strongly recommended.

What are the trails like?

Nyalaland Trail
This trail runs through one of the prime wilderness areas of South Africa. The base camp is on the banks of the Madzaringwe Spruit north of Punda Maria, near the Luvhuvhu River. Geologically the soils are sandstone and consequently many species of wildlife are unique to this area of the Lowveld.

Olifants Trail
The base camp of this trail is situated on the southern bank of the Olifants River, west of the Olifants/Letaba confluence. It offers a magnificent view of this beautiful stretch of river. The landscape varies from riverine bush and gorges to the foothills of the Lebombos. It supports varied wildlife.

Sweni Trail
The establishment of the new Sweni trail in the wilderness area near

Nwanetsi has been eagerly awaited by trailists. The base camp, which overlooks the Sweni Spruit, provides a view of the surrounding marula and knobthorn savanna. The area is known for its large herds of zebra, wildebeest and buffalo, and accordingly, predators such as lion and spotted hyena are never far away. On the floodplain of the Sweni unique communities of mlala palm (*Hyphaene natalensis*) can also be seen.

Metsi Metsi Trail
This is located in the area east of the Nwamuriwa mountain near Tshokwane, with the base camp at the foot of the mountain. A great variety of wildlife can be encountered here, including black rhino. The landscape varies from undulating savanna to rocky gorges and ravines.

Wolhuter Trail
The Wolhuter trail commemorates the legendary veteran father and son rangers, Harry and Henry, who for many years patrolled the southern section of the Park. The base camp is situated midway between Berg-en-dal and Pretoriuskop in the southern section of the Park, in the heart of white rhino country. The features of the area are gentle undulating bushveld plains with distinctive rocky outcrops.

Bushman Trail
This trail is situated in the south-western section of the Park near Berg-en-dal, with the base camp situated in a secluded valley, in a landscape characterized by awe-inspring granite mountains and hills. The plant and animal life is

representative of this type of habitat. Bushman paintings can be viewed in many of the hill shelters and are a feature of this trail.

Napi Trail
The Napi trail is situated in an undulating landscape with its base camp on the confluence of the Mbyamiti and Napi Spruits, southwest of Skukuza. It is characterized by bush savanna and is preferred habitat of elephant, white rhino, buffalo, sable antelope and reedbuck, among others.

How can I book for a wilderness trail?
Bookings for trails can be made a year in advance. Two consecutive trails in the same area may be reserved by any one group, provided that the second trail commences on a Friday. The party will then remain at base from Friday through to the following Thursday. Enquiries in this regard may be made at a National Parks Board reservations office.

School and student parties may apply for a reduced tariff through the reservations office in Pretoria; such groups must be accompanied by a responsible adult. Indemnity forms for such parties are available from the reservations office and must be completed and signed by the accompanying adult, and handed to the trails ranger before the group sets out on the trail.

Applications for wilderness trails must clearly state the number of trailists, their ages and sex. It is advisable to provide alternative dates and trail preferences. It is important that deposits should not be sent with applications; they will be requested when the booking is confirmed.

Proof of booking, which is issued when the booking is confirmed, must be shown on arrival at the Park.

What are the qualifications to become an honorary game ranger?
To become an honorary game ranger you must be a regular visitor to the Park, have a real interest in nature, have at least an above average knowledge of nature and must be fluent in English and Afrikaans. There are other requirements, but for further information please contact the Chief Executive Director, PO Box 787, Pretoria 0001.

Do all the rest camps have camping and caravan sites?
These facilities are available at the major rest camps, except at Olifants, Mopani and Orpen. The Maroela rest camp caters especially for caravans.

No ground sheets or tents with ground sheets allowed at Letaba, Berg-en-dal, Lower Sabie or Crocodile Bridge and Satara. If you have a ground sheet, contact the camp manager.

Are there any sports facilities in the Park?
No, and most visitors prefer it that way.

Do visitors from abroad get preference when reserving accommodation?
These visitors are most welcome to South Africa and to the Kruger National Park in particular, but they do not get preference at the expense of South Africans. Overseas visitors amount to about 10% of the total number of people visiting the Park every year and most of them travel with bus tours. These organizations have block bookings and take South Africans as well as foreigners.

How many people visit the Kruger National Park annually?
In 1927 only three cars entered the Kruger National Park. Since then the figure has steadily risen to 669 167 tourists in 1989/90.

How many entrance gates are there and what are the nearest towns and routes to follow?

There are eight entrance gates.

Gate	Nearest town/route
Crocodile Bridge	Komatipoort via Nelspruit
Malelane	Malelane via Nelspruit
Numbi	White River via Nelspruit or Sabie
Paul Kruger	Hazyview via Nelspruit or Sabie
Orpen	Acornhoek via Sabie or Hoedspruit
Phalaborwa	Phalaborwa via Hoedspruit or Tzaneen
Punda Maria	Thohoyandou via Louis Trichardt
Parfuri	Tshipise via Louis Trichardt or Messina

How much waste is generated by visitors?
Some 183 000 tons of waste material such as glass, tin, cardboard, paper and plastic is collected annually. This gives an average of 0,5 kg of litter per person per day.

NATURE CONSERVATION

How many different species of vertebrate animals are there in the Park?

Species and number of species
Mammalia (Mammals) 147
Aves (Birds) 507
Reptilia (Reptiles) 114
Amphibia (Amphibians) 33
Pisces (Fishes) 50

How many of the animal species represented in the Park are normally seen by a visitor?
Some animals are nocturnal in habit, some are very small, others are burrowers, and others still are very rare. About 50 of the more conspicuous species may be seen. A one-day visit could yield anything from about 10 to 20 or more of the larger mammal species.

Are any animals in the Park threatened by extinction?
Not at this stage. However, it would be more satisfactory if numbers of cheetah, wild dog, roan antelope and black rhino were to increase.

What does the National Parks Board do to ensure the survival of rare species?
A team of highly specialized scientists comprising zoologists, botanists and veterinarians are employed by the Parks Board. These people are constantly engaged in intensive research to ascertain the best methods of conserving the different species in general and rare species in particular. A number of cheetah, mountain reedbuck, eland and red duiker have been introduced to bring in new genetic material and so strengthen local populations.
   Breeding camps for sable, roan antelope, tsessebe, Lichtenstein's hartebeest and eland have been established in an area north of Shingwedzi, and near Pretoriuskop.

Has any species of game become extinct in the Park?
Yes. White rhino became extinct shortly before the Sabie Game Reserve was proclaimed, and black rhino disappeared in the late 1930s and early 1940s. Oribi also became extinct, but all three species were re-introduced some years ago from areas where they still occurred in fair numbers.

Is there an animal hospital in the Park?
No, but the Ministry of Agriculture has an experimental station for disease research at Skukuza. Occasionally animals are treated at this station, but it is not an animal hospital in the true sense of the word. It is not open to the public because of quarantine measures.

Seriously injured animals are usually destroyed to put them out of their misery. In exceptional cases, rare animals are treated, provided the prognosis is good.

In cooperation with the National Parks Board, the Ministry also takes the necessary precautions to curb the spread of diseases such as foot-and-mouth and anthrax within the Park. The National Parks Board also employs its own veterinary staff.

Are there many diseases that pose a threat to wildlife?
Wild animals are susceptible to a large number of diseases but only two of them, foot-and-mouth and anthrax, have posed a danger in recent years.

Are some animals more susceptible to these diseases than others?
All mammals are susceptible to anthrax, but roan antelope and kudu suffer most. Up to 47 fatalities amongst roan and more than 200 amongst kudu were reported in a single outbreak of this disease. Only a few other animals were affected in the same outbreak.

Foot-and-mouth disease is more prevalent amongst buffalo and impala, although most of the herbivores are susceptible to it.

Are these diseases highly contagious?
They are indeed. Anthrax is caused by a bacterium, *Bacillus anthracis*, while foot-and-mouth disease is caused by three different strains of virus.

What measures are taken to combat these diseases?
It is impossible to control foot-and-mouth disease within the boundaries of the Park and there is no effective measure to treat it. A fence was erected on the Park's western and southern borders in 1961 to prevent animals from leaving and so spreading the disease.

During an outbreak of foot-and-mouth disease – or anthrax – game inspections are intensified to keep track of the direction in which the disease spreads so that necessary steps can be taken in areas adjoining the Park. To prevent accidental spreading of the disease, no animal or animal product may be removed from the Park without the permission of the State veterinarian, even when there is no active outbreak of the disease. The exception to this rule is the zebra, which is immune to foot-and-mouth disease.

Additional precautions in the case of anthrax are the burning of all carcasses found and the disinfecting of waterholes in the area.

How do these diseases affect the animals involved?
Mortality from foot-and-mouth disease in wild animals is low, and most of the affected animals recover within about 24 days. Secondary infection of the hoof and mouth may have a more serious effect if sepsis sets in and the animal becomes crippled, and thus easy prey for predators.

Anthrax is a particularly unpleasant and a usually fatal disease which leads to death within a very short period.

Are there any prophylactic measures taken for these diseases?
The relatively mild nature of foot-and-mouth disease renders special measures unnecessary and uneconomical. Of course it is a different matter as far as domestic stock is concerned; contaminated meat is unfit for human consumption and many domestic animals die of the disease (De Vos, Van Rooyen and Kloppers, 1973).

Roan antelope are vaccinated against anthrax once a year. This is done from a helicopter by means of a dart gun and a disposable dart containing the vaccine.

Have there been any outbreaks of rinderpest?
The only known rinderpest epizootic occurred in 1896 when large numbers of buffalo, and many other game animals, were decimated.

Is the whole of the Park fenced in?
Yes. A 2,5-m high elephant-proof fence, strengthened with high-strain breaking cables, runs along the eastern and northern boundaries of the Park.

In the west and south of the Kruger National Park the area is completely enclosed with a 2m-high barbed wire fence.

Why is the whole of the Park not enclosed by the elephant-proof fence?
The high cost involved makes it impossible to achieve this ideal in the Kruger National Park in the foreseeable future.

Do larger animals often damage this fence?
Elephant, and to a lesser extent giraffe and buffalo, sometimes damage the fence along the western boundary. Even the fence on the eastern boundary, which under normal conditions could be called elephant-proof, has been damaged by these huge animals.

Does this fencing interfere with animal migrations or movements?
Before the erection of the fence between the Park and Mozambique some animal species, particularly elephant and eland, migrated to the latter area after good rains fell there. They usually returned during winter because of more permanent water in the Park.

Some other species, especially zebra and wildebeest, migrated westwards during late autumn or early winter, returning with the onset of spring. The development of farming areas and the fence put a stop to these migrations.

In its fenced-in state the Park is no longer a natural ecological unit, a fact recognized in its management programme.

Do animals move around in the Park?
Some animals show a tendency for seasonal movement. Large herds of zebra and wildebeest, for example, find their summer grazing in the Satara area and their winter food supplies in the Sabie River area. About 10% of the elephant population moves about seasonally. Other species usually leave an area only when scarcity of water or food forces them to do so.

Do certain game species frequent specific areas or habitats?
Predators are usually found near waterholes, where it is easier to surprise their prey. Lions can remain in one area for a considerable length of time, but if the herbivores move away in search of food and water, the lions will follow.

Waterbuck are very fond of water and will seldom wander far away from it. Impala, to a lesser extent, also frequent the vicinity of waterholes and rivers. Bushbuck and nyala are restricted to thickets, mostly along watercourses. Klipspringers are adapted to rocky habitats and are always found on koppies or nearby rocks. Zebra and wildebeest prefer open areas with short grass, while kudu keep to denser bush. Eland and wild dogs are nomadic, moving around constantly.

Some animals, like the leopard, are territorial and will defend an area against intruders of their own kind. Others, such as the giraffe, will stay in the same area for years without marking or defending it. In this case the area is known as a home range, as opposed to a territorium, which is marked or defended.

The highest density of lions is found in the Lower Sabie and Crocodile Bridge areas, while the northern part of the Park has the largest concentration of African elephants.

Is it worthwhile stopping at a waterhole and waiting for the animals to come and quench their thirst?
There are usually some animals to be seen at a waterhole, and even when it appears deserted it could be worthwhile stopping for a while and waiting for game to come and drink. During winter or periods of drought large concentrations of game are to be found at the more permanent watering points or rivers and pools.

After good rains many temporary waterholes appear all over the veld and the animals are therefore scattered over large areas. A slow drive along the roads could then be more rewarding than waiting at a waterhole.

What time of the day is best for spotting game?
During the summer heat it is advisable to go on early morning and late afternoon drives and to spend the hottest part of the day – from about 11:00 to 15:00 or slightly later – in the camp, resting or looking at and learning more about the trees and birdlife.

In the winter months more game can be seen throughout the day and early drives are not really necessary. Under cool conditions the game tends to come to the waterholes between about 08:00 to 12:00.

Which roads are the best for game viewing?
In contrast to the fire-breaks, which often cut across relatively waterless areas, the tourist roads either follow watercourses for some distance or have a number of dams or waterholes near them.

Some visitors believe that there is more game to be seen along the dirt roads than the tarred roads, while others prefer a smooth, dustless ride on the tarred roads.

Both types of road have their advantages: vegetation along tarred roads is relatively free of dust, whereas the more natural-looking, quiet dirt roads are more appealing to some visitors, especially keen photographers. There is no proof that more game can generally be seen from dirt roads.

Where am I most likely to see a kill?
Most kills take place near a waterhole, especially in times of drought.

Is the game evenly distributed throughout the Park?
The topography, geology, climate and biotic factors have been instrumental in creating many clearly defined plant communities. It is important to note that there is a very close correlation between soil type and the distribution of plant species.
    Animal distribution is affected by a number of ecological factors, such as the vegetation and the particular habits of the species – some prefer dense bush, some like more open areas, while others have very specialized habitat requirements. Further information on this topic can be found in the entries on the different animal species.

The Pretoriuskop area was once well-known as the haunt of large herds of wildebeest and zebra. Why are these species now scarce there?
Until 1924 farmers still had grazing rights in this area, and to ensure good grazing for the winter they burned the veld every year. Very little burning was carried out after 1924, and in 1943 Colonel Stevenson-Hamilton reported that a serious problem was being created by the encroachment of bush and by tall unpalatable grasses replacing the short grass. He stated on his report: 'The result is seen in the immense increase of the browsers – impala and kudu – and the decrease by emigration to more open country in the west, of the grazing species – wildebeest, zebra, sable, roan and waterbuck.'

Can previous conditions be restored?
Burning of the veld was re-implemented in the 1950s to establish more suitable conditions for the grazers, and there is now good reason to believe that the pendulum is swinging back. More dams were built and boreholes drilled to ensure that drinking water was not a limiting factor.

Will more waterholes be established?
There are more than 450 functional boreholes with windmills and/or diesel engines to pump water to reservoirs and troughs. There are also 86 dams and the dam-building programme, as well as the drilling of new boreholes, continues. Because of unfavourable rock formations, subterranean water is scarce and many dry holes have been drilled. Some boreholes dry up during prolonged spells of drought. Providing artificial waterholes cannot continue indefinitely, however.
    Nor is it the complete answer; even when the stage has been reached where there is enough water to drink from a sufficient number of waterholes and dams, rain for plant growth will still be necessary.

When was the water-provisioning scheme initiated?

Since the late 1930s boreholes have been sunk and dams built on a small scale. As the number of animals increased, progressively more water had to be supplied and the programme was speeded up, especially during the 1960s and 1970s.

Does the Park become drier?

In his reports during the 1920s and '30s, Colonel Stevenson-Hamilton expressed the opinion that a process of increasing desiccation was taking place. This has not been proven yet, but it is a fact that a number of perennial rivers have become seasonal rivers over the past 20 years or more.

Increased farming and industrial activities in the catchment areas of these rivers have caused a higher demand for water, which has therefore impaired the flow of rivers such as the Timbavati and Letaba. Although they still flow throughout the year, rivers like the Crocodile, Sabie and Olifants are also affected.

The drying up of springs could be attributed to erratic rainfall.

Is intensive research being done in the Park?

The National Parks Board's research team consists of trained and experienced workers. Research is not confined to the survival of rare species, but also involves the more prolific species and the control of their numbers. Zoological and veterinary research is supplemented by intensive study of plants and plant communities, with special reference to pastures. Soil types and their influence on vegetation are also studied.

What is the purpose of this research?

To conserve successfully one must have an intimate knowledge of the ecology of plants and animals. The Kruger National Park and most other nature reserves are not natural ecological units and nature must therefore be aided by man through sound nature management techniques.

The more prolific species in the park pose a threat to rare species by virtue of their numbers and the resulting over-utilization of available habitat.

Apart from the fact that there is still so much that we do not know, new problems arise all the time and they have to be solved.

How are the numbers of animals in the Park ascertained?

The census of game takes place during the winter months, when most of the trees are bare, the grass is short and the game is concentrated near permanent waterholes. The Park is divided into flying grids and counts are done from a helicopter and low-flying fixed-wing aircraft; the results are then correlated with censuses on the ground.

What procedure is used for counting a herd of elephant or buffalo on the run?

When the aircraft is directly above the herd, colour slides are taken and afterwards projected onto a screen and counted by two or more persons. Figures for elephant and buffalo are therefore very accurate.

It is obviously not possible to cover the whole of the Park in flying grids in one day. How are double counts avoided?
During the time of the year that the counts are carried out, the animals tend to remain in the vicinity of the permanent waterholes and do not move around significantly.

How long does the annual census take?
The census is undertaken from the middle of May to the end of August.

Have any rangers or other members of the staff been attacked or killed by animals?
Only a few persons, probably not more than 20, have been killed in the entire existence of the Park. Most of them were killed by lions, a few by crocodiles, one by a leopard and two by elephants.
Most of these people were out in the bush at night or early in the morning and were not pursuing their normal duties. Lion and leopard are bolder at night, partly because this is their normal hunting time, but probably also because their night vision is better than that of their normal prey as well as that of human beings. They are therefore more dangerous at night than during the day.

Have there been any exceptional encounters between humans and animals in the Kruger National Park?
Ranger Harry Wolhuter and his horse were attacked by two lions late one afternoon in August 1903. Keeping his presence of mind, Wolhuter killed one of the lions with his sheath knife and climbed a tree. As he feared, the other lion, which had unsuccessfully attacked the horse, soon returned and reared up against the tree trunk in an endeavour to reach the badly wounded man. Fortunately, Wolhuter's dog, Bull, also returned and started to distract the lion's attention by his barking. Meanwhile his black assistants, who had lagged behind owing to the slow-moving pack donkeys, arrived and managed to frighten off the lion. The full story is related in chapter six of Wolhuter's book *Memories of a Game Ranger* (1948).
The skin of the lion and the knife used to kill it are on display in the Information Centre at Skukuza.
In 1935 Mr Glen Leary, father-in-law of ranger Harold Trollope, was fatally injured by a wounded leopard. During the same year a black ranger on foot patrol was attacked by a lion. He managed to deliver a fatal stab to the lion but afterwards succumbed to haemhorrage and shock.
In 1963 a black ranger travelling by bicycle was killed by an elephant near Punda Maria. Judging by the signs, the man tried to run away but was overtaken. The elephant then gored him with one of his tusks, severed his right arm and also broke his leg.
Four years later, contrary to strict orders from the ranger, some black employees returned to Pretoriuskop early one morning by taking a short cut through the bush. One of them was attacked by lions and the rest fled to the camp to call the ranger. When he arrived at the scene, very little was left of the victim. Two lionesses were shot but the other three got away.

A few rangers have been injured by buffalo, none of them fatally. In 1970 a postal worker was fishing in the Sabie River with an employee of the National Parks Board. He waded into the river and swam for some distance before being attacked by a huge crocodile. He disappeared and his body was never recovered. It should be pointed out that employees are able to obtain a licence to fish at a few places along the river.

During March 1970 a black man trying to cross the Park's border with Mozambique encountered an elephant which trampled him to death. Also, an employee walking along the old railway line near Skukuza was killed by a lion.

Crocodiles also took their toll in 1974. An employee disappeared on the flooded causeway of the Olifants River, probably taken by a crocodile, while another black ranger was killed by a crocodile when he waded through the Sabie River. A hippo attacked a man and his wife and child on the banks of the Luvuvhu River, killing the woman. Her body was almost severed in two.

Taking into account the number of cases in which humans have been killed by wild animals since the proclamation of the Park in 1898, we find that this cannot compare with the number of murders and violent deaths that occur in a medium-sized town in one year. It should be added that in most of the cases sheer negligence was the actual cause of their fate. A number of non-fatal attacks by other animals, including leopard, have also occurred.

Viewed in perspective, it has been proved through the experiences of people living in the bush that wild animals, if left undisturbed, very seldom deliberately try to harm a human being.

How many rangers are there in the Park?
There are 283 people involved in ranger services in the Park.

What qualifications are required to become a ranger?
The following qualifications are required:
1. South African citizenship.
2. Efficiency in speaking, reading and writing English and Afrikaans.
3. A diploma in Nature Management, but preference will be given to applicants with higher academic qualifications.

In addition, applicants are recommended to have the following:
1. A knowledge of one or more of the Tsonga, Siswati or Zulu languages.
2. Proficiency in the use of firearms.
3. A practical knowledge of nature.
4. Experience in law enforcement.
5. Adaptability to a quiet life, often devoid of normal social life and amenities such as shops, medical services and service stations for vehicles. Rangers' quarters are often situated in remote parts of the Park.

It is also important to note that a ranger's child would have to attend a boarding school from an early age. Family life is restricted and rangers as parents must be prepared to accept this.

What are the general duties of a ranger?

A ranger is responsible for the implementation of all management activities in the area under his control. These include patrolling his section regularly and reporting on the condition of grazing and game, water resources, weather conditions, roads, fences and firebreaks.

He must execute a programme of controlled, rotational veld burning, prevent accidental fires, combat poaching, and attend to the culling programme. He is also responsible for law enforcement on the roads and within the rest camps, and if necessary, undertake other police duties as well. He is expected to assist the research staff during game censuses and epizootics as well as with scientific observations. Administrative work such as correspondence and keeping a diary, and the extermination of exotic plants and animals are also his responsibilities.

Are the rumours about mining activities in the north of the Park true?

Mining will probably not take place in the near future. If it is found to be in the interest of the Republic of South Africa, any economical mineral deposits in the Park will be mined, but before this can be done the law prohibiting prospecting and mining in a national park will have to be amended. Mining of the coal deposits in the northern part of the Park, a particularly beautiful area, could yield short-term benefits for the country, but would leave scars that would take centuries to heal. When trees a few hundred years old are removed one can imagine how long it will take to replace them.

If one considers that a small country like Japan has devoted proportionally twice as much land to nature conservation as South Africa has, then it is difficult to understand why we should destroy the little we have!

Will any more national parks be created?

The National Parks Board is continually negotiating for new parks. There are quite a number of biomes in South Africa which are still not sufficiently protected.

CULLING

What is culling?
Culling is the removal of excess animals from a population. In the Kruger National Park it takes place in three categories: firstly through predators; secondly through diseases and natural mortality factors; and thirdly when man reduces the number of animals by shooting or darting them.

Which species are culled?
From 1903 until 1958 predators such as lion, leopard, hyena and, unfortunately, cheetah and wild hunting dogs were hunted. In later years zebra, wildebeest, impala, buffalo, elephant, and occasionally hippo, also featured on the culling list. For some years the culling of predators ceased but was later resumed on a limited scale.

Some culling is also done on a small scale in certain areas to give rarer species a chance to establish themselves. This was done, for example, when mountain reedbuck were translocated from the Mountain Zebra National Park to the Malelane area in the Kruger National Park.

It seems strange that predators had to be culled. What was the reason?
When Colonel Stevenson-Hamilton arrived in the old Sabie Game Reserve herbivores had been severely depleted by hunting activities, and the effect of the rinderpest, too, had probably not been overcome. This led to the idea that predator numbers should be curbed to give the herbivore populations a chance to recover.

How many lions were destroyed during the period 1903 to 1958?
An average of 52 lions per year were culled, totalling 2 486.

What was the effect of this culling?
In 1925 it was estimated that the lion population in the central part of the Park, that is, the area between the Letaba and Sabie rivers, was 250. A survey in 1975 revealed some 708 lions in this area. Reports since 1925 indicate that despite the moderate culling of lions, the increase in herbivores also led to a satisfactory build-up of the lion population. The culling curbed their numbers to some extent but did not jeopardize their survival.

There were reports of another culling scheme for lion, as well as one for hyena, in 1975. Why was this done?
A number of exceptionally wet years prior to 1975 led to excessive growth of long grass and to other vegetation becoming increasingly dense. Because of this, populations of zebra and wildebeest concentrated in the remaining short grass areas. This in turn led to heavy predation by lion and hyena on the relatively crowded populations. It was therefore decided – after surveys had been carried out and intensively studied – to reduce the predator numbers by culling.

How many lions were culled in this operation?
A total of 62, or 8,75% of the population in the area.

How did this affect the visitor's chances of seeing lion?
Very little; the areas where culling took place were mostly far from tourist roads.

Could nature not be left to sort out the problem?
As the Park is fenced in, the area is not a natural ecological unit and man has to intervene. If any of the rarer species in the Park should become extinct, there are no other areas from which these species could be replenished through migration.

What norms are applied to determine whether culling is necessary or not?
It is the policy of the National Parks Board to allow only as many animals of a certain population or species as the area is able to support during the dry time of the year. If certain animals become too numerous, they endanger their own survival – and that of the rarer species – by overtaxing food and water supplies. Over-population of an area often causes irreparable damage to the vegetation, to the extent that soil erosion may result.

What about the balance of nature?
Nature is geared to balance itself over large areas and this also applies to ecosystems under natural conditions. Man has pushed wildlife back into small, often ecologically non-viable, units where it is difficult if not impossible to maintain a natural balance. The balance of nature has always been dynamic rather than static. Climatic conditions vary between droughts and times of good rain. When the number of herbivores rises in good years, the number of predators follows suit until the amount of available prey drops. It then becomes more difficult for them to obtain food and their number in turn must fall.

Man, the super-predator, has been eliminated as a mortality factor in nature reserves, bush fires and diseases are controlled, and many artificial waterholes have been established. All this leads to optimum conditions for some animal species, which then become too numerous.

Why do only some species become too numerous?
Some animals are better equipped for survival, and under favourable conditions, such as those created by sound nature management, will breed more efficiently than less well-equipped species. Animals with a high degree of habitat specialization, for example, are very susceptible to even small changes in their environment. Such specialists seldom, if ever, exist in large numbers.

Are there any other reasons for reducing animal numbers besides that of controlling over-population?
Badly injured animals are destroyed for humane reasons. Injured animals such as lion or elephant, or any others who could pose a potential threat to human safety, also have to be destroyed.

At times animals seem to be very scarce. Is this not due to over-culling?
The effect of culling is very small if one considers that in most cases less than
10% of a species is culled. Moreover, the culling is seldom done near tourist roads.

When animals appear to be scarce it will be noticed that just about all species are
scare, not only those subjected to culling.

For a number of years now, only elephant and buffalo have featured on the
culling list.

Is there a possibility that a species may be over-culled?
The authorities are very careful not to endanger the survival of any species.
However, even if buffalo, elephant or any other species were over-culled, the
population would be back to normal after one or two years of non-culling.

The possibility of a species becoming extinct would be greatly increased if
culling were terminated. There is very little likelihood that culling as such could
lead to the extinction of a particular species.

Are there not enough predators to control the herbivores?
Predators alone cannot control the numbers of their prey species. Nature has
many ways of preventing predators from over-utilizing their source of food. In
any natural ecosystem, predators do not account for the total mortality of their
prey – disease and lack of food are two other major factors that influence the
numbers of the prey species. When predators become numerous in an area, a stage
is soon reached where they find it difficult to kill because of the lower density of
their prey species and the fact that only the fittest of the prey are left. This in turn
leads to starvation amongst the predators.

Considering that the effects of drought and disease have been eliminated to a
large extent through nature management, it is obvious that conditions of
over-population could develop.

It should also be noted that some herbivores are not preyed upon. So lions do
not kill elephants, except perhaps – in exceptional circumstances – an elephant calf.

*A predator such as a lion produces two to five cubs at a time, while herbivores
usually produce one young per year. Why can lions therefore not increase their
numbers more rapidly?*
Mortality amongst young predators is very high. During times of food scarcity
many lion cubs die of starvation because the adults feed first and there is often
little left for the cubs. Many hungry cubs trying to feed with the adults are killed
in the process.

Lion cubs hidden by their mother for the first few weeks after birth often fall
prey to hyenas and other predators. Diseases and parasites also take a heavy toll.

Territorial fights between lions also account for a considerable number of deaths.
Because of their territorial behaviour, lions do not tolerate the presence of
strangers, especially members of the same sex. Lions that cannot find a suitable
territory often leave the Park and usually end up in confrontation with a farmer or
a hunter.

Who does the culling?
All culling is done by members of the Nature Conservation Department of the National Parks Board.

Why are professional hunters not allowed to cull under supervision?
This could mean extra revenue for the Park.

Trophy hunters who pay for their hunting tend to go for record trophies. In the culling process animals are culled at random to keep the composition of the herds as natural as possible. Selection of one sex or size of animal would lead to a disturbance in the herd composition.

Professional hunters are allowed to cull game on game farms. Why can this not be done in the Kruger National Park?
Farms are much smaller than the Park. On a farm the non-breeding animals can easily be herded into a camp where they can be culled, but this is not possible in the Park.

How are the animals culled?
Elephant, buffalo and other dangerous animals are killed by means of a dart, with a lethal dose of a paralysing drug, fired from a helicopter. This method eliminates the danger of wounding the animal, which in turn can be dangerous to personnel and tourists.

Rifles are used on animals that do not pose a danger to human beings.

What about the disturbance factor of culling?
When a culling operation commences, the required number of animals to be destroyed is separated from the herd by a low-flying helicopter. This group, normally consisting of animals from both sexes and different age groups, is then darted while the rest of the herd is undisturbed.

The authors do not claim that there is never any disturbance during culling operations, but both personal experience and scientific opinion has proved that the disturbance factor is negligible.

Do animals suffer when they are destroyed?
The drug used, scoline, is a paralysing drug which causes suffocation by affecting the respiratory muscles. The large dose of the drug injected paralyses the beast very quickly, enabling the ground crew to move in and kill the animal with a heavy calibre rifle.

To date this method has been found to be the most effective to cull elephant and buffalo in the Park.

Is this method fool proof?
It occasionally happens that the dart fails to inject a full dose of the drug. To prevent any suffering which may arise from such a situation, a loaded rifle is always kept on hand.

Will culling continue indefinitely?
The numbers of specific species on the culling list are determined by research and are controlled according to ecological requirements. The numbers and species might differ from time to time, but the culling process in the Park will continue for the forseeable future.

What happens to the carcasses of culled animals?
Carcasses are transported to the abattoir near Skukuza, where the meat of edible species is processed for human consumption. This meat is used in restaurants in the rest camps or sold in preserved form either in tins or as biltong.

Can one buy venison in the Park?
Unfortunately not. Veterinary restrictions prohibit the export of raw meat from the Park. Biltong – dried raw meat – is treated according to veterinary requirements and may only be taken out in the sealed bags in which it is sold.

It is said that the abattoir and meat-processing plant cost R1 million and still has to show a profit.
This plant is paid for and the National Parks Board does not intend to make a profit at any cost. If the culling quota for a year is completed ahead of schedule, the plant is idle for a period. This has happened in the past.

Why are surplus animals not sold to zoological gardens or other nature reserves?
Except for zebra and elephant, all other herbivorous animals have to be kept in quarantine for at least a month before they can be removed from the Park. This is done to eliminate the possible spread of diseases to other areas. Keeping animals in quarantine is very costly and therefore the disposal of surplus animals to other reserves is usually uneconomical.

More importantly, prolific species such as impala may be bought from private game reserves at a reasonable price. Veterinary restrictions such as those imposed in the Kruger National Park do not apply in these private reserves. It would have been economical to sell roan antelope because of the high prices they fetch, but it is common knowledge that the Park would rather buy than sell these rare animals.

Zebra have been sold in the past and are sold when necessary. Currently young elephants are sold from time to time.

THE ROLE OF FIRE IN ECOLOGY
AND NATURE MANAGEMENT

Parts of the Park have obviously been burned. Is this done deliberately?
A programme of controlled veld burning has been followed since 1954, when it
was decided that burning should take place as late as possible in spring or after
the first rains.

*Would it not be better for the vegetation in a nature reserve to be protected
against fire?*
Fire is a natural phenomenon, as is shown by the number of fires caused by
lightning every year. Like climatic factors, fire plays an important role in
developing and maintaining savanna conditions.

   Periodic burning prevents savanna areas from becoming decadent, helps to
maintain maximum productivity, and is important in retarding woody growth.

What would happen if fire was curbed in the Kruger Park?
The Pretoriuskop area was subjected to burning until about 1924 and then burning
was discontinued until 1954. During those years bush encroachment took place,
making the habitat unfit to a great extent for some animals. It has been proved in
the Park and elsewhere that complete protection from fire leads to an
accumulation of dead herbage which smothers new growth. If an accidental fire
then occurs it is usually devastating.

How is the burning programme carried out?
Using the tourist roads and fire-breaks, the Park is divided into about 300 blocks
of approximately 64^2 km each. These blocks are burnt on a rotational basis, so that
more or less one third of the area of the Park burnt annually.

Is a rigid pattern of burning followed?
The burning is carried out according to computerized programmes which are
adjusted from time to time, depending on circumstances, to ensure maximum
benefit to the plant communities in the Park.

   The nature conservation staff make it their duty to determine when and how
often fire should be applied to stimulate natural conditions and, if possible, to
improve these conditions.

Are some areas in the Park protected against fire?
The following areas are protected: the catchment areas of rivers, lakes, the valleys
of the larger rivers that originate in the Park, and river banks in general, to protect
the riparian vegetation. Also excluded are mountain slopes and mountainous
parts of the Park, as well as vulnerable areas with shallow stony soils on which the
plant cover is very sparse, and the sandveld areas of Punda Maria and Nwambia.

Why are these areas exempted?

Hippos grazing on river banks at night and animals visiting these watercourses keep excess grass and herbage in check.

Vegetation in the catchment areas curbs desiccation of the soil while plants on mountain slopes check soil erosion. The vegetation of the sandveld areas also curbs erosion.

Are some plants fire tolerant?

Savanna plants are mostly fire tolerant and even if they are burnt down to ground level are usually capable of sprouting again, while annual grasses and plants survive in the form of seed.

How much of the vegetation can be destroyed by a fire?

Fires in early winter are 'cool' because some green material is still present. Late burns, especially before any rain has fallen, can create very high temperatures and cause severe damage.

What temperatures could be created?

Depending on the amount of dry material present – such as in an area which has not been burned for a number of years – and on the presence of wind, temperatures of more than 500 °C can develop. This type of fire can destroy between 60 and 90% of the vegetation, including large trees. 'Cool' fires on the other hand destroy as little as 25% of the vegetation.

How are these temperatures measured?

Metal strips painted with thermo-sensitive paints are placed in the area to be burned. After the burn these strips are collected and inspected. The different heat-resistant paints have different colours and the paint colours not destroyed by the fire indicate the temperature range.

It is said that fire inhibits the growth of certain plants, while the growth of others is stimulated. Is this true?

The growth of most savanna plants is stimulated, provided the fire is not too severe. Unwanted vegetation is usually curbed.

What is the effect of burning at different times of the year?

Experimental plots in various parts of the Park serve as testing sites. The information gained from them is used to indicate the most suitable time and conditions for burning in a specific plant community.

Has the burning programme in the Park been a success?

Bush encroachment is a problem in certain parts of the Park, but remarkable success has already been achieved in reversing the process. It occurs over long periods and therefore burning programmes have to be amended from time to time to obtain maximum results.

What about small animals that succumb in these fires?

Investigations after fires reveal that very few small animals die. When the flames approach, many escape by moving away in good time, while most of them take refuge underground in holes and crevices. These fires usually progress fast and even though the temperatures at the soil's surface may be very high, subterranean levels are shielded by a few centimetres of soil.

What about big animals?

It can happen that the veld is set on fire by a number of lightning strikes, creating conditions in which animals could be trapped. During 1954 a total of 40 animals were found killed or had to be destroyed as a result of accidental fires. They were: six elephants, two lions, 12 impala, 10 kudu, three waterbuck, three steenbok, two roan antelope, one duiker and one warthog. More animals probably died but were not found.

This sounds grave, but averaged over the years, these casualties constitute a minute percentage of the larger animals. In relation to other hazards which can befall them, the number of animals that succumb to fire is indeed negligible.

What are the main causes of accidental fires?

Lightning is probably the main cause. The negligent behaviour of tourists is another cause. A number of fires are caused accidentally or deliberately, and arson in the Park has been proved on occasion. Poachers often set the veld on fire at the Park's borders to lure animals there with the young palatable growth of grass that follows.

To sum up, what are the benefits of veld burning?

Controlled burning of excess and redundant plant material at the right time has a most desirable effect. It disposes of old, unpalatable herbage, controls bush encroachment and other undesirable plants, and encourages healthy fresh growth. Parasites are destroyed, fire hazards are reduced, and the animals are better distributed. Seeding is stimulated and a better seed-bed results.

Early, dry-season burning encourages bush encroachment at the expense of grasses and causes exposure that could result in soil erosion.

POACHING

Is poaching a problem in the Park?
Poaching occurs from time to time, but regular patrols by rangers in the Park keep this activity to a low level.

How do poachers manage to enter the Park?
It is very difficult to seal the fence where rivers and rivulets enter the Park, and it is impossible to guard the fence at all times. Apart from using riverbeds to enter the Park, poachers cut the fence from time to time.

In which areas do these poaching activities mostly take place?
Most of the poaching is carried out in border areas. If the poacher is detected, his chances of escape are much better than in areas far from the border. It is also easier for him to remove his haul.

How do these poachers kill the animals?
The animals are killed mostly by snaring, but firearms are also used. The snares, of different sizes and strengths, are usually set in a game path leading to a drinking place. Some are tied between two shrubs or trees, while others are tied to a small tree which is bent down to provide a spring action when tripped. Depending on the type of snare, animals can be caught by the neck, in which case they die a slow death by strangulation, or they can be caught by the leg. The wire or thin cable used cuts into the flesh, causing severe wounds which leave the unfortunate beast crippled even if it manages to break the snare. Sepsis in the wound often leads to death or incapacitates the animal to such an extent that it falls victim to predators or dies of starvation due to immobility.

Which animals are mostly trapped by snaring?
Animals from the size of a hare to an elephant fall prey to poachers, but antelopes make up the bulk of the plunder.

Quite a number of elephants have lost part of their trunks, or have sustained serious injuries to their trunks. When an elephant gets a foot caught in a snare it is generally strong enough to break the thin cable used to snare big game. However, it usually sustains serious injuries because the cable cuts deep into the flesh and causes severe wounds which lead to sepsis and even gangrene.

Snares are also set for giraffes at about 3 m or more above ground level. Giraffes caught by the leg in snares suffer a lingering death.

Warthogs have been caught around the muzzle and, because their protruding, tusk-like canines prevent the snare from slipping off, they die of thirst and starvation. One former ranger told the senior author about a poacher who had a very shrewd way of capturing warthog. He even took special orders for Christmas! The warthogs were frightened, and when they took refuge in an old aardvark hole a funnel made from maize bags was secured around the entrance.

Beating and jumping around the hole made the animals try to escape. In their flight they landed in this funnel and were bludgeoned to death.

Many animals, amongst them lion and other predators, have been saved by darting them with a drug and then removing the snare and treating the wound.

The skeleton of a waterbuck bull was once found with a snare embedded in the skull. The thin cable had pulled tightly around the skull at the base of the horns, and although the buck had managed to break the snare, apparently by moving its head from side to side, part of the cable had cut a groove in the skull. The unfortunate animal then walked around with this noose for some weeks because it was later found to be partly covered with bone. Infection probably caused its death after weeks of agony.

In 1967 one of the research staff found a dying hyena with a broken snare around its neck. Apparently the poacher had reappeared on the scene while the hyena was still struggling to break the snare, and had knocked the animal unconscious with a heavy blow to the head. The pads under the feet and the lips were then cut off and the rectum removed. When the hyena regained consciousness, it must have licked its wounds and walked around on the bare bones of its feet for some time. The animal was put out of its misery.

A white rhino that strayed out of the Park some years ago became stuck in a small, muddy dam. A number of poachers hacked it to death with axes.

Do poachers kill animals mainly for food?
Few, if any, of the poachers really need to kill to eat, but they apparently regard poaching as a cheap and fairly easy means of procuring food. In a small percentage of cases animals are poached for trophies.

As was the case of the hyena mentioned earlier, animals are also poached for reasons of witchcraft. Crocodile fat and some of the organs are regarded as potent medicine for different ailments.

Are many of these poachers brought to justice?
About 50 convictions per year are recorded, with the average fine in the region of R150. Maximum fines could be much higher, depending on the circumstances. When poachers use a vehicle and a rifle, both items are confiscated.

Do Park employees and poachers often clash?
Poachers can be extremely dangerous and a number of Park employees have been killed with knives, axes and firearms. Fatalities have been suffered on both sides in skirmishes. Armed poachers usually do not hesitate to act violently and Park employees are in grave danger when they pursue or try to corner poachers.

Have poachers been killed by their victims?
It is not uncommon for a wild animal to break loose from a snare or a trap. The animal then takes flight or may attack its human enemy. In 1978 the remains of a poacher were found near a snare. He apparently went to inspect his snares when he was surprised and almost totally devoured by lions.

ANIMALS OF THE KRUGER NATIONAL PARK

CHACMA BABOON *Papio ursinus* (Kerr, 1792)

What is the distribution?
Papio ursinus orientalis (Goldblatt, 1926), which is dark in colour, is found in suitable habitats all over the Park except in the Pafuri area where it is replaced by the lighter coloured *Papio ursinus griseipes* (Pocock, 1911).

Are baboons well distributed in other parts of Africa?
The chacma baboon (*Papio ursinus*) inhabits extensive areas throughout southern Africa. The genus *Papio* is restricted to Africa.

How many baboons are there in the Kruger National Park?
It is not easy to count them but it is conservatively estimated that there could be some 4 000 animals in about 123 troops throughout the Park (according to the 1990 aerial survey).

What is the average size of a troop?
The number of individuals in a troop varies from 10 to 100 or more. The average size of a troop in the Park is 30 to 40 individuals.

What are their major physical features?
Baboons are medium-sized members of the order of Primates. The male, with a mass of 27 to 44 kg, is about twice the size of the female, which normally has a mass of 15 to 18 kg. The males also have much longer canine teeth than the females.

Are baboons intelligent?
Baboons are very cunning and intelligent, and their behaviour can be very human, making them most interesting animals to watch. Their proud, arrogant way of walking, with the tail in a swaggering loop, is impressive – and even hilarious at times!

Do baboons only live in troops or do some of them lead a solitary life?
Baboons are gregarious and have very strong social ties. They are very dependent on the protection afforded by numbers, and solitary animals are very seldom encountered. Males may, however, change from one troop to another.

Do they have a specific leader?
There is more than one dominant male in a troop, but there is always a supreme leader. A very strict hierarchical order is maintained.

How is the dominance amongst males established?
Fierce fights for leadership ensue from time to time, but dominance depends mostly on bluff. Baboons are masters of the art of bluffing and intimidation.

How do they go about this bluffing game?
A dominant male often intimidates others by a show of bravado. He will, for instance, try to get onto higher ground than his opponent, and an anthill often serves this purpose. By making his hair stand on end he also appears bigger and stronger. Chasing around members of lower rank in the troop is another way of intimidating them. This behaviour is accompanied

by grunts and barks and is meant to frighten potential rivals as well as lower-ranked baboons. He also shows intimidatory behaviour by running around barking and breaking branches from trees and shrubs.

Do males often kill each other in fights?
If every confrontation had to lead to a serious fight, mortality would be unnecessarily high. Natural selection provides the answer in the form of a ritual of bluffing and intimidation as mentioned above. Even if it comes to a real fight, the loser can still save his life by becoming submissive. This he does by presenting his hindquarters to his victor, a gesture which is usually accepted. Threats from a superior can also be warded off in this manner. But males do kill each other occasionally.

Is there also a dominance hierarchy amongst other members of the troop?
Dominance exists among females and juveniles as well. A female could temporarily dominate a rival female when she is accompanied by a dominant male during the few days she is on heat. Her male escort will intimidate other females that normally dominate her.

If a female dominates another female, her child will try to intimidate another grown-up female as long as his mother is nearby.

Does the mother's dominance affect her offspring?
In most cases, yes. Her dominance is based on her physical strength and self-confidence. When she mates with a dominant male her offspring has a very good chance of inheriting

dominating traits. Her confidence also encourages her young to act in a self-assured way. A mother low in the hierarchical order is usually more nervous and because she often yields to others in the troop, her young may adopt the same submissive attitude.

Do some baboons act as sentries?
It is alleged that baboons use sentries to warn a troop of danger but there is still no indisputable proof of an organized system of sentries. Baboons are very inquisitive by nature and for this reason members of the troop will from time to time climb a tree or rock to survey the surroundings. Individuals therefore act on their own accord in the capacity of sentries. Communication by sounds and 'body language' among baboons is highly developed and danger signals are therefore very effectively transmitted by a 'sentry' to the troop.

Are baboons territorial animals?
Each troop has its area and intruders are actively driven away. Troops in adjoining territories often threaten each other at the boundaries of their territories. They seldom really get to grips but usually hold their respective grounds in extensive rituals of bluff and even by chasing one another to and fro over the boundary.

For instance, troop A would cross the boundary and chase troop B for some distance into the latter's territory. The deeper they penetrate this territory the more they lose their confidence, while troop B gains more confidence and then reverses the chase. Territorial animals become bolder the nearer they get to the centre of their territory.

Where do baboons sleep at night?
They sleep in big trees, on rock ledges or in caves which are virtually inaccessible to most other animals. Even leopards find it difficult to reach them or surprise them in these abodes.

Are baboons active only in the day?
Baboons are diurnal and normally do not move around at night.

Will baboons defend their young against predators or human beings?
A baboon in a dangerous situation will usually escape if given the opportunity and space to do so. However, a cornered baboon will attack, and if a young one is being threatened by a predator or disturbed by a human being, the adult males will attack fiercely. Under such circumstances they are so dangerous that many a predator will be forced to keep clear. It is said that a leopard often has to retreat after killing a young baboon, waiting for the troop to leave before it can claim its prey.

Do they always take refuge in trees when put to flight?
Not always. They often scamper along the ground. It is interesting to note that if baboons are in an isolated tree they will leave the tree if a human being approaches. If you drive up to the tree in a motor vehicle and park below it, the baboons will literally fall out of the tree screaming and barking their discontent. Once on the ground they run away immediately.

Is the connection between mother and child very strong?
A baboon female is an excellent mother. During the first week or two she will not allow any other member of the troop even to touch her baby. Later she will allow other females to cuddle her baby and let juveniles play with it. The mothers are very devoted to their young and will defend them fiercely. Males are even more aggressive in this respect.

It is said that a baboon mother sometimes carries a dead baby for days on end. Is it true?
If an infant dies, the mother often carries the tiny corpse with her for a week or more, despite its advanced decomposition.

Are baboons nomadic?
They are not seasonal nomads but they will move away if food and/or water supplies become scarce in a given area. However, they normally live near permanent water where food is usually abundant, even in winter.

Are baboons' senses well developed?
They have keen binocular eyesight, good hearing and a fair sense of smell.

What habitats do baboons prefer?
They prefer a fairly open savanna ranging from sub-desert to light woodland, and are also found in riverine forests and rocky and mountainous country. The chacma baboon does not occur in rain forests or open grasslands.

What do they eat?
The baboon's omnivorous diet includes roots, tubers, fruit, berries, insects, scorpions and birds' eggs, and occasionally they attack and kill small antelope or lambs. In spite of this, game animals generally show no fear of baboons. The predation on young antelope may be due to a deficiency of proteins and usually occurs during periods of drought or at the end of winter, when food is scarcer.

Do they have a specific breeding time?
There is no fixed breeding season but there appears to be a birth peak during the summer months.
A single baby is usually born after a gestation period of 6 to 7 months. Twins are rare.

Why are the backsides of some baboons so swollen?
When a female baboon comes into season the bare reddish patches on either side of her tail become immensely swollen and bright pink in colour. After ovulation the swelling subsides.

Do baboons mate indiscriminately?
At the start of her oestrus cycle the female will allow any male to mate with her, but at the time of actual ovulation she will only mate with a dominant male. This behaviour has obvious advantages for the survival of the fittest of the species.

What is the lifespan of a baboon?
It is claimed to be about 18 years.

What are their major enemies?
The leopard is believed to be their major enemy, but lions apparently also kill quite a number of baboons. The sight of any one of these big cats causes hysterical outcries and grunts

from the baboons. On retreating to safety, they will keep the enemy in sight as long as possible. Other enemies include eagles, which kill young baboons, as well as pythons, poisonous snakes – of which baboons have an instinctive fear – crocodiles and possibly even caracals.

Can baboons get bilharzia?
Bilharziasis, caused by *Schistosoma mattheei*, has been recorded among the baboon population of the Park. Although human beings are usually infected by *S. mansoni*, *S. haematobium* or *S. japonicum*, they are also susceptible to *S. mattheei*. It is interesting to note that baboons in East Africa can be infected by *S. mansoni* and *S. haematobium*.

To what other diseases are baboons susceptible?
There's a high incidence of pleuritis and a pulmonary disease caused by mites entering the air passages and lungs.

Although indications of arteriosclerosis of the aorta and the coronary arteries have been found in 40% or more of the population, this still appears to be a minor disease confined to adults.

A mild form of nephritis occurs and quite a number of baboons show minor kidney lesions caused by this disease.

Tapeworms (*Bertiella studeri*) are found in about a quarter of the population, while other worm parasites such as the *Desophagostomum* species are found in more than 80%.

A number of parasitic and probably also some virus diseases can be transmitted from the baboon to man – one of several good reasons why these primates should rather be left alone by humans than interfered with.

What other members of the primate order are found in the Park?
Besides the chacma baboon (*Papio ursinus*) and the vervet monkey (*Cercopithecus aethiops*), the lesser bushbaby (*Galago moholi*), the thick-tailed bushbaby (*Otolemur crassicaudatus*) and the samango monkey (*Cercopithecus mitis*) are also found in the Kruger National Park.

Primates are not well represented in southern Africa – probably due to a scarcity of rain forests – and the great apes such as the gorilla (*Gorilla gorilla*) and chimpanzee (*Pan troglodytes*) are totally absent from this region.

VERVET MONKEY *Cercopithecus aethiops* (Linnaeus, 1758)

What is the distribution?
Vervet monkeys are distributed in suitable habitats throughout the Park as well as the northern and eastern parts of South Africa. Wooded or savanna country close to water is preferred, and they are more arboreal than their cousins, the baboons.

How do monkeys differ from baboons?
They are much smaller, light greyish in colour with relatively longer tails. Their tails, like those of baboons, are not prehensile, as are the tails of many of the New World monkeys. The Afrikaans name 'blou-aap' is probably derived from the brilliant greenish-blue colour of the scrotum.

What is their general behaviour?
In many respects their behaviour is like that of baboons. They are sociable, with a hierarchy like baboons, and gregarious. The troop is generally smaller in size, comprising some 15 to 30 individuals, but can occasionally be as large as 50 or more. Males stay with the troop until they are about four years old when they are chased off by the leader. They are extremely cunning and can be destructive on farms and in gardens.

Monkeys show territorial behaviour and will not move away unless forced to do so by a scarcity of food.

Where do they sleep?
They sleep huddled up together near the tops of large trees.

How well are their senses developed?
Like baboons they have very keen eyesight and a good sense of hearing and sense of smell.

Are they dangerous to humans?
When fed they become aggressive and their formidable canines can inflict serious wounds. A large male can give a good account of himself when attacked by a dog.

What do they eat?
They are omnivorous. As well as seeds, fruit and other vegetable matter, they eat eggs, nestling birds, insects and spiders. Growing crops, especially maize, are also relished. When fed near a farm house they can become a nuisance and will try to enter and raid the house for food.

Are they intelligent?
They are very intelligent and cunning, but highly strung and very nervous by nature. In the wild they have a gentle disposition. It is easy to tame them but this is a dangerous practice because they can become very treacherous when mature. They should therefore not be kept as pets. A special permit is needed to keep them in captivity, but this practice is not recommended at all.

What is the gestation period?
It is about 7 months. One young is usually born and twins are rare. Babies are born at any time of the year, but there appears to be a peak during December and January.

What is their lifespan?
It is considerably less than that of the baboon, possibly up to 12 years.

What are their major enemies?
Leopards and other smaller members of the felid family. When the monkeys spot a leopard they become almost hysterical and will follow its prowling movements, barking and coughing at it from the trees. In this way they make the presence of the enemy known to other animals. Leopards probably kill quite a number of monkeys as they sleep huddled together in large trees.

Eagles, particularly Crowned Eagles, and pythons also take their toll. When an eagle is spotted, its arrival is signalled from the tops of the trees.

Are there samango monkeys in the Park?
The samango monkey (*Cercopithecus mitis*) was previously not a permanent resident of the Park but has now been re-introduced. These monkeys also occur in northern Zululand, Mozambique and eastern Zimbabwe.

How do samangos differ from vervets?
Samangos are slightly bigger than vervets and have longer, darker fur. The face is dark brown rather than white, and more than two thirds of the long tail is black.

They are shy and elusive animals, not as noisy as the vervets, and they prefer evergreen montane or riverine forests. The troops are usually smaller than those of vervets, often consisting only of a family group. Samangos and vervets seldom share the same habitat and the former are less destructive to farm crops and gardens than vervets.

Little is known about the samango's feeding habits but it subsists primarily on seeds, wild fruit, leaves, insects and birds' eggs.

THICK-TAILED BUSHBABY   *Otolemur crassicaudatus* (Geoffroy)

What is the distribution?
There are six species of bushbaby, or Galago, all confined to Africa. The Thick-tailed bushbaby is restricted to the far-eastern parts of South Africa and it is sparsely distributed throughout the Kruger National Park, with a greater concentration appearing in the Pafuri area.

Are these animals often seen?
These primates are nocturnal, and are naturally secretive, so they are not often seen by visitors to the Park.

What are their characteristic features?
The Thick-tailed bushbaby, largest of the *Galago*-type bushbabies, sometimes attains a weight of 2 kg, and males may grow to a total length of 74 cm (including the tail). When seen on the ground, the Thick-tailed bushbaby is superficially cat-like, but its hindquarters are higher than its shoulder region and its long tail is held erect, so its stance reminds one of a lemur. The fur and tail are woolly. There are five digits on both hands and feet, all provided with nails, except for the second digit on the hindfoot which has a long, curved claw that is used to groom the fine greyish, soft fur. Its eyes are large and conspicuous, as are its ears.

What are their habits?
Thet are primarily nocturnal and arboreal, and live in small groups of 2 to 6 animals. They forage on their own. Their daytime resting- and hiding-places are scent-marked with a secretion from a gland on their chests, and they dribble urine onto their hands and feet and tread it into the branches of the well-foliated trees that they frequent.

What do they eat?
Thick-tailed bushbabies subsist on wild fruit and the gum exuded from trees. They also take insects, an occasional lizard or a fledgling bird.

What is known about their reproduction?
Mating takes place during June or July and births occur during summer. Usually two young are born after a gestation period of some 130 days.

Can you hear bushbabies in the Park?
Yes, their presence is revealed by a loud, screaming call that resembles a human baby in distress. This may explain why they are commonly known as 'bushbabies'.

LESSER BUSHBABY *Galago Moholi* (A Smith, 1836)

What is the distribution?
In South Africa, these attractive little fellows are restricted to the northern and north-eastern parts of the country. You will find them sparsely distributed throughout the Kruger National Park, with greater numbers in *Acacia* woodland savanna and in riverine woodland.

How do we recognise the animal?
This nocturnal species is seen more often than the Thick-tailed bushbaby. It is considerably smaller than the latter, averaging 150 g in weight, and reaching 30 to 40 cm in total length (including the tail). Its fur is fine and woolly, and it has a fluffy tail. The Lesser bushbaby's ears are large and very mobile. It can move them to help locate the barely audible sounds made by the insects upon which it preys. Its limbs are relatively long and its legs are powerful, which makes the animal a very effective leaper. This ability is enhanced by its large eyes and excellent vision that facilitates landing in the right place, even in the dark. The second digit of the hindfoot is endowed with a claw (instead of a nail) which is used to groom the fur.

What are their habits?
Lesser bushbabies live in areas that are divided up by the complex and rather rigid rules that are characteristic of their society. Top-ranking animals are known as territorial or *alpha* males. They have well-developed glands on the scrotal and throat skin, resulting in a smelly coat, while their urine also has a distinct odour.

A subordinate class of *beta* males (less smelly and usually smaller) are tolerated in *alpha* male territory, as long as they remain submissive. Sooner or later, after migrating up to 2 km (or more) away from their place of birth, many of the *beta* individuals find a place where they can set themselves up as *alpha* males.

Lesser bushbabies mark their home range by urinating on their hands and feet, and treading it onto the branches of trees. Groups occupy home ranges of about 3 ha in extent.

When do they reproduce?
A female may have two litters per season, with the second born in late summer. The gestation period lasts some 121 to 124 days. Usually, two young are born, in nests lined with freshly-picked leaves.

What noises do they make?
This species has a wide range of vocalizations, varying from a low croaking to chittering.

Where do they spend the daylight hours?
They hide away in dense foliage or in holes in tree trunks. Some 2 to 8 animals may sleep together, but they usually forage on their own.

What do they eat?
Gum or the sap exuded by trees is an important dietary component, but they also eat insects which they catch with their agile little hands.

Lesser bushbabies also consume wild fruits and growing buds of vegetation.

BUSHPIG *Potamochoerus porcus* (Linnaeus, 1758)

What is the distribution?
Bushpigs are found in the eastern
Cape Province, Natal and the
Transvaal, Namibia, Botswana,
Mozambique, Zimbabwe and parts of
East and Central Africa. The Park
population belongs to the subspecies
P. p. koiropotamus (Desmoulins, 1831).
In the Park, the highest concentration
is found along the Luvuvhu River and
in the riparian forest along the
Limpopo River.

What type of habitat do bushpigs prefer?
Dense bush and forest, particularly
near rivers, are preferred.

What do they eat?
Although vegetable matter
predominates in their diet, these omni-
rous animals also devour birds' eggs,
reptiles, insects and carrion.

What are their main physical features?
Bushpigs look very much like their
domestic counterparts but have more
body hair and an erectile crest of long
hair along the head, neck and
shoulders. This crest is dirty white in
colour, with black hairs mixed in, and
the flanks are reddish brown to dark
brown or even black. The ears are
pointed; the tail is tufted, but when the
bushpig is running it does not hold the
tail erect as the warthog does. The
tusks, or canine teeth, are much
smaller than those of the warthog, but
are very sharp and therefore
dangerous weapons.
 The body mass is approximately
60 kg, with a shoulder height 75 cm.

Are bushpigs solitary or gregarious?
They are gregarious and run
in sounders comprising 5 to 10
individuals or more.
 Solitary animals also occur, as
well as bachelor groups.

Do they have a social hierarchy?
A hierarchy exists among boars and
it accords the most dominant one
the best food sources and
mating privileges.

Are they territorial in habit?
According to Astley Maberly (1967)
they are territorial animals and
intolerant of intruders. On the other
hand, their territory could shift to
some extent due to the availability of
food. Dorst and Dandelot (1972) refer
to a large home range rather than a
specific territory.

Where and when can one see bushpigs?
To some extent they are rare in the
Kruger National Park, and owing to
their habitat preference and nocturnal
habits are seldom seen by visitors or
even rangers. The most likely place to
see bushpigs in the Park is in the
Pafuri area.

Are they clumsy animals?
Their physical appearance might
suggest that they are cumbersome, yet
they are fleet-footed and surprisingly
strong swimmers.

What sounds do they make?
They grunt and squeal very much like
domestic pigs and, unlike warthog,
often grunt continuously as they feed.

Do they cause damage to crops?
Bushpigs are very destructive to
cultivated crops, devouring large
quantities and trampling even more
underfoot. They will, for instance,
scrape the soft stem of a papaw tree
until the tree falls over so that they can
get at the fruit. Crops such as carrots
and potatoes are uprooted and
relished by the animals.

Where do they hide during the day?
Usually in dense undergrowth.

Are they dangerous to man?
Although bushpigs will normally flee
from human beings, they will not
hesitate to charge when cornered or
wounded. The boars are particularly
courageous and will often charge dogs
on sight, especially when there are
piglets in the sounder. Their short
tusks are very sharp and can cause
slash wounds. A dog has little or no
chance against an infuriated boar.
Cases have been reported where a
leopard has come off second best in an
encounter with a bushpig.

What are their breeding habits?
The majority of piglets are probably
born during the rainy season, which
lasts from about September to March.
In areas with a high rainfall and
sufficient food throughout the
year, birth peaks might be small or
even absent.

Three to six young per litter
appears to be the average. The piglets
are dark brown with pale yellow or
buff longitudinal stripes, which
disappear when the piglets are about
three months old.

What are their major enemies?
Leopards are probably their most
important natural enemies. The
leopard usually pounces on its victim
and then retires to a tree as quickly as
possible to escape the wrath of the
bushpigs.

According to Pitman (1944), lions
became confirmed bushpig killers in
parts of Zambia and Uganda. This,
however, is exceptional, as bushpigs
are generally not plentiful in typical
lion country.

WARTHOG *Phacochoerus aethiopicus* (Pallas, 1776)

What is the distribution?
Warthogs occur throughout most of
the savanna regions of Africa and are
well represented in the Kruger
National Park by the subspecies *P. a.
sundevalli* (Lonnberg, 1908). They are
particularly abundant in the Satara,
Skukuza and Crocodile Bridge areas.

What type of habitat do they prefer?
Warthogs prefer open savanna and are
fond of water, but strangely enough
are also found in areas where open
water is absent for several months of
the year.

What do they eat?
They live predominantly on grass but
also root for grass rhizomes and eat
bark and wild fruits. They kneel to
root for underground food, their
'knees' becoming calloused in the
process (Smithers, 1986).

Are warthogs also destructive to crops?
They do damage crops but as a rule
are not as destructive as the bushpig.

Are they dependent on water?
They like water and mud to wallow in
but if necessary can do without water
for long periods by eating bulbs and
tubers.

What are the main physical features?
In contrast to the hairy coat of the
bushpig, the warthog appears naked
except for a long crest of bristly hairs
down the back of the neck to the
shoulders and very sparse short hairs
along the back and the flanks. The
general skin colour is grey but could
appear quite different, depending on
the colour of the mud in which the
animal last wallowed. The head is
large, with huge, widely curved upper
tusks or canines. Large wart-like
protuberances project laterally from
the flattened face (two pairs in the case
of boars and a single pair in sows) and
the eyes are situated high on the face.
The long, thin tail has a tuft of dark
hairs at the tip. The tail is held upright
when the warthog runs.

The body mass is 80 to 90 kg for
males and 55 to 70 kg for females.
Dorst and Dandelot (1972), however,
quote a mass of up to 136 kg for a
large boar. Sizes probably vary in
different parts of the range. The
shoulder height is about 75 cm for
a male and slightly less for a female.

What is the origin of the name?
The wart-like protuberances must
have led to the name. These 'warts' are
not real warts and are not pathological
in origin.

What length can the tusks attain?
A length of more than 60 cm could be
attained by the upper tusks, while the
lower tusks are seldom more than 15
cm long.

What is the purpose of such large tusks?
The size of the tusks obviously has
survival value for the animal. Roots,
bulbs and tubers are dug out with the
upper tusks, while the very sharp
lower tusks are used for fighting and
self-defence. It is interesting to note

that the upper and lower tusks rub against each other in such a way that the lower ones are kept sharp. The tusks of the sow are considerably smaller than those of the boar.

Are warthogs dangerous to man?
They will usually flee from humans, but when at bay or wounded they may become dangerous.

Are they gregarious?
Warthogs usually run in family groups of less than 10 individuals, consisting of a male, a female and the piglets of one or two successive litters. Old boars can become solitary.

Are the senses well developed?
The sense of sight appears to be poor, but the senses of hearing and smell seem to be acute.

Are they diurnal?
Warthogs are mainly diurnal, in contrast to the nocturnal bushpigs. They sometimes feed on moonlit nights and where they are hunted may become more nocturnal than diurnal. On very hot days they often lie in old antbear burrows or a secluded, shady place.

Do warthogs make sounds?
Although normally silent, they occasionally utter soft grunts to maintain group contact as they feed. They give a long-drawn grunt of alarm when startled and will snarl and snort when defending themselves (Goss, 1986).

Are they plentiful in the Park?
They are common in the Park and are often seen by visitors.

Do they live in burrows?
They often live in burrows and readily retreat to them when pursued by predators. They are very sensitive to low temperatures and require the warm shelter provided by the hole.

How does a warthog enter a burrow?
It has the peculiar habit of swinging round when it reaches the burrow so that it can enter backwards. In this position it can defend itself against most of its enemies, as its back is covered and the predator has to reckon with its dangerous tusks.

Can they run fast?
They are deceptively fast and can reach a speed of 50 to 55 km/h.

Are warthogs territorial in habit?
They are not strictly territorial but do have a home range. The availability of food, and to a lesser extent water, determines the size and locality of the home range. Fighting for dominance between boars and subsequent mating opportunities takes place during April and May.

Are the warthogs that can be seen in some rest camps tame animals?
They are to some extent used to the presence of human beings but are not really tame. People, and especially children, feeding them have been seriously injured. Left alone, they will seldom become aggressive towards Park visitors.

Why do they run with their tails erect?
It appears to be a way of keeping contact between the piglets and their mother, as well as between adults.

Does their wallowing in the mud serve a specific purpose?
When the mud dries on the skin and falls or is rubbed off, the warthogs get rid of ectoparasites such as ticks and insects. At the same time the mud covering affords protection against stinging flies.

Warthog meat is supposed to be delicious. Is this true?
All African predators (including man) seem to savour warthog flesh.

What are their breeding habits?
The average litter consists of four piglets, usually born between October and December. The gestation period is 167 to 175 days, and the mother usually gives birth in an old aardvark hole. A ratio of 112,6 juveniles per 100 adult females pertaining to August-October 1990 is suggested by the 1990 aerial survey. Survival of piglets seems to be better in the southern half of the Park than in the area north of the Olifants River (Mason, 1991).

What are their major enemies?
Lion, leopard, cheetah and wild dogs are the warthog's major enemies, although fully grown boars are rather difficult customers for any of these predators.

ANTELOPES – GENERAL

How many different species of antelope occur in the Park?

There are 22 different ruminant species in the Kruger National Park.

They are: suni, steenbok, Sharpe's grysbok, red duiker, common duiker, oribi, klipspringer, mountain reedbuck, reedbuck, grey rhebok, impala, bushbuck, nyala, kudu, eland, waterbuck, tsessebe, Lichtenstein's hartebeest, blue wildebeest, roan antelope, sable and buffalo.

Are antelope well adapted for survival in the wild?

The antelopes in southern Africa are mostly adapted to savanna and even more open types of habitat. They possess sharp vision with a wide angle of view, and their senses of hearing and smell are superb.

Antelope are also very fleet-footed, and some are so big and powerful that as adults they have few enemies apart from lions.

If their vision is so sharp, why do they fail to recognize humans in a motor vehicle?

Antelopes, like most other animals, recognize human beings by their upright stance. Their lack of binocular vision may further impair their ability to recognize a person in a vehicle, when only his head and part of his shoulders are visible.

Antelopes also rely to a large extent on the movement of an object to detect it. Most predators make use of this phenomenon and, by freezing during a stalk, manage to get close enough to the animal for an attack.

Are antelopes very dependent on water for survival?

Some species, such as the waterbuck, are very dependent on water; the impala less so, while the steenbok can probably exist without water for months on end.

Most antelopes, however, will drink readily if water is available. In general, antelopes are adapted to survive in drought conditions. Water is efficiently extracted from their food; they do not sweat much and their faeces are usually deposited as dry pellets.

Are antelopes territorial in habit?

All antelopes show some kind of territorial behaviour. Some, such as klipspringers, may actively defend a territorium, while others live in preferred areas called home ranges. Many antelopes use scent glands to mark their territories or home ranges.

Do the males often kill rivals in territorial fights?

Fighting behaviour is highly ritualized, relying on displays of aggression, and many fights are avoided by one male out-bluffing his opponent. Even in real fights, relatively few combatants are killed.

Do antelopes and other herbivores know when a lion is not hungry?

Herbivores maintain certain flight or escape distances from their enemies. This distance varies from species to species, or even amongst members of the same species. Larger animals usually have a shorter flight distance than smaller species.

It is difficult to determine whether herbivores actually know when a lion is hungry or not. When herbivores have an enemy in sight they are not unduly alarmed because they can maintain a safe flight distance. But they tend to become very nervous when they hear or smell a predator without being able to locate it visually.

What is the general lifespan of an antelope?
Claims for longevity vary considerably. Some authors base their claims on lifespan in captivity, while others attempt to estimate what it could be in the wild. To establish average lifespans is very difficult. Factors such as the influence of different habitats, number of enemies, incidence of diseases and climatic conditions all play a part in an animal's survival.

In general, small antelopes live 5 to 10 years, medium-sized antelopes 10 to 15 years and large ones up to 20 years or slightly more. They also live longer in captivity than in the wild, where they are subjected to predation, diseases and food shortages.

Do springbok and gemsbok occur in the Kruger National Park?
No, they prefer the drier and more open parts of South Africa. To the best of our knowledge, these antelopes were never indigenous to the Lowveld.

To keep the Park natural, only animals which previously occurred in the area are re-introduced, if necessary.

Have any antelopes been introduced into the Park?
Oribi, red duiker, mountain reedbuck, grey rhebok, Lichtenstein's hartebeest, roan antelope, eland and suni have been translocated to the Park from areas where they still exist in fair numbers.

Were all these antelopes extinct in the Kruger National Park?
No, only oribi, grey rhebok and Lichtenstein's hartebeest were extinct. The others were translocated to the Park to strengthen the numbers of existing populations. Lichtenstein's hartebeest became extinct as a result of hunting during the last century, and oribi became extinct in about 1943. Suni were thought to exist in small numbers in the Nyandu bush in the remote north-eastern border area of the Park. To supplement their small numbers, suni were translocated from northern Natal during 1979 and 1981. All the antelope species previously found in the area are now represented in the Park.

Will more antelopes be translocated to the Park?
Yes, this would be done if the need should arise to augment the numbers of the rarer species.

Which antelope is the biggest?
The eland (*Taurotragus oryx*), with a mass of about 700 kg, is the largest antelope in southern Africa. The Lord Derby eland (*Taurotragus derbianus*) is the largest antelope in the world, with a mass of up to 1 000 kg and a shoulder height of up to 2 m. It is found in Cameroon, Nigeria, Ghana and Togo.

Which is the smallest?
In southern Africa there are two tiny antelopes, the suni (*Neotragus*

moschatus) and the blue duiker (*Cephalophus monticola*). Most authors regard the suni, at 3 to 8 kg, as the smallest.

One of the suni family, the Royal antelope found in Ghana and Sierra Leone, is the smallest in the world. It is said to have a mass of 3 to 4 kg and a shoulder height of 25 cm.

Which is the fastest antelope?
It is commonly believed that members of the hartebeest family are the fastest, and speeds of up to 80 km/h have been claimed.

The speed of wild animals is a controversial topic and exaggerations are the rule rather than the exception. How does one measure a wild animal's speed accurately? Are the speeds claimed for different animals a record, or just a rough estimate? Has any species of wild animal ever been tested thoroughly, in other words was a representative sample of the population tested by a foolproof method?

The common method of chasing an animal with a vehicle only gives a rough estimate of the speed of that particular animal.

Which antelope is the best jumper?
Of the African antelopes, the impala is probably the champion long jumper, with a reputed leap of approximately 10 m. The springbok can jump higher than the impala and it is claimed that it can clear 3 m.

Are there any gazelles in the Park?
No. The only gazelle species that occurs in southern Africa is the springbok, which isn't found in the Park.

What is the difference between a gazelle and an antelope?
Gazelles belong to a sub-group of the antelope family and are mostly confined to the more open savannas and grasslands. They are fleet-footed and usually possess lyre-shaped horns.

Is the deer family found in the Park?
No deer are found naturally in Africa south of the Sahara.

How do antelopes and deer differ from each other?
Antelopes have horns, bony structures consisting of an inner core of porous bone covered by an impervious bony sheath. The horns are unbranched, never shed, and if broken are never replaced. Deer have antlers which are branched structures of solid bone shed annually.

Can antelopes be dangerous to man?
Astley Maberly gives the answer: 'Like roan, sable are courageous and high-spirited, very dangerous and apt to charge when wounded or bayed.' Gemsbok and bushbuck are also dangerous when wounded. A few hunters have been killed by bushbuck.

Which antelope is regarded as the most beautiful in Africa?
Most people regard the sable as the most magnificent of the African antelopes. The kudu and the gemsbok, however, are also strong candidates.

Do the antelopes migrate in the Park?
Although wildebeest move seasonally, large-scale migrations such as those that occur in Serengeti do not occur in the Kruger National Park.

SUNI *Neotragus moschatus* (Von Dueben, 1846)

What is the distribution?

Suni, or Livingstone's Antelope, are extremely rare in the Kruger National Park, and are confined to the far north-eastern part. During 1979 and 1981 a number of them were translocated to the Park from northern Natal. However, due to their habits and small numbers, visitors are not likely to see them. The Park population belongs to the subspecies *N. m. zuluensis* (Thomas, 1898). These tiny antelope are also found in parts of Mozambique and eastern Zimbabwe.

What type of habitat do suni prefer?

They generally prefer dry country with thick bush, but are also found in dense vegetation along rivers. They are always associated with dense cover.

What do they eat?

They are mainly browsers. Most of their moisture requirements are obtained metabolically from the food they eat and they are therefore fairly independent of free water.

What are the main physical features?

The shoulder height is 33 to 38 cm and the average mass about 5 kg. The colour is dull fawn to a rich chestnut, with white-tipped hairs giving it a slightly speckled appearance. The horns, borne only by the males, have an average length of 8 cm. The tail is fairly long, the upper part being dark brown and the tip white, and it is regularly flicked from side to side (Stuart & Stuart, 1988).

What are the suni's habits?

Suni occur singly, in pairs, or even in small family groups. Territories are marked with a musky secretion from two large facial glands which are situated in front of each eye in the ram. These secretive little antelopes are seldom seen even where they are fairly plentiful.

What are their breeding habits?

A single lamb is born, usually during summer. The gestation period is about 120 days.

What are their major enemies?

Most of the smaller felids, leopards, other carnivores such as jackals, the larger eagles (such as the Crowned Eagle) and pythons all prey upon suni.

STEENBOK *Raphicerus campestris* (Thunberg, 1811)

What is the distribution?
Steenbok are widely spread throughout southern Africa and the subspecies *R. c. capricornis* (Thomas and Schwann), 1906, is well represented in the Park and may be found particularly on the open flats along the Lebombo Mountains.

What habitat do steenbok prefer?
They occur in a variety of habitats, from open plains to open woodlands and thickets, and from undulating terrain to hilly areas.

What do they eat?
Steenbok are predominantly browsers but will also eat roots, tubers and grass. However, they are selective feeders. They will drink water when it is available, but obtain enough moisture from food when it is not.

What are the main physical features?
The steenbok is one of the most beautiful of the small buck. This graceful antelope is rufous brown on the back and sides, with white underparts and white on the inside of the legs. Its eyes and ears are large, and the inside of the ear has a distinct leaf-like pattern of dark blood vessels. Facial glands are visible at the lower edge of the eyes. Their mass is about 11 kg. Only the males have horns, and rams are lighter and smaller in stature than ewes.

What are their habits?
This beautiful antelope is a very clean-living animal and even digs a hole in which it deposits its dung, which it afterwards covers with sand. When walking, it stretches its neck forward to form a straight line along the back. Despite its careful, dainty way of walking it can dash off with surprising speed. It usually runs for about a 100 metres and then stops and veers around to establish whether it is being followed – a dangerous habit if it has been flushed by a hunter.

Steenbok lead solitary lives, except when mating or when a ewe has a lamb. They have well-defined territories which may be some 30 ha in extent – a large area for a small antelope.

What are their breeding habits?
A single lamb is usually born after a gestation period of 5 to 6 months. The young may be born at any time of the year. The mother hides the lamb until it is about three months old.

What are their major enemies?
They are cheetah, leopard, wild dog, hyena, jackal, serval, caracal, Martial eagles and even pythons.

SHARPE'S GRYSBOK *Raphicerus sharpei* (Thomas, 1897)

What is the distribution?
Sharpe's grysbok are found in the northern parts of the Transvaal, Zimbabwe and Mozambique. In the Park they are mostly confined to the Pafuri area and more sparsely to the north and south of the Olifants River.

What type of habitat do Sharpe's grysbok prefer?
They usually inhabit broken, hilly areas, preferring thorny scrub and areas with a low vegetation cover. Visitors seldom see them because of their nocturnal habits and timid ways.

What do they eat?
They are mainly browsers, feeding on leaves, shoots and also fruit, but they eat grass too.

What are the main physical features?
This antelope is slightly smaller and darker in colour than the steenbok. It is chestnut to fawn-coloured, with intermingling white hairs giving it a grizzled appearance. The horns (in rams only) extend vertically from the forehead and are about 36 mm long. The ears are large with light-coloured hair on the inside and dark hairs at the edges. The very short bushy tail is the same colour as the coat. The shoulder height is about 45 cm and the mass some 9 to 12 kg.

What are their habits?
These elusive, shy little antelopes are nocturnal and seldom seen, although they may occasionally emerge on cool, overcast days. Like the steenbok, they are either found singly or in pairs.
    When disturbed they lie quietly until the last moment and then dash away, twisting and turning to avoid obstacles such as rocks, stones or bushes, and not stopping to look back until they feel safe to lie down and hide again.

What are their breeding habits?
According to Stevenson-Hamilton, they have a summer breeding peak, especially in the months of October and November. However, young may be born at any time throughout the year.
    A single lamb is born after a gestation period of 7 months.

What are their major enemies?
Wild dog, jackal, cheetah, leopard, caracal and hyena are probably their most important enemies.

RED DUIKER *Cephalophus natalensis* (A Smith, 1834)

What is the distribution?
Red duiker occur in Natal, Swaziland, Eastern Transvaal and the southern parts of Mozambique. In the Park they are confined to the Pretoriuskop area.

What type of habitat do they prefer?
They prefer evergreen bush and a humid forest habitat with ravines overgrown with dense vegetation.

What do red duiker eat?
They are browsers, and also eat wild fruit and berries; grass is also taken on occasion.

What are the main physical features?
Short, ridged horns about 8 cm long are carried by both sexes. The body colour is reddish brown, slightly paler on the underparts, and lacks the flecking of either Sharpe's grysbok or the suni. A typical feature of the species is a well-developed crest of hair between the horns. The ears are small, and the tail is short, with a tuft of dark and white hair. The shoulder height is between 40 and 46 cm and the mass is 12 to 14 kg.

What are their habits?
Although mainly solitary, these small antelopes are also found in pairs or small groups. They are very wary little creatures and expert in threading their way through thickets, especially when escaping from enemies. Because of their secluded habitat and a tendency to be nocturnal, little is really known about them. Communal dung heaps are utilized.

What are their breeding habits?
The gestation period has not been established beyond doubt but could be roughly four months. Lambing seems to occur throughout the year, with a summer peak. A single lamb is born.

What are their major enemies?
Probably leopard, the smaller felids and eagles.

COMMON DUIKER   *Sylvicapra grimmia*   (Linnaeus, 1758)

What is the distribution?
Common duiker are found throughout Africa south of the Sahara, except in the rain forests of central Africa. *Sylvicapra* is probably the antelope genus with the widest distribution and, at 19, the largest number of subspecies in Africa. However, the boundaries between the subspecies are not well defined.

The local population consists of the subspecies *S.g. caffra* (Fitzinger, 1869), which is also found in northern Natal, northern Transvaal, eastern Zimbabwe and southern Mozambique. They are widely distributed in the park.

What type of habitat do they prefer?
They inhabit more or less wooded country, but are the only duiker that also occur in fairly open habitats. In fact they may be found virtually anywhere that provides cover in which to rest.

What do they eat?
They are almost exclusively browsers, feeding on leaves, pods, seeds and wild fruit, but rarely taking grass. They have also been known to take animal matter such as insects and even guineafowl chickens. They are not dependent on a regular water supply (Smithers, 1986).

What are the main physical features?
The colour may vary, from a grizzled grey to a brownish or yellowish fawn. Both sexes have a narrow but conspicuous tuft of long hair on top of the head; in the female, which does not have horns, this sometimes looks like a single horn. The ram's horn is 7 to 15 cm long.

The shoulder height is about 50 cm and the mass is 18 to 20 kg. The female is slightly bigger than the male.

What are their habits?
Like other duiker species, the common duiker is mostly nocturnal, and lies in long grass or thickets during the day. On cool or cloudy days, however, it may be seen at any time of the day. Duikers are found singly or in pairs. They frequent game paths and are therefore often caught in poachers' snares. When fleeing from an enemy, a duiker runs in a characteristic zigzag fashion that is interspersed with plunging leaps – hence the name 'duiker', the Afrikaans for 'diver'. It will seldom run far before stopping to turn around, trying to ascertain the nature of the danger. This most adaptable antelope often survives where other species have been unable to.

What are their breeding habits?
Lambs are born at any time of the year, after a gestation period of three months; there appears to be no specific breeding season. Usually a single lamb is born, and it can actively run within 24 hours of birth. Twins are very rare. Ewes can conceive at the early age of eight or nine months.

What are their major enemies?
Leopard, cheetah, serval, caracal, wild dog, jackal, hyena, eagles and pythons.

ORIBI *Ourebia ourebi* (Zimmermann, 1783)

What is the distribution?
Oribi are found in many nature reserves and are indigenous to grassland areas of the Cape Province, Orange Free State, Natal, Transvaal, Swaziland, parts of Mozambique and the eastern parts of Zimbabwe up to the Zambezi River. The Park population belongs to the subspecies *O. o. ourebi* (Zimmermann, 1783) and is limited to the Pretoriuskop area.

What type of habitat do they prefer?
Although mainly associated with grasslands, the oribi is also found in a variety of other well-watered habitats, including rocky outcrops and fairly open parkland.

What do oribi eat?
They are primarily grazers, but browse occasionally and they are independent of drinking water.

What are the main physical features?
The oribi, the largest of the 'small' antelopes, stands 56 to 66 cm at the shoulder and has a mass of up to 14 kg. Only the males have short (10 cm), straight horns. This handsome antelope is bright rufous-brown with white underparts and has a short bushy tail with a conspicuous black tip. It also has a well-marked, bare glandular spot below each ear.

What are their habits?
Oribi occur in pairs or small groups. When alarmed they start off at a brisk gallop and then proceed with a curious 'stotting' action, jumping into the air with all four legs straight and stiff and displaying the conspicuously black-tipped tail.

During the heat of the day they prefer to lie in long grass.

What are their breeding habits?
A single lamb is born after a gestation period of 210 days, usually during the summer months. The lamb remains hidden for as long as three to four months before joining the group.

What are their major enemies?
Leopard, cheetah, the smaller felids, hyena, wild dogs, jackal, eagles and probably pythons.

KLIPSPRINGER *Oreotragus oreotragus* (Zimmermann, 1783)

What is the distribution?
Klipspringer are found in many localities in southern and eastern Africa, where suitable habitats occur. The subspecies *O. o. transvaalensis* (Roberts, 1917) occurs throughout the Park, with higher concentrations along the eastern boundary to the north of Olifants rest camp, and to the north of Punda Maria.

What type of habitat do they prefer?
They are very specialized in habitat preference and are found only on rocky hills, rocky outcrops and mountains.

What do they eat?
They are mainly browsers. If water is available they drink freely, but if necessary can cope with little water.

What are the main physical features?
The klipspringer is a small, stoutly built antelope with rough spinous hair. The general body colour is more or less greyish brown speckled with yellow, although albinism is not uncommon. The peculiar spinous and brittle-haired coat may afford protection when the klipspringer comes into contact with sharp rocks.
   The shoulder height is 50 to 60 cm and the body mass is approximately 12 kg. Only the males carry short, spiky horns that are about 10 cm long; the record length is 15,88 cm.

What are their habits?
This charming little antelope adopts a most characteristic pose, standing on a boulder with its four hooves bunched together and its back conspicuously arched. It actually stands 'on tiptoe' and its hooves are specially adapted for its rocky habitat. The klipspringer is unbelievably agile and can jump from one rock to another or even run up gradients which appear inaccessible to anything else but a baboon. Although it is often seen poised on rocks or ledges, it may just as frequently be found grazing at the foot of its hilly habitat. They live in small territorial family groups.

What are their breeding habits?
A single lamb is born after a gestation period of seven months. Lambs are born throughout the year.

What are their major enemies?
Leopard, the smaller felids, pythons and the larger eagles are the klipspringer's most important enemies.

MOUNTAIN REEDBUCK *Redunca fulvorufula* (Afzelius, 1815)

What is the distribution?
Although once fairly widespread in suitable habitats, mountain reedbuck are now restricted to a few reserves in Natal and the Orange Free State, the Mountain Zebra National Park in the Cape Province and a number of private farms. In the Park they are confined to the mountainous area near Malelane and the Lebombo foothills just north of the Sabie River.

The local subspecies is *R. f. fulvorufula* (Afzelius, 1815).

What type of habitat do mountain reedbuck prefer?
As the name implies, they prefer a more or less mountainous habitat, especially on slopes where they can take cover among rocks and undergrowth. They shun open grassland and flats.

What do they eat?
They are mainly grazers and are fond of the fresh green shoots that sprout after veld fires. Access to water is essential for the animal.

What are the main physical features?
This small to medium-sized antelope stands about 70 cm at the shoulder and has a mass of 28 to 30 kg. The horns, carried by males only, are generally 13 to 18 cm long, the record length being 25,5 cm.

The body colour is greyish fawn with white underparts, and the neck is yellowish to reddish brown. The mountain reedbuck lacks the black markings on the legs that the reedbuck has. The tail is short and bushy, greyish above and white below.

What are their habits?
These animals are to some extent gregarious and are often found in small groups of up to about 10 individuals.

They are shy animals, usually feeding and showing activity in the early morning and evening. Territorial males occupy territories up to 28 ha in area on a year-round basis. During the dry season they are more active during the day than during the summer months, when they are predominantly nocturnal (Smithers, 1986).

What are their breeding habits?
A single lamb is born mostly from September to March of each year, after a gestation period lasting anything from 236 to 251 days.

What are their major enemies?
Leopard, the smaller cats and, in the case of lambs, jackal and eagles.

REEDBUCK *Redunca arundinum* (Boddaert, 1785)

What is the distribution?
Reedbuck occur in most game reserves and a number of private farms in Natal and the northern half of the Transvaal. The local subspecies is *R. a. arundinum* (Boddaert, 1785). Within the Park they show a fairly wide distribution, but are absent from the area between the Letaba and Olifants rivers. They are probably most abundant in the Pretoriuskop-Malelane area and in the Nshawu valley to the north of Letaba.

What type of habitat do reedbuck prefer?
As the name suggests, they prefer thickly overgrown patches of reeds near vleis, where their buff-coloured coats blend very well with the grassy background. This antelope is very dependent on its particular habitat and when this is destroyed by human interference, drought or fire, the reedbuck suffers severely because exposure makes it easy for it to be run down by dogs and other canids. Sufficient drinking water is another essential requirement.

What do they eat?
The reedbuck is a grazer and particularly partial to young grass.

What are the main physical features?
This antelope stands 84 to 94 cm at the shoulder and attains a mass of up to 70 kg or slightly more. Only the males have horns, which are about 38 cm long, with a record length of 45,7 cm. The ridged horns curve upwards and backwards, with the tips directed forward, and resemble those of the waterbuck in miniature.

The coarse coat is yellowish to reddish brown on the back, but paler on the sides of the head. The belly is white and the tail short, thick and somewhat bushy.

What are their habits?
Reedbuck are seen singly or in pairs and also in small groups of up to six animals. During the heat of the day they tend to lie up in reed-beds or tall grass, usually near water. In the dry season they are more active during the day than they are in the summer months, when they are predominantly nocturnal (Smithers, 1986).

When alarmed or calling each other, reedbuck utter a whistling sound. They run with a distinctive rocking-horse gait, stiffly kicking out the fore- and hindlegs with each leap.

What are their breeding habits?
There appears to be a lambing peak between December and May, but young can also be born at other times of the year. One lamb is born after a gestation period of 235 to 240 days.

What are their major enemies?
Leopard, cheetah, wild dogs, caracal, serval, jackal and probably also hyena.

GREY RHEBOK *Pelea capreolus* (Forster, 1790)

What is the distribution?
Grey rhebok are confined to South Africa, Swaziland and Lesotho. This antelope became extinct in the Kruger National Park and during May 1978 20 animals were translocated from the Golden Gate Highlands National Park and released on the Kandizwe plateau near Malelane.

What habitat do they prefer?
They prefer rocky hills, mountain slopes and good stands of grassland on mountain plateaus.

What do they eat?
Grey rhebok appear to be exclusively grazers by nature.

Do they drink water regularly?
They are able to go without water for long periods.

What are the main physical features?
Grey rhebok are slender, medium-sized antelopes about 75 cm tall at the shoulder, and have a mass of about 20 kg. The males carry horns which are ridged halfway along their length from the base. The record length for the horns is 29,2 cm.

These antelope have a short, thick, woolly coat which is buff-grey to greyish brown in colour, with white underparts. The eyes have a conspicuous white ring around them. The ears are long and narrow, with white hairs on the inside. Unlike the mountain reedbuck and the reedbuck, the grey rhebok has no glands below the ears. They do, however, have glands between the hooves which secrete a light-coloured fluid with an unpleasant odour.

What are their habits?
They may be found in small groups of up to about 12 individuals which comprise an adult ram and a few ewes and lambs. Rams may become solitary. Territorial in habit, they will defend a specific area, and make snorting and groaning noises when marking it off. They are active for most of the day but rest when it becomes hot. They are good jumpers and run with a distinct rocking-horse gait, stiffly kicking out the fore- and hind-legs with each leap.

What are their breeding habits?
One lamb is born after a gestation period of about 261 days. The mating season is around April and the lambs are born during November and December of each year.

What are their major enemies?
Leopards and the smaller felids.

IMPALA *Aepyceros melampus* (Lichtenstein, 1812)

What is the distribution?
Impala are found in south-eastern Angola, Botswana, Zimbabwe, southern Mozambique and the northern parts of the Transvaal and Natal, as well as in Malawi, Zambia, Tanzania and Kenya. The black-faced impala *A. m. petersi* (Bocage, 1879) is confined to the extreme northern area of Namibia and the extreme south-western parts of Angola. The local subspecies is *A. m. melampus* (Lichtenstein, 1812) and is found throughout the Kruger National Park. Larger concentrations are found along perennial rivers.

What type of habitat do impala prefer?
They prefer open bushveld with sufficient water, but are also found in a variety of other habitats. Although found throughout the Park, they are more plentiful in the acacia savanna of the south than in the mopane veld of the north. They avoid areas with long grass and therefore occur only in small numbers in the Pretoriuskop area.

What do they eat?
Impala are both grazers and browsers and the proportion depends on the area and the season (Stuart & Stuart, 1988). They feed during the day and the night and will drink water daily if it is available.

What are the main physical features?
The body mass varies in different areas and could be anything from about 40 to 60 kg, or even more. The shoulder height is approximately 84 to 95 cm. The lyrate horns, carried by the males only, are about 50 cm long, although the record length is 91,76 cm. The glossy body coat is rufous-fawn above, darker along the back and creamy white below. Very characteristic features are the tufts of black hair just above the hooves of the hindlegs, and a vertical black blaze on each buttock.

What are their habits?
Impala are gregarious, very social and occur in herds of 10 to 50 or more. In fact, herds of a few hundred animals are not uncommon, especially during the winter months. They often associate with other herbivores such as blue wildebeest, zebra, giraffe and baboons. They adapt well to overgrazed and trampled areas.

During the breeding season dominant males fight to establish territories and harems of females, which may number anything up to 30 individuals. The males without harems form smaller bachelor herds. A male with a large harem lives a very active life: it is not easy for him to keep the ewes together, fight off other intruding males and, above all, to inseminate the females.

The impala is normally a silent animal, uttering a blast-like snort only when alarmed. During the rutting season – in southern Africa from April to May – the rams utter a loud grunting and snarling sound.

What are their breeding habits?

A single lamb, or occasionally twins, is born from about the end of October to the beginning of February. The gestation period is about 196 days.

What are their major enemies?

Lion, leopard, cheetah, wild dogs, hyena, jackal, caracal, serval, pythons and crocodile.

Is there more than one species of impala in the Park?

Young rams with horn tips pointing inwards give people the impression that there is another subspecies. In the Kruger National Park there is only one subspecies of impala, namely *A. m. melampus* (Lichtenstein, 1812). The 1990 aerial count total of 116 223 impala in the Kruger National Park was 3,6% lower than in 1989.

BUSHBUCK *Tragelaphus scriptus* (Pallas, 1766)

What is the distribution?
This species has a very wide distribution in the Afro-tropical region, being absent from the rain forests and the drier open areas. Bushbuck are found in the whole of the Kruger National Park, where the subspecies *T. s. roualeyni* (Gray, 1852) occurs. They are well-represented in suitable habitats, the largest concentrations being found in the riparian vegetation along the Sabie, Luvuvhu and Limpopo rivers, as well as in dense bush near Pretoriuskop.

What do bushbuck eat?
They are mainly browsers, feeding on leaves, tender shoots, seed pods, tubers and roots. Nevertheless, grass may contribute some 33% of the total food intake.

What are the main physical features?
A bushbuck stands about 80 cm at the shoulder. The ram may attain a mass of 30 to 50 kg. Spiralled, 40-cm sharp-pointed horns are carried by males. The general colour varies from chestnut to dark brown. The white markings comprise a conspicuous 'collar', spots on the cheeks and the flanks, and sometimes stripes on the flanks and the hindquarters.

What are their habits?
Bushbuck live singly or in pairs and occasionally in small family groups. Old rams are solitary in habit and may live in the same area for many years. These antelope are most active at night, but may also be seen in the early morning or late afternoon, often adopting a conspicuous hunched-up stance. They have acute senses of sight and smell and persist in close association with human development.

Rams are extremely pugnacious and brave when wounded or cornered, and may become treacherous and dangerous in captivity.

In areas where bushbuck abound their loud hoarse bark, uttered by both sexes, is a common nocturnal sound.

What are their breeding habits?
A single lamb is born after a gestation period of 180 days. Births occur throughout the year. The lamb follows its mother around after remaining hidden for four months.

What are their major enemies?
Probably leopard, and also wild dogs if they encounter a bushbuck in the open. When danger threatens, bushbuck often take refuge among reeds or move through water to escape.

NYALA *Tragelaphus angasii* (Gray, 1849)

What is the distribution?

Nyala are confined to a few reserves in northern Natal, the northern part of the Kruger National Park, south-eastern Zimbabwe and southern Mozambique. In the Park they are normally not found south of the Olifants River, although some have strayed as far south as the Sabie River.

What type of habitat do they prefer?

They are found in low-lying savanna areas where they frequent dense bush along watercourses. In the Kruger National Park they roam along the Luvuvhu and Shingwedzi rivers and to a lesser extent the banks of the Letaba and Olifants rivers. They are also found in broken mountainous terrain north of Punda Maria and east of Shingwedzi.

What are their habits?

Nyala are usually found in small herds of about 5 animals, occasionally more; a herd of 12 to 15 animals is a rarity. A herd sometimes consists of females and young only, or it may include one or more males. Old males tend to roam singly or in pairs and they are not territorial.

Although feeding normally occurs from late afternoon to early morning, nyala are not strictly nocturnal and may be seen at any time of day. They become very secretive when hunted. Like bushbuck, they have a deep bark and hoarse grunt.

What are their breeding habits?
A single calf is born after a gestation period of just over 220 days. There appears to be a calving peak in spring, in September and October. The calves remain hidden for the first two weeks.

What are the nyala's major enemies?
Leopard, lion and wild dogs appear to be its main enemies. Like the bushbuck, it is a formidable and dangerous quarry.

What do nyala eat?
Although they are mainly browsers, feeding on leaves, pods, fruit and twigs, they also graze to a fair extent.

What are the main physical features?
The nyala is a medium-sized antelope, halfway between the bushbuck and the kudu in size and with similar features of both. The male has a shoulder height of up to 1,12 m and an average body mass of 108 kg, and is a slender, narrow-bodied antelope with a shaggy purplish to slate-coloured coat. Eight to 14 vertical white stripes – sometimes indistinct – run down the sides of the body and there are also a number of white spots. A distinct chevron found between the eyes of the male is absent in the female. A conspicuous crest of long hairs from the occiput to the root of the tail may be raised when the animal is alarmed or frightened. There is also a heavy fringe on the throat and underparts. Orange 'socks' on the lower legs distinguish a young nyala male from a bushbuck ram. Only the males carry the beautiful lyre-shaped horns which may vary from about 56 to 71 cm in length. The record length is 83,5 cm, from an animal shot in Mozambique.

The female, with a shoulder height of 97 cm and an average body mass of 62 kg, is much smaller than the male. Orange-brown in colour with a black stripe down the back, she has more distinct stripes and spots, but no chevron on the forehead.

KUDU *Tragelaphus strepsiceros* (Pallas, 1766)

What is the distribution?
Kudu may be seen in most game reserves and on many farms in South Africa. The species is furthermore distributed throughout northern Natal, the northern parts of Transvaal and the Cape Province, Swaziland, Botswana, Namibia, Zimbabwe, East Africa and as far north as Ethiopia and the Sudan. The subspecies *T. s. strepsiceros* (Pallas, 1766) is evenly distributed throughout the Park.

What type of habitat do they prefer?
They prefer well-wooded savanna or hilly country, usually not far from water. However, they can also exist in very dry areas and their wide distribution implies a wide habitat tolerance.

What do kudu eat?
They are essentially browsers, feeding on leaves, pods, fruits and twigs, but will occasionally also take grass. They are also attracted to burnt areas where they feed on the newly-sprouted herbs and forbs.

What are the main physical features?
This is large, slender and very elegant antelope. The bull stands about 1,4 m at the shoulder and attains a mass of 250 kg, while the cow is much smaller (160 kg) and does not have the massive neck that characterizes the bull. Only the male carries the magnificent spiralled horns. These vary in length from 1,14 to 1,52 m, the

average being 1,2 m, and the record standing at 1,82 m.

The body colour varies from bluish grey to greyish brown and rufous. Cows and calves are more rufous-brown than the bulls. The sides of the body are marked with six to ten vertical white stripes. Bulls have a heavy fringe of hair from the chin to the throat, and both sexes have a mane from the occiput to the root of the tail.

What are their habits?

Kudu associate in small herds of about five to seven animals, although larger herds of six to 20 cows and calves are sometimes encountered. Mature males are usually found in pairs or in groups of up to about six animals, while very old males often become solitary. The call in both sexes is a loud, hoarse bark, that of the bull being deeper and harsher than that of the cow.

When dashing through thick bush, the bull tilts his chin up so that the horns lie back, almost along the shoulders.

Startled animals will flee by running in a zigzag fashion, breaking through thickets with amazing ease. Kudu are very agile jumpers and it is claimed that they can clear a fence higher than 2 m.

Is the kudu dangerous to humans?

Despite their size and formidable horns, kudu are normally inoffensive and rarely charge even in self-defence. Like most other animals, however, their behaviour can be unpredictable in captivity.

What are their breeding habits?

There is a calving peak in March and April. Normally a single calf is born after a gestation period which is usually about 210 days.

What are their major enemies?

Adult bulls are seldom attacked by predators other than lions or occasionally wild dogs.

Females and calves are preyed upon by leopard, cheetah and wild dogs. Very small calves may be attacked by hyena, jackal and the smaller felids. The kudu is also very susceptible to anthrax.

ELAND *Taurotragus oryx* (Pallas, 1766)

What is the distribution?

The eland's range extends over the northern parts of the Cape Province, north-eastern Namibia, most of Botswana, Zimbabwe, the northern part of the Kruger National Park, Mozambique, Tanzania, Kenya, Uganda and southern Sudan.

The subspecies *T. o. oryx* (Pallas, 1766), is represented in the Park and is confined to the area north of the Olifants River. The largest concentrations occur in the well-wooded savanna towards the western boundary of the Park, the open, eastern flats to the north of the Shingwedzi River and between the Luvuhvu and Limpopo rivers. A small population has been resettled near Pretoriuskop. The 1990 aerial census revealed the presence of 744 animals in the Park. Eland are found in many other game reserves, having been re-introduced into a number of them.

What type of habitat do eland prefer?

Savanna, dry forests and open plains are preferred. They can also survive in semi-desert areas where free water could be absent for many months of the year. Where water is available they will drink regularly.

What do they eat?

They are mainly browsers but will also graze on young grass. Eland also eat fruit and use their hooves to dig out bulbs, especially in dry areas.

What are the main physical features?

The eland is very large and bulky, with ox-like features. Bulls can attain a

body mass of 700 kg and cows 460 kg. The shoulder height of bulls varies between 1,5 and 1,9 m, the average being 1,7 m. Horns are carried by both sexes; those of the male are more massive and often shorter than the more slender ones of the cow. The average length of horn for both sexes is about 60 cm, while the record for a bull's horn is 81,9 cm. The horns extend straight back from the back of the skull and are ruggedly twisted and spiralled at the base.

The general body colour is fawn, turning blue-grey with age. The sides of the body can be lightly striped, but the stripes are often so faint that they seem to be absent. A large dewlap with tufts of black hair along the edge is especially prominent on the bull, which also has a short, brown mane on the back of the neck and a mat of dark hair on the forehead.

What are their habits?
Eland are gregarious, forming herds of anything up to a few hundred in areas where they are still abundant. They are usually more timid than the other large antelopes and are very nomadic in nature. Although very wary in the wild, they are easily domesticated. There are several captive herds in South Africa, and Zimbabwe.

Like kudu, eland are very strong jumpers and can clear 2 m – an extraordinary feat for such massively imposing animals.

Are they territorial in habit?
No, they are nomadic and move over large areas.

Could the eland be used for meat production?
Eland could probably produce more meat under drought conditions than cattle, but with intensive feeding cattle still exceed eland in meat production. If eland ever become a viable source of meat, it would probably only be in our arid and semi-desert areas.

What are their breeding habits?
A single calf is born, usually in spring, after a gestation period of 271 days. Twins are rare.

Cows will only suckle their own calves, and the latter grow fast, achieving a mass of 450 kg by the end of their first year.

What are their major enemies?
Lions are the principal enemies of eland but calves fall prey to leopard, cheetah and other predators.

Is the eland a dangerous animal?
The eland is one of the most gentle of wild animals and will seldom charge except when wounded or cornered and threatened by dogs.

WATERBUCK *Kobus ellipsiprymnus* (Ogilby, 1833)

What is the distribution?
Waterbuck occur in the Hluhluwe and Umfolozi game reserves in Natal, in eastern and northern Transvaal, northern Botswana, Mozambique and through to East Africa.

The local population in the Park consists of the subspecies *K. e. ellipsiprymnus* (Ogilby, 1833).

What type of habitat do they prefer?
They are confined to well-watered savanna areas and are usually found reasonably close to water. However, they avoid riparian forest and dense bushveld, preferring areas with medium to tall grass (1 to 1,5 m high) broken topography.

What do they eat?
They are normally grazers but will occasionally browse.

What are the main physical features?
This is a robust antelope with coarse, long hair that is grey to greyish brown in colour. A conspicuous white mark on each buttock jointly forms a white circle around the base of the tail. The long, impressive horns, carried only by the bulls, project backwards, curving upwards, outwards, and finally forward at the tips. Their length varies from 70 to 85 cm, with a record length of 99,7 cm.

The waterbuck's shoulder height is 1,2 to 1,35 m and the mass of an average bull is 250 to 260 kg.

Are waterbuck territorial in habit?
A dominant territorial bull will not tolerate other males in his range, which varies in diameter from 1,2 to 2,8 km throughout the year. The rest of the social organization consists of

nursery herds of female and juveniles and bachelor herds of non-territorial and juvenile males and occasionally juvenile females (Smithers, 1986). The herds, comprising any number from about 10 to 30 animals, tend to fragment during the winter months when food is scarce. According to the 1990 aerial census, some 3 203 waterbuck were counted in the Park.

Do they migrate?
If water is available they will seldom move to another area, and seasonal migrations do not occur.

Can a waterbuck bull be dangerous to a human being?
A wounded or cornered bull will not hesitate to charge and is therefore a dangerous opponent.

What are their breeding habits?
A single calf is usually born and there appears to be a summer calving peak. The gestation period is about 240 days.

It is said that crocodiles do not kill waterbuck. Is it true?
No. They are prey to crocodiles like any other antelope.

Do waterbuck easily take to water when pursued by predators?
They readily take to water when pursued by predators such as wild dogs. In the process they may even submerge their bodies, leaving only their nostrils above water.

Predators usually do not follow them into the water.

Are waterbuck preyed upon by many predators?
Adult bulls are seldom attacked by predators other than lion and crocodiles. Cows and calves are preyed upon by leopard, cheetah and wild dogs. As discussed in the section on lion, these big cats kill many waterbuck.

How do they defend themselves?
They are strong runners, their senses are well developed, and bulls can put up an effective fight when cornered.

Some people claim that their meat is inedible. Is this true?
An oily secretion of the skin gives it a musky smell and, although the meat is not inedible, it is reported to have an unusual taste. It is rarely eaten by man.

TSESSEBE *Damaliscus lunatus* (Burchell, 1823)

What is the distribution?
Tsessebe are found in parts of Zambia, Zimbabwe, Mozambique, Namibia, Botswana and the northern Transvaal. In the Kruger National Park they are mostly restricted to the area north of the Letaba River and represent the subspecies *D. l. lunatus* (Burchell, 1823). A small herd occurs in the Mlondozi area near Lower Sabie and from time to time small groups are also found near Tshokwane.

What type of habitat do they prefer?
These antelope prefer open plains and lightly wooded country. They will drink regularly when water is available but can exist in areas where water is absent for long periods.

What do they eat?
They are mainly grazers.

What are the main physical features?
This fairly large, awkward-looking antelope has a long face and a sloping back. An average bull stands 1,15 to 1,2 m at the shoulder and attains a mass of 140 kg or more. The body colour is reddish brown with a distinct purplish sheen, but the rump is paler and there are dark patches on the thighs and upper front legs.

Both the males and females have rather short, lyre-shaped horns; the horns of the females are shorter than those of the males.

The horns' average length is 30 to 40 cm; the record length is 46,9 cm.

Can tsessebe run fast?
They have the reputation of being the fastest antelopes in the Park, and speeds of up to 60 km/h can be maintained for long stretches. They also possess great stamina and once they break into a steady, bouncing gallop they can continue for many kilometres.

Are they gregarious?
Yes, they are gregarious, forming small herds or family groups numbering about 10 animals. Larger herds may be formed at the end of the dry season. Old males however often become solitary.

Are they territorial in habit?
They have a home range and activity zones, and each group or small herd usually has a dominant male in attendance. The territorial bulls patrol their territories, marking the latter by manoeuvring grass stems into their pre-orbital glands, which exude a transparent, sticky secretion. These bulls often exhibit their presence by standing on termite hills or rises.

Do they migrate?
Usually not on a seasonal basis, but if food becomes scarce in their normal home range they will move away in search of better pastures.

Are they easy to spot?
They are very inquisitive, and if they are not disturbed will often stare for some time before moving off. In areas where they are hunted, they become wary and wild.

Do they associate with other animals?
They sometimes associate with zebra, wildebeest and other herbivores.

What are their breeding habits?
A single calf is born in September or October after a gestation period of just on 240 days. Calves can run with the herd shortly after birth. Cows are sexually mature at the age of about three years.

What are their major enemies?
Lion, leopard, cheetah and wild dogs are their major enemies.

Why are tsessebe so rare in the Kruger National Park?
Apart from predation, the scarcity of suitable habitats in the Park is probably the main reason. The aerial survey of 1990 indicates a population of about 711 animals.

Are any measures taken to try and increase their numbers?
Intensive research and breeding programmes are carried out in camps built specially for this purpose. The idea is to build up breeding herds and release them in the southern part of the Park. The veld-burning programme will hopefully establish more suitable conditions for this antelope in different parts of the area.

LICHTENSTEIN'S HARTEBEEST *Sigmoceros lichtensteinii*

What is the distribution?
Lichtenstein's hartebeest are found in parts of Tanzania, Zaïre, Angola, Zambia and northern Mozambique as well as on privately owned land in south-eastern Zimbabwe.

In the previous century the Lichtenstein's Hartebeest were also found in the north-eastern Transvaal, the old Pongola Reserve and northern Zululand, where they were ruthlessly hunted (Milstein, 1989).

They were re-introduced to the northern part of the Park in July 1985, when six animals were successfully transferred from a population in Malawi, the nearest from which a number of animals could be obtained.

The hartebeest were released in a camp some 25 km south of Punda Maria on the eastern basaltic flats. In November 1986 an additional 15 animals were introduced (Pienaar, Joubert, Hall-Martin, De Graaff & Rautenbach, 1987).

What type of habitat do they prefer?
They prefer parkland savanna and marshy grasslands.

What do they eat?
Lichtenstein's hartebeest are grazers, browsing occasionally. They are usually found to feed in the early morning and late afternoon in the Kruger National Park.

Do they drink water regularly?
Where water is freely available they drink daily, usually in the morning.

What are the main physical features?
A definite hump and sloping back are characteristic features of Lichtenstein's hartebeest.

They stand approximately 1,25 m high at the shoulder and the bulls have a mass of 160 to 200 kg, the cows about 11 kilograms less. Both sexes have short, sturdy, S-shaped horns approximately 50 cm long, the record length being 60,6 cm. The body colour is yellowish brown, with a red brown 'saddle' stretching from the shoulder to the base of the tail.

Are their senses well developed?
Their senses of sight and hearing are well developed, but their sense of smell is not.

Are they gregarious?
They move around in small groups of up to 10 animals which come together to from larger herds seasonally.

Are they territorial in habit?
A dominant bull leads each group and defends its territory (about 2,5 km^2 in extent in Zambian populations) against other bulls. He marks off the territory by gouging out the soil with his horns and rubbing a secretion from the pre-orbital glands onto the soil. He also defecates in certain areas to further mark off the territory.

The dominant bull also guards the group, usually standing on higher ground a little way from the cows and their calves. When the herd is threatened and they flee, he takes up a position at the rear and stops every so often to check whether they are still in danger. When the cows are in season the bull will often leave his domain to acquire females from another herd, giving rise to fights amongst the bulls.

These hartebeest can often be distinguished by their habit of rubbing their faces on their flanks; after grazing over burnt areas they often leave a distinct black blotch just behind the shoulders which washes away after rain (Smithers, 1986).

What are their breeding habits?
A single calf (approximate mass 15 kg) is born after a gestation period of 240 days. Although the mother does not hide the calf after its birth, she will leave it in long grass while she grazes.

What are their major enemies?
Lion are the major enemies of adult hartebeest, while young animals are preyed upon by wild dogs, leopard and cheetah.

BLUE WILDEBEEST *Connochaetes taurinus* (Burchell, 1823)

What is the distribution?
Blue wildebeest are well represented in the northern Cape, the Transvaal bushveld, Natal, Mozambique, Tanzania, Zimbabwe, parts of Zambia, Kenya, Namibia and Angola. The subspecies *C. t. taurinus* (Burchell, 1823) is represented in the Park, and occurs widely throughout the area. There are three major areas of concentration south of the Olifants River namely:

   i) the area north-east of Satara (Mavumbye/Gudzani), towards Bangu

   ii) the area between the Sweni River and the Mlondozi Dam

   iii) the open flats between Lower Sabie and Crocodile Bridge.

   According to the 1990 aerial census, there are some 14 293 blue wildebeest in the Park, showing a sex ratio of 1,47 females per male for animals aged one to two years and older.

What type of habitat do blue wildebeest prefer?
They prefer open plains or lightly wooded savanna with short grass.

What do they eat?
Wildebeest are grazers and are particularly attracted to recently burnt veld where they nibble the sprouting grass. They drink regularly where water is freely available, but in arid habitats they are able to go without water for a considerable time.

What are the main physical features?
This boisterous, robust-looking antelope stands about 1,25 to 1,42 m at the shoulder and attains a mass of about 180 kg for females and 250 kg for males. The record mass for an animal in the Kruger National Park is 307,5 kg. Both sexes carry horns, those of the bulls being more massive than

those of the cows. The general colour is dark brown to slate grey, with more or less black facial parts. A number of vertical dark stripes are visible on the neck, shoulders and body.

A drooping mane on the neck reaches to the withers, a 'beard' hangs below the so-called animal's chin, and the tail is long and bushy. The back is sloping and the legs appear to be thin compared with the size of the body. The broad, flattened muzzle and large nostrils are conspicuous.

What are their habits?

Wildebeest are highly gregarious, forming large herds and often associating with other animals such as impala, giraffe, ostrich and especially zebra.

The males show territorial behaviour during the rutting season and they are then even more noisy than usual, uttering deep grunting sounds. Old males often become solitary and moody.

Wildebeest appear to be very restless. Is this so?

They are very inquisitive, and when they run away from an enemy or even suspected danger they will not go very far before halting and turning around to try and locate the cause of concern. This, of course, makes them easy quarry for hunters. Their continuous snorting and blowing through the nostrils while running in circles creates the impression that they are nervous. They certainly are very nervous at a waterhole, and on approaching the water will stampede away at the slightest hint of danger. Drinking often commences only after a number of trials.

Are they dangerous to human beings?

These antelopes are very tenacious and tough, and can be dangerous when wounded or cornered, although in the wild they are normally timid and inoffensive.

Do they migrate?

Wildebeest are well known for their very strong migratory instinct. On the Serengeti plains in central Africa they migrate in their thousands over hundreds of kilometres. Because of the fences and neighbouring farmlands, long-distance migrations are not possible in the Kruger National Park, but seasonal movements for food and water do occur within the Park.

Are wildebeest territorial in habit?

During the breeding season bulls establish a small territorium to which they lure the females.

Why are wildebeest less common in the Pretoriuskop area than earlier?

Bush encroachment was responsible for this state of affairs, and as pointed out in the section on veld burning, action is being taken to restore the habitat to a condition reflecting the original situation.

What are their breeding habits?

There is a summer calving period that lasts from about the end of November to the end of January. A single calf is usually born after a gestation period of about 250 to 260 days. The calf is able to run with the mother a few minutes after birth.

What are their major enemies?

Cows and especially calves are vulnerable to hyena, wild dogs, cheetah, leopard and lion.

ROAN ANTELOPE *Hippotragus equinus* (Desmarest, 1804)

What is the distribution?
Roan antelope occur in small, scattered groups over most of their range in the savannas of Africa and may be regarded as a rare species. In southern Africa they are confined to southern Angola, northern Namibia and Botswana, a few game reserves in the northern Transvaal, and the western parts of Mozambique.

The Kruger National Park population is mostly confined to the basalt flats along the Lebombo range north of the Olifants River, while a small remnant population is still found near Pretoriuskop. It represents the subspecies *H. e. equinus* (Desmarest, 1804).

What type of habitat do they prefer?
They prefer open, well-watered grassland savanna with easily accessible woodland to which they may revert for shelter.

What do they eat?
Roan antelope are primarily grazers, but will also to a certain extent browse on young shoots of shrubs and trees. They are also dependent on a regular supply of water.

What are the main physical features?
This antelope reaches a height of 1,4 m at the shoulder. A large bull may attain a mass of 250 to 270 kg or even more, while the cow is about 45 kg less.

The most striking features are the exceptionally long ears (about 25 to 30 cm long) and the facial coloration which consists of a black background with a white snout and half-circles around the eyes, creating the impression of a mask. The general

body colour is greyish brown or roan, with dark brown legs. There is also a well-developed mane.

Both sexes have heavily ringed horns that curve backwards like those of the sable, although they are somewhat shorter. The record length is 99 cm, but the horns normally vary in length between 66 and 76 cm.

Are they gregarious in habit?

Roan antelope are semi-gregarious and usually associate with small herds of five to 12 animals in the Kruger National Park. Larger herds of 15 to 25 and more are also encountered. It is said that in some other parts of their range (e.g. Angola) they can congregate in herds of 50 to 80 animals. A normal herd consists of a dominant bull and a number of cows and calves.

Is the dominant bull the leader of the antelope herd?

Young bulls are evicted from the herd at the age of two-and-a-half to three years. They form bachelor groups and when fully mature will try and secure a harem of their own by challenging an old herd bull. The old bulls usually become solitary or may even associate with other herbivores.

Bulls are dominant as far as breeding is concerned and keep other bulls out of their activity zone. Leadership of the herd is actually the duty of the dominant cow.

Are they territorial in habit?

According to Joubert (1970) no proof could be found that territories are in fact delimited by definite and rigid borders. The herd bull, however, actively defends an area around the herd within a radius of approximately 300 to 500 m, also referred to as an intolerance zone. A herd can meander over an area 60 to 100 km^2 in extent.

What are their breeding habits?

A single calf is born at any time of the year, although there appears to be a summer peak. The gestation period lasts 270 to 280 days. The newly born calf is concealed for a few weeks before it joins its mother.

Are roan antelope aggressive animals?

Normally not, but when at bay or wounded they are apt to become dangerous and defend themselves viciously. According to Astley Maberly (1967), they kick and bite when tackling an assailant and at such times will utter squeals of rage and hissing sounds. Apart from uttering a horse-like snort when alarmed or suspicious, they are normally silent creatures.

What are their major enemies?

Lions are the principal natural enemies of adult roan antelope, although a single lion facing a roan at bay has to be careful not to be gored by the antelope's horns.

Calf mortality is probably high owing to the mother's habit of hiding the calf for the first few weeks of its life. During this period it is very vulnerable to sniffing predators such as jackal, hyena, leopard, cheetah and some of the other felids. A young calf freezes when an enemy approaches and, if spotted, makes easy prey.

SABLE *Hippotragus niger* (Harris, 1838)

What is the distribution?
Sable occur in the northern and south-eastern Transvaal, Zimbabwe, northern Botswana, the Caprivi in Namibia, Zambia, south-eastern Zaïre, Malawi, Mozambique, southern Angola, north-eastern Tanzania and the south-eastern parts of Kenya. The local subspecies is *H. n. niger* (Harris, 1838).

According to the 1990 census some 1 877 sable occur in the Kruger National Park. They may be encountered in a suitable habitat in any part of the Park, except in the area between Lower Sabie and Crocodile Bridge. The greatest concentrations may be found in the Pretoriuskop area, the Manzimhlope area on the Nhlanguleni Road, and in the western half of the Park north of the Letaba River.

What type of habitat do sable prefer?
They like open, fairly dry savanna of mixed bush and grassland near water.

What do they eat?
Grass is the staple diet, but leaves and fruit are also taken when the nutritional value of the grass drops off at the end of the dry season.

What are the main physical features?
This magnificent antelope stands about 1,35 m at the shoulder and attains a mass of 230 to 250 kg. The general colour of the bulls is brown to

black, with pure white underparts and a conspicuous white facial marking. The cows are more or less chestnut-coloured, while calves are fawn-coloured. Both sexes have a heavy mane down the back of the neck to the withers.

The horns, which rise vertically and then sweep backwards, are carried by both sexes, although those of the cow are smaller and less curved. The bull's horns are about 102 cm long.

Are sable gregarious?

They are gregarious, running in herds that may comprise any number between 10 and 40 animals, although the average herd size is 14.

Who leads the herd?

An average herd consists of a number of cows and calves and one large bull. The latter is dominant as far as breeding is concerned, but the dominant cow leads the herd. Young bulls are evicted from the herd by the dominant bull when they are two-and-a-half to three years of age. Old bulls often take to a solitary life.

Do sable migrate?

As selective grazers subsisting on various types of grasses and drinking regularly, sable do undertake migrations. Years ago they would migrate westwards to the foothills of Transvaal Drakensberg, an area outside the present borders of the Kruger National Park.

Since the erection of the boundary fence these migration routes have been severed and movement is now restricted to areas within the Park.

Do they associate with other game?

Sable rarely associate with other game species in the veld. At a waterhole they will temporarily mingle with other species, but having finished their drinking they usually move away without lingering at the waterhole, as do waterbuck and blue wildebeest.

Are they territorial in habit?

They do not defend territories but they have activity zones (some 200 to 400 ha in extent) which are the areas in which they happen to be at a specific time. The herd bull wards off intruders, in much the same way as the roan antelope herd bull does.

Are sable dangerous to humans?

These courageous and beautiful antelopes can be very dangerous and will charge with little provocation when wounded or at bay.

What are their breeding habits?

A single calf is born, usually between February and March. The gestation period is about 240 days. The calf is suckled in the early morning for about two weeks after birth, being hidden away in dense undergrowth for the rest of the day. Cows are sexually mature when they are three years old.

What are their major enemies?

Sable can defend themselves ably against predators. Even lions have to be careful when attacking a fully grown bull, and there have been instances of sable killing lions. Cows and calves are more vulnerable, and occasionally also fall prey to leopard, cheetah and even wild dogs.

AFRICAN BUFFALO *Syncerus caffer* (Sparrman, 1779)

What is the distribution?
Buffalo are encountered across the whole of central and West Africa south of the Sahara, and formerly along the entire eastern side of southern Africa. Within the Park they are evenly distributed, and are usually found near permanent water.

What type of habitat do buffalo prefer?
Although they have adapted to quite a wide range of habitats, they prefer river valleys, grassy plains or parkland savanna near water.

What do they eat?
They are principally grazers.

What are the main physical features?
They are cattle-like in form, very bulky, and stand about 1,4 m or slightly more at the shoulder. Bulls are much larger than cows and may attain a mass of 600 to 800 kg.

Both sexes have massive horns with broad bases, but the bull's horns are larger than those of the cow. They average 91 cm in length, measured along the outer curve of the horn. Apart from the horns, the large drooping ears are also very conspicuous.

Bulls are blackish in colour, while cows and calves are dark reddish brown. Their spoor and dung are very similar to those of cattle.

How can one distinguish between buffalo and wildebeest?
From a distance the two species are very similar in colour, and both have ox-like features. There are, however, marked differences. Firstly, the wildebeest is a slenderly built animal in contrast to the massive, stout appearance of the buffalo. Also the horns of the wildebeest are much smaller, and its back has a distinct slope in profile.

Are buffalo gregarious?
They are gregarious, forming large herds that often consist of more than a hundred animals. Herds of more than a thousand head have been observed in the Kruger National Park. Old bulls often become solitary or roam around in small groups ranging from 2 to about 10 individuals.

Is the dominant bull the leader of the buffalo herd?
Fierce fights during the rutting season determine the dominant hierarchy amongst the bulls. However, as in the cases of many other bovids, it is a dominant cow that leads the herd.

Are they diurnal or nocturnal animals?
Buffalo tend to be more nocturnal than diurnal. Most of the grazing is done during the night, early morning or late afternoon. They often drink water twice a day.

Their habit of spending the hot hours of the day in dense vegetation often makes it difficult to spot them, giving the impression that there are not many of them in the Park.

Are their senses well developed?
Their senses of sight and hearing are not acute but their sense of smell seems to be well developed.

Are they territorial in habit?
Although not territorial in habit, they will frequent a specific home range for many years.

What sound do they make?
Buffalo are silent animals except during the mating season, when they grunt and bellow hoarsely. When stampeding they utter snorts of alarm. Buffalo calves bleat like cattle calves.

Are buffalo nomadic?
They frequent well-watered areas where there is sufficient food and therefore probably move away only under extreme conditions.

Are they dangerous to man?
They are extremely dangerous when wounded or cornered, but if left in peace they seldom pose a threat. Hunters in general regard a wounded buffalo as one of the most dangerous animals. Once a buffalo charges its adversary, only a well-placed bullet fired from a heavy calibre rifle can stop it. During the charge the head is held high to keep the adversary in sight and only at the last moment is the buffalo's head lowered for the physical attack.

It is said that a wounded buffalo tends to ambush its pursuer. Is this strictly true?
Many hunters have made this claim, but it is doubtful whether it could really be proven. What probably happens is that the hunter chases his wounded quarry for some distance until the latter, exhausted and feeling cornered, then charges.

Is the buffalo as tough as it is made out to be?
Yes, indeed, and a number of hunters have found that out too late! A charging buffalo presents a very difficult target for a brain shot, and the massive horn bosses often deflect the bullet.

Can a buffalo run fast?
It is claimed that a buffalo can attain a speed of 50 km/h.

A herd of buffalo looks frightening.
Will it charge a vehicle?
Buffalo are very inquisitive and will
often stare, nose raised high, at a
vehicle or other object. At the same
time they may take a few steps
forward accompanied by snorts and a
defiant sweeping motion of the
massive head and horns. When not
threatened they are almost as harmless
as cattle. On the other hand, their
tendency to stampede when alarmed
could be dangerous if one happens to
be in their way.

What are their breeding habits?
The gestation period is about 330 to
346 days. A single calf is born at any
time of the year but in the Park there
seems to be a peak calving period
between March and May.

The calf may remain with the mother
for two years.

What are their major enemies?
Lions are their only significant natural
enemies, although adults as well as
immature animals sometimes fall prey
to crocodiles. Old, solitary bulls are
quite often killed by lions, usually in a
team effort. Young animals may be
killed by the other larger predators,
and figures indicate that only six to
nine calves of every 20 born reach
maturity.

A single lion facing a buffalo has a
formidable task. Unless he can
surprise or outwit the buffalo in some
way, he stands a good chance of losing
his own life. It has often been observed
that a bull, or a small party of bulls,
charges and frightens off lions. If
attacked, a bull will go down fighting
fiercely and virtually to the last breath,
which is usually in the form of a

coarse, grunting sound. Many a lion
has been injured in such battles, a
number of them fatally.

When a herd is threatened by lions it
forms a protective circle with the bulls
on the perimeter. To circumvent this,
lions usually try to surprise and
frighten the animals. In the stampede
that follows, one is separated from the
herd and is then attacked.

The senior author once watched a
herd of buffalo with a number of lions
nearby. Every few minutes one or
more bulls left the herd and charged in
the direction of the lions, which then
fled for some distance. At a certain
point the buffalo, getting too far away
from the herd, turned back, promptly
followed by the lions up to a few
metres from the herd. This went on for
a few hours until one buffalo went a
little too far and was attacked and
killed by the lions.

Do buffalo suffer from cattle diseases?
They are susceptible to most of the
cattle diseases. Mortality in this
respect does not seem to be high if one
considers the sharp rise in the
numbers of buffalo over the past
decade or so. Foot-and-mouth disease
is at times quite common amongst
these bovids. Anthrax, although a
highly fatal disease, has up to the
present not been a significant factor in
mortality.

During the latter part of the 19th
century, buffalo populations in many
parts of Africa, including the Kruger
National Park, were nearly wiped out
by rinderpest.

The 1990 census results indicated
some 25 738 animals in 89 breeding
herds with a mean herd size of 289,2
animals, within the Park.

GIRAFFE *Giraffa camelopardalis* (Linnaeus, 1758)

Were giraffes at any time widely distributed in Africa?
Giraffes were once widely found in savanna areas from the Sahara southwards to the Orange River, but now occur only in numerous isolated populations. The subspecies in the Park is *G. c. capensis* (Lesson, 1842).

Where can one see them in the Park?
The Satara and Crocodile Bridge areas have the bulk of the population, with approximately one giraffe in every 2 km^2. North of the Olifants River they are quite rare (one giraffe per 6,2 km^2). North of the Letaba River there is only one giraffe to about 50 to 100 km^2.

Why are they so rare in the northern part of the Park?
Mainly because of the scarcity of their favourite food plants.

How many giraffes are in the Park?
According to the 1990 aerial census there are 4 719 giraffes in the Park.

Are giraffes well represented in South Africa outside the Park?
Large populations exist in the private game reserves west of the Park, and smaller populations are to be found in a large number of the smaller provincial and private game reserves. They were also re-introduced in the Willem Pretorius Game Reserve in the Orange Free State and in Hluhluwe Game Reserve in Natal.

What type of habitat do they prefer?
They prefer more open, flat parkland savanna, especially where *Acacia* trees are abundant. Bulls are sometimes encountered in light forest, but they usually only stay there temporarily. Cows and calves show a definite preference for more open country.

Is there any specific reason why giraffes prefer more open areas?
Dense forest impairs their vision, making them more vulnerable to predators.

Are they able to negotiate uneven terrain?
They are sometimes found in the foothills of the Lebombo Mountains, where they go for the fresh spring growth on the *Combretum* trees, but the uneven terrain impairs movement.

What do they eat?
They are normally browsers, grazing only in very exceptional circumstances. Even at times when they appeared to be eating grass, close investigation proved that the plant eaten was a small creeper of the genus Cucumis. Their favourite food is the foliage of Acacia trees and in the Park about 30% of their intake is made up of knobthorn *(Acacia nigrescens)*, while about 20% comprises other acacias, nearly 20% Combretum species, and 7% is made up of wait-a-bit *(Ziziphus mucronata)*. Giraffes utilize some 70 or more species of trees and shrubs in the Park.

Why do they show such a marked preference for certain plant species?
Taste and/or smell could play a role, but the exact reason remains unknown.

Does the composition of their food vary during the different seasons?
Their favourite food trees are deciduous and so they have to compensate by feeding on less palatable evergreen trees during the winter.

Do they get enough food in winter when many trees are bare?
The amount of food available in winter is a limiting factor in their survival. They are naturally forced to feed on evergreen substitutes such as *Euclea* species, but even this source of food is limited. Many of the deciduous trees are, however, only bare for a short time of the year.

Does heavy browsing by giraffes have an influence on their food trees?
In many parts of Africa it has been found that heavy browsing by giraffes has led to the stunting of certain trees. The 'pruning' of their favourite food trees into various shapes, such as dome, pyramid, hour-glass or even cigar shapes, is quite conspicuous in many areas in Africa, including the Kruger National Park. Twigs are pulled into the mouth by the lips and long prehensile tongue (which may reach 45 cm long) and the leaves are shredded off into the mouth. Between 15 and 20 hours of each day may be spent browsing.

Where can these tree shapes be seen?
They are quite conspicuous where *Acacia* species are the dominant or sub-dominant trees in a veld type. The Satara and Crocodile Bridge-Lower Sabie areas have many examples. They are also found in the vicinity of Tshokwane and just north of Satara.

Is it not strange that giraffes prefer thorny food plants?
The evolution of some African plants, especially the genus *Acacia*, appears to have been influenced by the giraffe and other large browsers that are now extinct. The development of thorns and spines was probably to protect these plants from the browsers. It is interesting to note here that Australia, where there is the largest variety of thornless *Acacia* species, has no large browsing herbivores.

Are Acacia *species the only trees that are 'pruned'?*
With a few exceptions, yes. A very small number of combretums show signs of giraffe browsing. The basic form of more than one stem does not lend itself to 'pruning' in different shapes. In about 90% of cases, an obviously 'pruned' tree will be an *Acacia nigrescens*, and in a few cases probably an *Acacia welwitschii* subspecies *delagoensis*.

At what height do giraffes normally feed?
This depends on the type and amount of food available. In winter, when they are forced to feed on some evergreen shrubs, they come down to almost ground level and thus compete with browsers of lesser height. A comfortable feeding height would probably be 2 to 5 m, depending on the individual's size.

Do they compete with other herbivores during times of abundant food?
Their feeding overlaps to some extent with browsers such as kudu and eland, and even more so with elephant when grass becomes scarce and the

latter revert to browsing. An elephant has, with the aid of its trunk, about the same reach as a giraffe. To determine the exact amount of competition between giraffe and elephant is very difficult owing to differences in food preferences and the fact that elephants often consume more grass than leaves.

Are there any peculiar plants that giraffes feed on?
They feed on the tamboti tree (*Spirostachys africana*) which is very poisonous to human beings. *Combretum* seeds, which are also poisonous but less so than tamboti, are also taken frequently.

Do giraffes ruminate?
Yes. They have four-chambered stomachs like other ruminants.

Are they very dependent on water?
It is generally accepted that they can go without drinking water for long periods, but if it is available they will drink regularly.

How much water can a giraffe drink at a time?
A big bull may drink up to 25 litres or more per day.

Can they store water to see them through periods when no water is available?
They cannot conserve water, but they probably get additional moisture from their food and, to a lesser extent, from dew on the plants they eat.

What are the main physical features?
The main physical features of this unique animal are so obvious that they hardly need be given in detail. They have a distinctive patchwork body patterning, large brown eyes with long eyelashes, a long neck and legs, a relatively short body and a long tail. The sloping nature of the back is mostly due to the long dorsal spines of the thoracic vertebrae, to which the strong neck muscles are attached. The forelegs are longer than the hindlegs.

How did the giraffe get its name?
In early times people thought the giraffe was a cross between a camel because of the way it walked, and a leopard because of its blotches. This led to the word '*camelopardalis*'. The Arabs called it '*xirapha*', which means 'one who walks fast'.

Is the giraffe related to any animal?
It is only related to the okapi (*Okapia johnstoni*) which occurs in the central African rain forest. Although this animal's neck is longish, it is not nearly as long as that of the giraffe. The okapi is very dark brown in colour, with a few vertical stripes and a few small spots. It looks very different from the giraffe, but the layman could still see the relationship between the two animals.

How many cervical or neck vertebrae does the giraffe have?
Seven, like most other mammals. The exceptions are the sloths, which have six or nine cervical vertebrae, and the manatee species which have six.

What is the purpose of the relatively small horns?
We do not know. They are useless against predators and although bulls use them in fights, they appear to do little harm.

Are the bulls' horns different from those of the cows?

The cow's horns are shorter and more slender than the bull's and have a tuft of hair at the tip; the tip of the bull's horn is bare. Thus it is possible to identify the sex of a giraffe even if only the animal's head is visible.

Why are the tips of the bulls' horns bald?

Probably because the bulls become involved in many fights and mock fights in which the horn tips frequently come into contact with the opponent's body. It has also been suggested that keratin deposits could be a contributory factor.

Are the calves born with horns?

Yes. At birth the horns are cartilaginous and about 25 mm long. They ossify as they grow, and their bases fuse completely with the parietal bones of the skull.

Is it true that some giraffes have more than two horns?

Some subspecies of giraffe show a tendency to develop more knobs, or so-called horns, on the skull. Besides the two parietal or main horns, a frontal horn and occipital horns can develop. The frontal horn of the subspecies *G. c. giraffa* is poorly developed and usually not much more than a slight knob. The Baringo giraffe is called the five-horned giraffe, while the other subspecies usually have either two or three horns.

There are authors who claim that some giraffes have seven horns. This is due to bony structures that sometimes develop on the Zygomatic arch of the skulls of old bulls. It is not a constant feature and should therefore be disregarded. Extra bony outgrowths on the face commonly occur in males and are probably caused by head-hitting during fights.

How many subspecies of giraffe are there in the world?

There is only one species, but this is divided into a number of subspecies based on minor differences. Some taxonomists describe 11 or more subspecies, but Meester & Setzer (1971) recognize only nine subspecies. The giraffe in the Park belong to the subspecies *G. c. capensis*.

Why are some giraffes darker than others?

They usually become darker with age and this is more pronounced in males than females. A very dark giraffe is usually a male.

Is the blotch pattern of giraffes in the Park more or less the same?

Yes, but no two individual giraffes have exactly the same pattern. It is, however, interesting to note that a small percentage have a star-like configuration on the buttocks, while a few have blotches that bear a strong resemblance to the star-like patterning of the Kenyan giraffe *G. c. tippelskirchi* (Matschie, 1898).

Are there albino giraffes in the Park?

Yes, but such individuals are fairly rare. About ten cases are mentioned in the literature, and some of them have been documented photographically.

How tall can a giraffe grow?

Bulls grow to a height of about 5 metres to the top of the head, and cows to about 4,4 m.

What is their mass?
Bulls can weigh up to 1 200 kg or
more, and cows up to about 900 kg.

How fast can giraffe run?
Approximately 48 km/h.

How far can they run?
They can keep a brisk pace over a
distance of up to 7 km, according to
hunters in the previous century who
ran them down with horses. It is said
that a horse had to be very fit to
out-distance a giraffe.

*Have giraffes very strong hearts to
pump the blood up their long necks?*
In relation to other mammals, their
hearts are not exceptionally big but
they are very strong. The blood
pressure at the heart is about 260/160,
compared to the 120/80 in a healthy
human being. The neck arteries also
have valves like the veins to prevent a
back-flow of blood.

*Why does a giraffe not become dizzy
when it lifts its head after drinking?*
A network of blood vessels at the base
of the brain, called the *rete mirahele*,
serves as a mechanism to prevent too
great a back-flow of blood. When the
giraffe bends down this mechanism
reduces the pressure of the blood at
the base of the brain to about 120/80.

How fast does the heart beat?
About 60 beats per minute.

*Why is it so difficult for the giraffe to
bend down its neck?*
The neck muscles connected to the
dorsal spines of the thoracic vertebrae
make it difficult for the giraffe to lower
its head and neck to ground level.

Do giraffe migrate?
They do not show distinct migration
patterns, but move from one area to
another for food and water. During
spring they move around to feed on
the flowers and young leaves of their
preferred food plants.
    They will remain in the same area
for years if food and water are always
available.

*What is the average size of a giraffe
herd?*
Giraffes have a very loose herd
structure and the composition and
number of animals in a herd varies
from day to day and even in a single
day. The largest herd recorded in the
Park numbered 46 animals. In other
parts of Africa larger herds have been
reported and some authors claim
figures of up to 70 animals in one herd
of giraffe.
    A herd is often spread over such a
large area that it is difficult to decide
whether it is one large herd or merely
a loose congregation of smaller herds.
Herds in the Park usually consist of
less than 20 animals.

Why are bulls often alone?
Males of many animal species tend to
be solitary when they cannot compete
successfully for females, and this is to
a certain extent also true for the giraffe.
    Solitary males often move from one
giraffe herd to another in search of
females on heat. They mate
throughout the year.

Do old bulls have a pungent smell?
It is said that old males do have a
peculiar smell, and hunters of the 19th
century called them by the evocative
name of 'stink bulls'.

Does a herd have a dominant bull?
Bulls move around so much that a
herd can have a different dominant
bull at different times.

Who is the actual leader of the herd?
It is difficult to say when both bulls
and cows are present in a herd.
Sometimes a cow and sometimes a
bull will lead the way to a new feeding
area or a waterhole.

*Does the composition of a giraffe herd
vary a lot?*
Yes. Within their home range
members of different herds mix freely.
Family groups are more stable.

Are they territorial in habit?
They do not defend a territory but
usually have a home range of
anything between 20 and 70 km^2, in
which they may remain for years.

Do bulls often fight?
They frequently indulge in fights
ranging from low-intensity sparring to
serious fights for dominance.

How do the bulls fight?
They usually stand side by side facing
in the same direction or in opposite
directions, and then hit each other
with sweeping blows of the neck and
head. These fights are seldom fatal
and usually end when one or both
animals become too exhausted to
continue.

*Does the mother defend her calf
against predators?*
During the first few weeks after the
birth of the calf the mother will try to
manoeuvre it between her front legs
when confronting an attacker. Cases

have been recorded of a cow beating
off a lion attack.

*When does the calf become
independent?*
The mother-calf relationship is very
loose. When the calf is about six weeks
old the mother no longer defends it
and it has to watch and follow her
when she moves on or flees from
danger. The young grow fast – females
can reach a height of 4,3 m in five years.

*How long does the calf stay with the
mother?*
Usually for more than a year and even
up to maturity. A mother and one or
more daughters with their own offspring is not an uncommon social
grouping. But calves a few weeks old
can stray from their mothers and
survive in a strange herd with other
adults.

*One often sees a few young giraffes
with an adult. Do they have
'baby-sitters'?*
As the young ones have to fend for
themselves from a very early age, they
feel more secure in the presence of
adults. This type of 'baby-sitting' is
therefore fairly frequent. An adult
male with a number of calves
accompanying him is not a rare
occurrence. The young ones
continually change their 'baby-sitters'.

Are giraffes very inquisitive?
They are probably amongst the most
inquisitive of animals in the Kruger
National Park and will stare at strange
objects for a long time.

Do they have 'sentinels'?
No, but every member of a herd is

constantly on the lookout for enemies. If one sees something suspicious, it will stare at it or even move to a position where it will have a better view of the object of concern. When other members of the herd notice this behaviour, they also try to locate the cause of the suspicion.

Because of their good vision and lofty view, giraffes often locate danger before most other ungulates become aware of it. If one is looking for predators it could be worthwhile watching giraffes, because when members of a herd stand motionless and erect and face one direction, it is often an indication of the presence of one or more predators.

Are their senses well developed?

Their sense of sight is very well developed. Their hearing seems to be adequate, but is probably not as well developed as their sight. There is still controversy about their sense of smell; some authors claim that it is well developed, while others deny it. The nostrils can be closed voluntarily, but the reason for this is unknown.

Are giraffes mute?

For many years it was believed that giraffes were mute. Normally they are quiet animals, but they do possess vocal chords like other mammals which enable them to utter grunting or bellowing sounds, usually under stress.

Can giraffes swim?
Giraffes are among the few species of mammals which apparently cannot swim. It has been observed in the Park and elsewhere that they occasionally wade through fairly deep water, but rivers often serve as an efficient barrier to their movements.

How do giraffes sleep?
Usually standing up, but they also lie down to sleep. They probably do not sleep more than about 20 minutes in 24 hours. Most of their rest is attained through many short doses of light sleep, called a polyphase sleep pattern. This contrasts with the monophase sleeping pattern of carnivores whereby the animals sleep for a long period and then become active for another long period.

Have they got specific breeding peaks?
Calves are born at any time of the year, although there may be a peak in late winter or spring, in about August and September.
Gestation is about 457 days.

How big is the calf at birth?
It could stand as high as 1,5 m or slightly more. The birth weight is about 100 kg.

How long does the calf suckle?
Usually about a year, but sometimes longer. From the age of about one month the calf starts to supplement its milk diet with leaves.

How does the mother give birth?
Standing up, so the calf drops more than 1,5 m to the ground. Parturition can take from 1 to 2 hours; it usually takes the calf another hour to stand up.

What is the lifespan of a giraffe?
The record is 28 years (attained in a zoo), and in the wild the lifespan is probably up to 27 years. One of the Park's rangers observed two giraffes with distinct markings over a period of 19 years. When he first saw them they were fully grown, and when they were last seen they must have been in their mid-twenties. Giraffe are sexually mature at about three-and-a-half to five years, and fully grown at about seven years of age.

How long is the calving interval?
The calving interval is about 20 months. A female can probably reproduce up to the age of 20 years or even longer, giving birth to 10 calves.

Are giraffe susceptible to diseases?
They are vulnerable to sudden spells of cold weather, especially if their condition is poor due to a scarcity of food at the end of winter or early spring. There are indications that many of them died of rinderpest during the last few years of the previous century. A few cases of death caused by anthrax have been recorded. In general, however, high mortality due to diseases has not been experienced in the Park.
Giraffes harbour quite a number of endo- and ectoparasites, and according to surveys, eggs of *Schistosoma matheei*, the bilharzia parasite, were found in the faeces of 19% of giraffes in the Park.

Why do giraffes sometimes chew bones?
Like many other wild herbivores, and cattle, giraffes sometimes chew or eat strange objects such as soil, faeces and

bones. This behaviour is called pica; the chewing of bones in particular is called osteophagia. This usually happens at the end of winter when the giraffes' diet is deficient in calcium, phosphorus or trace elements. Chewing bones can be dangerous because they sometimes harbour the bacterium *Clostridium botulinum* which secretes a most potent toxin. This causes botulism, a fatal disease.

Are they vulnerable when drinking?
They are vulnerable and they fully realize it. On approaching a waterhole a giraffe will stop frequently to scan the surroundings. It usually drinks for about 10 seconds and then lifts its head and neck to check for potential danger. When satisfied that it is still safe, it will proceed to drink again. The slightest sound or movement will make it jerk up its head and move off.

Some giraffes appear to suffer from a skin disease. What is it?
These are wart-like outgrowths caused by a virus. They are very unsightly, but not fatal unless secondary infection sets in.

Were giraffe heavily hunted in Southern Africa in the past?
Yes. They were killed mostly for their meat and for their skin, which was used for sandals and whips.

Is giraffe meat tasty?
The meat of cows and young animals is quite tasty, but no better than that of beef or mutton.

How were they hunted in the past?
They were often shot from horseback after they had been run down. The hunter had to have a good horse with a lot of stamina. In the days of the muzzle-loader it often took a number of shots – sometimes up to a dozen – before the giraffe died.

Are giraffes aggressive towards human beings?
They are very docile creatures and will rarely try to attack humans. On a few occasions cars have been damaged by bull giraffes kicking at the vehicles. This behaviour is highly exceptional, however, and visitors need not be alarmed. However, if a giraffe is cornered it will defend itself like any other threatened beast.

What are their major enemies?
Young animals are occasionally killed by leopard, cheetah and crocodile, while hyena and wild dogs pose a minor threat. Lion are practically the only natural enemy of adult giraffes.

How do lions kill a giraffe?
Different methods are used. Often a number of lions will surround the giraffe and make short charges at it, enticing it to chop at its attackers with its hooves or hindlegs. It eventually becomes so exhausted that it topples over, and the lions then seize it by the neck and soft parts of the body. A lion has been known to jump onto a giraffe and clamber up its back to bite it at the base of the neck.

It has also been observed how lions have tried to herd a giraffe towards uneven terrain, where it could easily lose its balance. Once the giraffe is down it has difficulty in getting up, even under normal circumstances, and it is relatively easy for the lion to grasp its prey by the throat and suffocate it.

Can lions easily kill giraffes when they sleep?
They sleep very lightly and normally only for a few minutes at a time. It seldom, if ever, happens that all the individuals in a herd sleep at the same time. Solitary animals are vulnerable.

Can a giraffe defend itself when attacked by lions?
When cornered by lions it will chop or kick at the predators. When a lion leaps onto the back of a giraffe, the giraffe will run underneath branches in an effort to dislodge its assailant.

Do lions kill many giraffes?
It is not known exactly how many are killed in the Park annually, but according to Smuts (1975), the number could be considerable. In fact, as far as biomass is concerned, the lion's most important food is giraffe.

Are cows more vulnerable to lion attacks than bulls?
Twice as many bulls are killed by lion than are cows in the Kruger National Park. Although a bull, by virtue of his greater size and strength, can put up a more efficient fight than a cow, he follows certain behaviour patterns that render him more vulnerable.

There are twice as many solitary bulls than there are solitary cows. Animals in a herd are safer than loners simply because there are more eyes, ears and noses to detect possible danger. Bulls show a tendency to move into thickets at times, while cows and calves usually keep to the more open areas where predators can be spotted more easily and there is less

chance of being cornered.

Like the males of many other herbivores, bulls have a shorter flight distance than cows and allow a lion to come closer than a cow would. In flight the males usually run at the rear of the herd where they are more vulnerable to attack than the cows and calves would be.

Is calf mortality high?
Yes, higher than that of adults of either sex. In the Eastern Transvaal the calf mortality can be as high as 48%. The loose mother-calf relationship definitely plays a role in this respect.

Can a giraffe out-distance a lion?
The lion may be faster over a very short distance, but the giraffe has much more stamina and is a strong runner. It is almost impossible for a lion to get hold of a running giraffe.

Are giraffes killed by poachers?
Giraffes with broken snares around their legs are found from time to time, but this is relatively rare. Before the Park was fenced, giraffes which moved outside it sometimes got entangled in snares set at their normal feeding level.

How does a giraffe walk?
A giraffe swings its two legs on one side of the body forward more closely together than most other quadrupeds. The right foreleg leaves the ground soon after the right hindleg has begun its forward swing (Dagg & Foster, 1976). This gait is similar to that of the camel and is quite different from the way an antelope walks.

HIPPOPOTAMUS *Hippopotamus amphibius* (Linnaeus, 1758)

What is the distribution?
Hippos once inhabited just about
every river in Africa from north to
south. According to Stott, the last
hippo in the Nile Delta was shot in
1851, although Buchardt gives the date
as 1816. The last hippo in the Orange
River was shot in 1825.
Hippos are still present in many rivers
in the Afrotropical region. In South
Africa they are more or less confined
to game reserves in the Transvaal and
Natal. About 2 500 animals are found
in the Kruger National Park, especially
in and along the perennial rivers and
larger dams.

**Are hippos very dependent on their
water habitat?**
They spend most of the day in the
water, although on cool, overcast days
they sometimes leave the water for
considerable periods to rest on
sandbanks.

**Do they have any special adaptation
for an aquatic life?**
Their elongated bodies with rounded
contours help them to move easily in
the water. The eyes, ears and nostrils
are positioned so that they are above
the surface when the rest of the
hippo's body is submerged in water.

Do they graze during the day?
The habitat of hippos extends quite a
distance from water. At night they
come out to feed on land and in the
process may wander as far as 30 km
away before returning to the river at
dawn. On cool, overcast days they
may leave the water to graze nearby.

How long can a hippo live on land?
This depends on weather conditions,
but would probably be for no longer
than a few days. Prolonged exposure
to the hot sun causes severe blistering
of the skin, which in turn causes
festering sores.

Do they eat fish?
No. They are grazers, feeding mostly
on grass, but to some extent also on
the young shoots of reeds.

**It has been observed that hippo are
sometimes surrounded by black fish.
Why is this so?**
The fish belong to the genus *Labeo* and
feed on vegetable matter stirred up by
the hippo.

How much does a hippo eat per night?
An adult can eat more than 130 kg of
grass a night.

Do they destroy cultivated crops?
They are destructive and where farms
border on game reserves they compete
severely with man for his crops.

**Why does a herbivore need such large
and impressive teeth?**
When a feature is as extraordinarily
well-developed as the hippo's teeth, it
is an indication that it has survival
value. The canines and, to a lesser
extent the incisors, are used in fights
with rivals, often with deadly effect. In
most of these fights the victor is the
contestant with the largest canines. He
is usually also the one who mates
successfully and passes his genes on to
the offspring.

How do hippos graze with teeth that seem to be in their way?
Grass is plucked with the strong lips and not the teeth. The molars masticate the food.

What is the mass of a fully grown hippopotamus?
Bulls attain a mass of approximately 1 500 kg and cows about 1 300 kg.

The highest recorded mass for a bull hippo in the Kruger National Park stands at 2 005 kg.

How thick is the hide?
The hide with its fatty tissue is about 50 mm thick and is said to make up about 16% of the animal's body mass.

Do hippos have any hair?
The skin is virtually naked apart from a scattering of bristles around the lips, the ears and the tip of the tail.

What is their shoulder height?
It is about 1,5 m for bulls and 1,4 m for hippo cows.

What is their body colour?
It is brownish grey to nearly black, with a pinkish tinge around the muzzle, eyes and throat.

Do hippos sweat blood?
No, but sometimes the hide shows a reddish colour due to a glandular secretion that serves to protect the skin against the rays of the sun. This secretion has led to the belief that they can sweat blood.

How many toes do they have?
There are four toes encased in rounded hooves on the end of each of their short legs.

What is the record length of their canine teeth?
According to Astley Maberly (1967), the longest normal canine measured was 105,4 cm. Rowland Ward (1986) quotes a malformed canine that was 121,9 cm long. The length of a tooth is measured on the outside curve and nearly half of it is inside the jawbone. Average canines are around 60 to 80 cm long. Incisors normally attain a length of up to 50 cm.

At what age do the canine teeth reach their maximum length?
This is difficult to determine. The teeth continue to grow throughout the hippo's life and are subjected to considerable wear. It is interesting to note that with the movement of the jaws, the smaller, upper canines move over their lower counterparts so as to keep them sharp all the time.

Are these teeth ivory?
Yes, and it is claimed to be finer and of better quality than that of the elephant.

Can a human being outrun a hippo?
Most probably not. The hippo is deceptively fast for an animal of its size and mass and could probably reach 30 km/h.

Some hippos have terrible scars. How did they get them?
When bulls fight they often seriously injure one another. Many a victor of such a fight subsequently dies from the wounds inflicted by his opponent.

Do they make any sounds?
Snarling roars, accompanied by rumbling snorts. When surfacing they snort and make blowing noises.

Are hippos strictly gregarious?

Hippos normally live in herds of 10 to 30 individuals, but much larger herds have been reported from different parts of their range. Old bulls evicted from a herd usually become solitary, although such individuals are rare.

Are they nomadic?

Seasonal movements do not occur, but when waterholes and rivers dry up during droughts they move to more permanent watercourses.
Overcrowding can also lead to activity in search of new habitats, and distances of 20 km per night can be covered under these circumstances.

It has been noticed that hippos are found in man-made dams. Were they introduced there?

No, not necessarily. They move fairly long distances overland, usually during the night, to dams and even temporary pools.
When the latter dry up they return to permanent water.

Are hippos territorial in habit?

The aquatic part of their habitat is defended as a territorium, while the land part where they graze is their home range. The latter is pear-shaped with the narrow end at the water, and is usually 3 to 8 km long.

Bulls defend their territories fiercely against male intruders. These fights are amongst the most vicious in the animal world and are accompanied by loud grunts and raucous cries. The neck, with its large blood vessels, and the forelegs and flanks are prime targets in these fights.

Do they follow certain routes to their grazing ground?

Hippos like to follow well-beaten paths to and from feeding grounds. These paths consist of a very characteristic double trail – each one made by the feet of one side of the body.

Why do hippos yawn so much?

Besides the physiological reasons responsible for yawning in other animals and also humans, hippos use their yawning to intimidate others. The extent to which they can open their mouths is amazing and at the same time shows off their huge teeth to any possible contestant.

Hippos appear to dive and surface continuously. Why do they do this?
They do it for the cooling effect and also to prevent skin damage from the rays of the sun.

How long can a hippo stay submerged?
Claims of up to 12 minutes have been made, but it is doubtful whether a hippo can submerge for more than five to six minutes. The animal normally submerges for no more than a minute or two.

Can they walk on the riverbed?
They are capable of walking on the riverbed and do so frequently.

Why do hippos swish their tails when defecating?
It probably has some territorial implication, but the reason for this behaviour is not clear.

Hippo faeces scattered in the water serve as a fertilizing agent. Rich in nitrogen, they encourage the growth of a wide variety of water plants, especially algae, which forms a nutritive base for many aquatic organisms on which fish feed.

What type of hierarchy exists in a hippo herd?
Mature hippo males jealously guard and defend their territories and a herd of hippo usually has one single dominant bull.

It is said that females will only tolerate a bull's attention when they are on heat. Young males are driven out of the herd before they can compete with the dominant bull.

Is a hippo dangerous to man?
An enraged hippo is capable of launching an attack without warning and all hippo should therefore be treated with the utmost caution.

It is justifiably claimed that the hippo is one of the most dangerous of wild animals.

Hippos are especially dangerous when they return from their grazing grounds and find a human being between them and their aquatic territorium. Many women and children fetching water in rivers where hippos abound have been killed or maimed by a returning hippo.

Is a camp fire a deterrent to hippos?
It was once believed that a camp fire would scare off hippos, but a camp and/or fire often receives hostile attention from a resident hippo, especially if it is a solitary bull.

What are a hippo's major enemies?
Apart from lions and crocodiles, which occasionally attack young stray hippos or weakened adults, the hippo has hardly any other enemies apart from man.

Would a crocodile attack a hippo?
The large size, thick hide and death-dealing canines and incisors of the hippo make it far superior to a crocodile, which seldom if ever takes a chance with a fully grown hippo.

How are hippo numbers regulated in a natural ecosystem?
Lack of food, disease and to some extent fights amongst bulls keep their numbers under control. During the severe drought of 1969 to 1970 more than 140 carcasses of hippos that died from starvation were found in the Letaba-Olifants area of the Park.

Why were these animals hunted so frequently in the past?
They were hunted for their meat, fat and hides, and also to stop their raids on farm crops. The thick parts of the hides were used for sjamboks, while the rest of the hides made good leather when tanned.

Is hippo meat tasty?
Many people regard it as tasty, but beef and mutton have more flavour.

Do hippos have to be culled?
Yes, but only occasionally. When rivers become overcrowded with hippos, considerable trampling is caused to the vegetation on and near the river banks.

How long is the gestation period?
Surprisingly for such a large animal, it is only 240 days. Large animals usually have a longer gestation period than this.

What is mass of the calf at birth?
About 30 to 40 kg.

Can hippos have twins?
Twins are rare. The cows usually have one calf at a time.

Where are the calves born?
They can be born either on land or in the water. The birthing process is fast, which enables calves that are born in water to immediately surface and get their vital first breath of air.

Can calves suckle under water?
Yes, but they have to surface frequently to breathe. They are also known to suckle on land.

At what time of year are the young born?
In the Kruger National Park they can be born at any time of year, but most births take place during the summer months.

Do hippos mate in water or on land?
They mate either in water or on land.

What is the potential lifespan?
Approximately 40 to 50 years. The record was set by 'Peter the Great', a hippo bull that lived in a New York zoo from 1903 to 1953 and died at the age of 49.

How many hippos are there in the Park?
Approximately 2 575, according to the 1990 census, but their numbers fluctuate.

It is doubtful whether the Park could accommodate many more than this figure without causing problems of overcrowding in the rivers and dams and serious damage to vegetation on the river banks.

How are hippo counted?
From a low-flying helicopter.

What are their closest relatives?
Hippos belong to the order Artiodactyla, or even-toed mammals, having four toes on each foot. They are further classified under the suborder Suiformes, which includes pigs. There are only two genera, each with one species, namely the ordinary hippo (*Hippopotamus amphibius*) and the pygmy or dwarf hippo (*Choeropsis liberiensis*) from Liberia. Had it not been for the sterling work done by zoological gardens, *Choeropsis liberiensis* would probably have been extinct by now.

BURCHELL'S ZEBRA Equus burchellii (Gray, 1824)

What is the distribution?
Burchell's zebra occurs throughout the savanna regions from the Sudan in East Africa to South Africa. The subspecies *E. b. antiquorum* (H Smith, 1841) is represented and distributed throughout the Park.

The mountain zebra (*E. zebra zebra*) Linnaeus, 1758, is restricted to the Mountain Zebra National Park near Cradock and isolated areas in the Cape Province. Slight differences occur between the Cradock populations and those in Namibia and Angola, where Hartmann's mountain zebra is found.

Are zebras restricted to certain areas of the Park?
They are found throughout the Park in the more open areas, with high concentrations along the eastern boundary. The 1990 aerial census indicated that there were 31 910 zebra in the Park, with the heaviest population (12 176 animals) in the central region (Mason, 1991).

What type of habitat do they prefer?
They prefer open grassy plains and parkland savanna with shortish grass.

What do they eat?
Zebra are essentially grazers, but do browse occasionally.

Are they dependent on water?
They are very dependent on water and as a rule do not wander very far from waterholes. They drink daily and regularly, with an average intake of water of about 14 litres per day.

Zebras drink mainly during the day, especially between about 09:00 and 12:00 in winter and a little earlier in summer. In winter they also tend to spend more time around the waterholes than in summer. Drinking at night is rare and usually occurs only on moonlit nights.

How do they manage to keep in good condition, even when food is scarce?
The fact that zebra are always fat and look well-nourished stems from their adaptability. Most other grazers use their tongues to crop the grass and feed it into their mouths, but zebra use their front teeth. They can therefore graze down to soil level and at times even dig up corms and rhizomes, particularly during times of drought.

What are the main physical features?
This stockily built member of the horse family attains a shoulder height of 1,26 to 1,46 m and a mass of 270 to 380 kg. Females are slightly heavier than males and the record mass for the Park is held by a mare at 429,4 kg. The maximum shoulder height is attained at about three years of age and the maximum mass at five years.

The most striking physical feature is the pattern of black stripes on a white or buff background. These stripes are very broad and oblique over the hindquarters, with lighter shadow stripes visible on the rump and sometimes the shoulder. The ears are short and an upright mane of stiff hairs reaches along the neck to the shoulders. The outer parts of the leg are lightly striped.

Is there much variation in the stripe patterns of individual zebras?
Zebras are well known and easily recognizable by their characteristic stripes. Just as humans all have different fingerprints, so no two individual zebras have the same stripe pattern.

How many different zebra species are there in the Park?
Basing their opinion on the fact that no two animals have exactly the same stripe pattern, some taxonomists have considered the possibility that there could be two subspecies. However, it is now generally accepted that there is in fact only one subspecies in the Park (*Equus burchelli antiquorum*).

How does the mountain zebra differ from Burchell's zebra?
The stripes of the mountain zebra are narrower and do not meet on the belly. Shadow stripes are absent and the stripes on the rump form a 'grid-iron' pattern. A loose piece of skin on the ventral side of the neck, called a dewlap, is present and the ears are relatively larger than those of Burchell's zebra.

What are the habits of Burchell's zebra?
These zebra are restless, noisy creatures, which utter a characteristic barking whinny. They are highly sociable and live in family groups, which in turn can form fairly large herds. The average size of a family unit varies from one distribution area to another; in the Kruger National Park it may be three to seven animals. Family groups account for about 85% of the zebra population in the Park.

How is a family group composed?
It consists of an adult stallion and a couple of mares with their offspring.

How stable are these family units?
It is not uncommon that when a stallion dies, another stallion takes over the whole group.

Where do the stallions without a family group fit in?
Stallions that are not able to secure family groups of their own join up to form stallion groups.

Do stallions fight for mares?
They do fight, but fatalities are rare. A sex ratio of 1,51 mares per stallion has been determined for adult zebra.

How do they fight?
They chop, kick and bite each other. These fights occur frequently and are accompanied by a lot of neighing and kicking up of dust.

Is the stallion the leader of the group?
As is the case with many other herbivores, the dominance of the stallion is more or less restricted to mating and keeping the mares together. The actual leadership is bestowed on the dominant mare.

Does a mare sometimes leave her family group?
When young mares reach sexual maturity they are often abducted from their families by other stallions to form a nucleus for a new family group.

What happens to the young stallions?
They leave the family groups of their own accord or are actively forced out by the dominant stallion.

Do zebra move about?
In the Kruger National Park zebra, especially those of the central area, undertake summer and winter movements.

What is the reason for these movements?
Their seasonal and local movements are closely correlated with the distribution and palatability of grasses and the availability of surface water. Predator pressure, density of the bush and inter-specific competition also affect their movements. Before moving off they congregate in large numbers and afterwards move in long files to their new grazing areas.

Do they often associate with other animals?
The fact that zebra are highly gregarious leads to their frequent association with other species, especially wildebeest. Some stallions and small herds of zebra frequently associate with species such as impala, waterbuck, kudu and wildebeest.

Do they derive any benefit from this association with other animals?
In these mixed groups the additional sensory receptors of the different species augment each other, especially in the detection of predators.

Zebra and wildebeest are very often found together. Is there any specific reason for this?
Many people believe that one of the two species – it is not always clear which one – can hear or see better than the other. The one with the poorer hearing or sight will therefore benefit from this association.

But their association is probably more fortuitous than anything else due to their similar habitat preference and gregarious habits.

Do they have specific breeding seasons?
They are seasonal breeders with a clear mating and foaling season. The latter period occurs in summer, from October to March, in the Kruger National Park, when more than 80% of the foals are born.

How long is the gestation period?
The gestation period varies between 360 and 390 days, with 375 days as the mean. Foals follow the mares directly after birth and are not hidden away for a while.

What is the birth mass?
It varies between 30 and 40 kg.

Can a mare produce twins?
In a study conducted over a number of years, Smuts (1974) found no indication of twins.

How long do foals suckle?
Weaning can take place between nine and 16 months of age, with the average about 11 months.

At what age do mares produce their first offspring?
Mares produce their first foals at about three-and-a-half years of age and can continue to breed until old age, which can be considered to be between 18 and 20 years.

How can one determine their age?
Rings resembling the year rings of trees can be counted when teeth taken from skulls are ground down.

According to this method it has been established that zebra can live for 20 years or more.

Which predators are their major enemies?

In the Park zebras are chiefly preyed upon by lions, which account for more than 90% of zebra kills. Leopard, cheetah, hyena and wild dogs are responsible for a small percentage of kills, mostly non-adults.

Are zebra very susceptible to diseases?

Zebra are free from many of the diseases common to wild bovids, particularly foot-and-mouth disease.

Have they been hunted heavily?

Because of their excellent senses of hearing, sight and smell, zebras are very difficult animals to approach. It therefore requires skill and cunning to hunt them on foot.

The adult stallion of a family group is more susceptible to being hunted than the mare. This is largely due to the investigatory and protective role assumed by the stallion when danger threatens. The mares and young will be the first to flee from any danger, whereas the stallion takes up his position behind them, often stopping to face the suspected danger. Because of this he is exposed to danger more often than the mares and young ones. The mortality rate for stallions is roughly twice that of mares. Generally, however, zebras are better adapted to escape from danger than most of the other herbivores.

Do they defend themselves against predators?

Usually not when lions are concerned, but they will often attack smaller adversaries. Stallions sometimes chase hyenas for up to a hundred metres or more. Hyenas usually try to dodge the stallion and concentrate on the rest of the family group. Lions kill more stallions than mares, while hyenas kill more mares than stallions in the few cases where they do kill adult zebras.

Is foal mortality high?

Mortality due to predation and to a lesser extent diseases could be as high as 60 to 80% in the first year of life.

Does the zebra have any relatives in the Park?

The zebra belongs to the order Perissodactyla (uneven-toed mammals), which includes three recent families: the Equidae, or horses, the Tapiridae, or tapirs, and the Rhinocerotidae, or rhinoceroses. Of the last-named, the black and the white rhino occur in the Park.

BLACK RHINOCEROS *Diceros bicornis* (Linnaeus, 1758)

What is the distribution?
In the past rhinos were widely distributed in suitable habitats south of the Sahara, excluding the rain forests. Their range of distribution was, and still is, much wider than that of the white rhino.

In South Africa at present members of the subspecies *D. b. minor* (Linnaeus, 1758) are restricted to the Kruger National Park and some of the Natal parks. The subspecies *D. b. michaeli* (Zukowski, 1964) is found in the Addo Elephant National Park (introduced in 1961), while *D. b. bicornis* (Linnaeus, 1758) can be seen in the Augrabies Falls National Park and the Vaalbos National Park (both these populations were re-introduced from Namibia).

Are there rhino species outside Africa?
There are three more species, all in danger of becoming extinct. They are the two single-horned rhinos, *Rhinoceros unicornis* from India and *Dicerorhinus sumatrensis* from Sumatra, and the Javan species *Rhinoceros sondaicus*.

Where can one see black rhino in the Kruger National Park?
They are found mostly between Skukuza and Pretoriuskop. A few have crossed the Sabie River, but they are seldom seen.

When did black rhinos disappear from the Park?
A black rhino, a cow, was seen between Skukuza and Lower Sabie in the Nwatimhiri bush in 1936 (Braack,

1988) by ranger Harry Kirkman. He followed her spoor for days on end and eventually saw her for only a few minutes before she disappeared into the thickets, never to be seen again.

Have black rhino always been in the Kruger National Park?
At the proclamation of the old Sabie Game Reserve there was still a small number of black rhinos in the area. These animals moved from the Kruger National Park to Mozambique and back at times, but by 1946 the last of them had definitely disappeared (Pienaar, *et al.* 1987).

How did they become extinct in the Kruger National Park?
There were very few of them left and breeding opportunities were therefore most unfavourable. Black rhinos also roamed extensively over large areas and probably often found themselves outside the Kruger National Park, where they fell prey to hunters.

When were they re-introduced?
Twenty were brought from Natal in 1971, 12 from Zimbabwe (then Rhodesia) in 1972, while a further translocation programme, comprising 38 animals from Natal, was started in 1977 and undertaken again in the period 1980 to 1982.

Have the re-introduced animals settled down well?
Yes. Breeding herds occur in the Lubyelubye area near Lower Sabie and also between Tshokwane and Satara.

Were there any fatalities among them?
Of the few that died after they were
re-introduced, one was trapped in a
cable snare and killed by poachers,
one was badly injured by a hippo and
another one was fatally mauled by
lions. Two more died in the antelope
camp near Pretoriuskop as a result of
botulism, and one was killed in a fight.
It is also believed that one or more
strayed out of the Park and were killed
by poachers. However, their numbers
are increasing and at present there are
some 125 black rhino in the Park.

*Were all the black rhinos released
immediately after translocation?*
After arrival in the Park they were first
kept in bomas, or pens, to allow them
to get used to their new environment.
Some were kept in camps near
Skukuza and Pretoriuskop, but
eventually all were released. The latest
arrivals were released directly in the
Kruger National Park.

What type of habitat do they prefer?
They have a wider habitat range than
the white rhino and are found in many
different types of terrain, including
savanna, bush and wooded mountain
regions.

What do they eat?
Black rhinos are browsers, utilizing a
wide variety of trees and shrubs. Their
food plants include the euphorbias
such as tamboti (*Spirostachys africana*)
and the candelabra tree (*Euphorbia
ingens*), both poisonous to humans.

What are the main physical features?
With a mass of 800 to 1 100 kg, the
black rhino is less bulky than the
white rhino. The head is relatively
short, without a hump at the back of
the neck, and the rhino usually carries
it more or less horizontally, especially
when walking. The rear horn is
sometimes nearly as long as the front
horn. The upper lip is pointed and
prehensile, and adapted for browsing.
The shoulder height is 1,5 to 1,6 m.
The three-toed foot, with the middle
toe larger than the other two, leaves a
spoor shaped like the ace of clubs.

What are the horns made of?
The horns are outgrowths of the
dermal papillae of the hide which in a
way resembles compressed hair. They
are therefore not true horns, which
have bony cores and bony sheaths.

Can a broken horn grow again?
Yes, a new horn can replace an old
one, which usually breaks at the base.

*Some rhinos seem to be lighter in
colour than others. Why?*
The colour of the mud of their last
mud bath is usually responsible for
this difference. Their normal colour is
light to dark grey.

*Where does the name 'black rhino'
come from?*
The origin of the name is not clear, but
it is claimed that black rhinos were
first seen by white hunters at the Black
Umfolozi River in Natal. They were
apparently called black rhinos to distinguish them from the other rhino species,
the square-lipped or white rhino.

How fast can they run?
Probably 30 to 40 km/h. Claims of up
to 50 km/h have appeared in the
literature, but no proof of this speed
has been found.

It is claimed that they are short-sighted. Is this true?
They are very short-sighted and must therefore rely on their excellent sense of smell and fairly well-developed hearing.

Are black rhinos solitary or gregarious?
There is a strong tendency towards a solitary way of life, but it is quite common to find a bull and a cow or a cow and one or more calves of different ages together.

Are they territorial in habit?
Not in the true sense of the word, because they do not defend an area against other members of the same sex. They do, however, frequent and mark certain areas which can be regarded as their home range. Variation in the availability of food and water could force them to wander considerably within the boundaries of their home range.

Do the bulls fight frequently?
Fights for the favours of a female occur fairly often and are fatal in a small percentage of cases. When a bull and cow encounter another adult male, a fight may ensue. The cow takes little or no interest in the fight and will accept the winner without any fuss.

Does the black rhino calf follow its mother, or does it run ahead of her?
The black rhino calf runs behind its mother, in contrast to the white rhino calf which runs ahead.

How strong is the relationship between the mother and her calf?
A very strong bond exists between them. The mother will defend her calf fiercely and the latter will defend its mother if she is wounded. If the mother dies for any reason, her calf may remain with her carcass for a few days and try to chase away any animals that approach it.

Calves usually stay with their mothers until they are sexually mature, even if the mother has given birth to another calf in the meantime.

Is the black rhino really as aggressive as people believe?
The black rhino has been singled out by many hunters as one of the most unpredictable and short-tempered beasts of the African bush. This picture suited hunters very well as an excuse to kill the animals and above all to appear to be a hero for killing such a 'dangerous' quarry. Its huge horns hardly seem to be designed for peaceful purposes, but on the other hand it is not as dangerous as generally believed. It is nevertheless aggressive and temperamental to some extent, and one should not take any liberties.

Why are rhinos so fond of mud baths?
Apart from the cooling effect on a hot day, the mud also affords protection against stinging insects and ticks. Many of their ectoparasites become dislodged when the mud dries.

One often sees big dung heaps along the road, especially between Skukuza and Pretoriuskop. Were they left by rhinos?
Rhinos often defecate in the same spot and then kick open the dung as a means of marking their home range.

What is the difference between rhino and elephant dung?
The dung balls of rhino are smaller and darker than those of elephant.

Is there a noticeable difference between the dung of black and white rhinos?
The heaps of dung are about the same size and shape, but the dung of the black rhino is not as dark as that of its white cousin and the remains of twigs and leaves are quite conspicuous.

When do black rhino drink water?
Although they have adapted fairly well to hot, dry conditions, black rhino still have to drink frequently, preferably every day. They usually drink at night, but it is not uncommon to see them at a waterhole in the early morning or late afternoon.

Are they active during the hot part of the day?
No, they prefer to lie in the shade or immerse themselves in a muddy pool.

It is therefore not so easy to spot them, especially wheyn they are in fairly dense bush.

Do they move about?
They wander about a lot and are not territorial in the true sense of the word. Scarcity of food and water may force them to move to better areas.

Are they nocturnal in habit?
To a certain extent, yes. They feed and drink mostly at night or in the early morning or late afternoon.

When does mating take place?
There seems to be no peak period and young ones may be seen any time of the year.

How long is the gestation period?
Approximately 450 days.

What is the mass of the calf at birth?
About 30 to 40 kg.

How long does the calf suckle?
For up to two years.

How many teats has the mother?
Two, between the hindlegs.

When are black rhinos fully grown?
Sexual maturity is reached between five and seven years of age, but maximum mass is probably attained a few years later.

How long do they live?
Up to 40 years.

What are their major enemies?
Lions occasionally kill a sickly adult or a stray calf. In the past, and to a great extent in the present, too, man has been their principal enemy.

Why were they hunted so heavily?
Powdered rhino horn is regarded as an aphrodisiac by many people from Africa and the Orient and has always fetched high prices. This fallacy has almost led to the extinction of black rhino and still poses a serious threat to their survival.

What gave rise to this strange belief in the supposed properties of rhino horn?
It could be due to the animal's prolonged sex act, which may last for more than half an hour.

Is disease an important mortality factor?
Mortality due to disease, starvation and parasites seems to be fairly low.

What birds are often associated with rhinos?
Oxpeckers, particularly the Redbilled Oxpecker (*Buphagus erythrorhynchus*), which rid the animal of ticks and at the same time serve as sentinels.

To which other animals is the rhino related?
It is related to the horse and the tapir.

They look prehistoric. Did they evolve a long time ago?
They do have a long prehistory and have probably existed in their current form for many millions of years.

WHITE RHINOCEROS *Ceratotherium simum* (Burchell, 1817)

Did the white rhino ever enjoy a wide distribution in Africa?
At one time the white rhino had a wide area of distribution, ranging from north-west Africa to the Cape. Man's conflict with these animals has led to their distribution shrinking alarmingly. A form that some taxonomists consider to be a separate subspecies, *Ceratotherium simum cottoni* (Lydekker, 1908), inhabits a small area near the source of the Nile comprising the north-western part of Uganda, southern Sudan and Zaïre. This population is virtually extinct. The subspecies found in the Park is *C. s. simum* (Burchell, 1817).

Where do we find them in southern Africa?
It has been claimed that by 1920 there were only 20 left in southern Africa, all of them confined to parks in Natal. About 50 years later, there were more than a thousand as a result of intensive conservation practices by the Natal Parks Board. They are now found in many reserves in South Africa.

When did the white rhino become extinct in the Transvaal?
According to the hunter Vaughan-Kirby, the last white rhino in the Transvaal was seen near the Sabie River in 1896, some two years before the proclamation of the Sabie Game Reserve.

Why did the white rhino disappear before the black rhino?
The virtually non-aggressive white rhino frequented the more open areas and was easier to hunt than the more aggressive, bush-living black rhino. The latter was also found in greater numbers in larger areas of Africa.

When was the white rhino re-introduced into the Kruger National Park?
The historic event took place on 14 October 1961, when two bulls and two cows from Natal were released near Pretoriuskop in the south-western section of the Park. 341 rhino were translocated between 1961 and 1972.

Are they widely distributed in the Kruger National Park?
Fairly, but they are mostly confined to the area between the Sabie and Crocodile rivers. There is a small group along the Tsende River between Letaba and Shingwedzi, and some in the Satara area.

Were all the translocated white rhinos kept in a camp for some time before they were released?
The first group was kept in the camp near Pretoriuskop, but later arrivals were released in the wild immediately.

What type of habitat do they prefer?
They prefer well-watered grassland and lightly wooded or open savanna.

What do they eat?
They are essentially grazers, and the broad square mouth is very well adapted for their method of feeding.

How much do they eat?
Probably 100 kg of vegetation (especially grass) per day.

When do they visit the waterholes?
Usually at night or early morning. The warmer part of the day is spent in the shade of trees.

What are their main physical features?
They are very bulky, with a pronounced hump at the neck; the head is carried low and the front horn is noticeably longer than the rear one; the ears are somewhat trumpet-shaped and fringed with hair. The colour is grey to dark grey and can differ in shade depending on their last mud bath.

White rhinos are second in size only to the elephant as far as land mammals are concerned.

How large can a white rhino get?
The shoulder height is 1,6 to 1,7 m. The mass of a bull is 2 000 to 2 300 kg and that of a cow 1 400 to 1 600 kg.

What is the size of the horns?
The horns are bigger and longer than those of the black rhino. The average length of the front horn is 60 to 90 cm, although the record length is an incredible 158,12 cm.

The record for the rear one is 56,52 cm. The front horn is usually smooth from being rubbed against anthills, stones or trees, whereas the rear one appears coarse.

What are the horns made of?
Like those of the black rhino, the horns of the white rhino are outgrowths of dermal papillae in the skin, i.e. bundles of stiff hairs.

Is there any difference between the horns of males and females?
The horns of the females tend to be more slender and sometimes longer than those of the males.

Can broken horns grow again?
Yes, a new horn can replace one that
has been broken off. If it breaks, the
fracture usually occurs at the base
where it is attached to the nasal bones
of the skull.

*What speed can this heavyweight
achieve?*
Unsubstantiated claims indicate about
40 km/h. Whether or not it could
really reach this speed, this huge
animal is nevertheless very agile and
amazingly nimble on its feet.

Are their senses well-developed?
White rhinos, like black rhinos, are
short-sighted. Their sense of smell is
excellent and their hearing is also well
developed.

*Why is it called a white rhino when it
is not white in colour?*
There are various explanations for the
origin of the name, but the most
acceptable is that the Dutch word
'wydmond', meaning wide mouth,
became 'white rhino'.
    As in the case of the black rhino, the
name has nothing to do with the
colour of the animal's hide.

*What are the differences between the
white and black rhino?*
The white rhino is a grazer with a
broad, square muzzle, while the
browsing black rhino has a pointed
muzzle with a prehensile upper lip
which it uses to strip leaves from
branches and twigs. The latter usually
keeps its head in line with its back and
can also lift its head higher to feed on
leaves. The white rhino, with its longer
head carried low most of the time, has
a different profile from that of the

black rhino. Apart from the
pronounced hump on the back of its
neck – absent in the black rhino – the
middle of the back is slightly arched in
contrast to the more or less concave
back-line of the black rhino.
    There is little or no difference in skin
colour. The black rhino also tends to
appear more aggressive than the white
rhinoceros.

*Are white rhinos solitary or
gregarious?*
They are not gregarious in the true
sense of the word but like to form
small groups of up to six or more
individuals.

Are they territorial in habit?
A territory is marked and defended by
a single territorial bull.
    Each group, family or solitary
individual has its own preferred
grazing and watering area.

Do they mark their territory?
Bulls do mark their territories and, like
the black rhino, defecate in the same
locality, creating a large dung heap.

Do they have a social hierarchy?
A hierarchy which we find with true
herd-forming animals is absent, but
there is a definite order of dominance.
Bulls often fight fiercely for the
favours of a female, and in a family or
social group the dominant bull will
drive away any young mature bulls if
he is able to do so.

Are they aggressive?
They are placid, even-tempered
animals. One can approach them quite
closely, but it is advisable to keep a
safe distance.

Do they like mud baths?
Yes. White rhinos enjoy wallowing.

Are they, like black rhinos, accompanied by tick-eating birds?
They are, and although these birds are called 'renostervoëls' ('rhino birds') in Afrikaans, they are by no means restricted to rhino alone; many other herbivores, such as giraffe and antelope, are visited by them.

How long is the gestation period?
It is about 16 months. One calf is usually born and the mass at birth is around 40 kg.

How long is the calving interval?
A calf is born roughly every three to four years.

How long does the calf suckle?
Probably for about 18 months.

Do white rhino have a specific breeding period?
They breed throughout the year, but in Natal birth peaks occur in March and July of a year.

At what age is sexual maturity reached?
Between five and seven years of age.

How many teats does the mother have?
Two, situated between the hindlegs (inguinally).

Does the white rhino calf follow its mother?
No, the white rhino calf usually runs slightly ahead of its mother.

Is the relationship between mother and calf strong?
The bond is very strong. The mother will fiercely defend her calf, and the latter will also defend its mother should circumstances arise.

What is the lifespan of white rhinos?
About 40 to 50 years.

Do they have natural enemies?
Not really. Stray calves could fall prey to the larger predators, but a healthy, fully grown rhino is more than a match for a lion. Man still remains the biggest enemy of the white rhino.

AFRICAN ELEPHANT *Loxodonta africana* (Blumenbach, 1797)

How many elephants are there in the Kruger National Park?
The figure varies from year to year, but the Park's biologists try to keep it at about 7 500 by means of culling.

Are they evenly distributed throughout the Park?
Although they are found everywhere in the Park, they are concentrated mostly in the central and northern sections.

The area from the Olifants River to the northern boundary accommodates about 70% of the population, while 24% are found between the Olifants and the Sabie rivers, and only about 6% south of the Sabie.

How many were there when the old Sabie Game Reserve was proclaimed in 1898?
There were none left. Even the Shingwedzi area, which was proclaimed a game reserve shortly after the Sabie Reserve, had no resident elephants.

Small numbers of these animals migrated between Shingwedzi and Mozambique.

It was only around 1912 that Stevenson-Hamilton could report a resident herd of about 25 elephants along the Shingwedzi River.

Did the current population come from this small herd?
They contributed to the population, but large numbers of elephants entered the Park from Mozambique before the completion of the elephant-proof fence in 1976.

What is the status of elephants in the rest of Africa?
Their range is more restricted than formerly, but they occur throughout central, East and West Africa. They are considered endangered and, although a fairly substantial population remains (about 600 000 animals), illegal hunting and poaching for ivory as well as the demand for more agricultural land and competition with domestic stock – which are allowed in many parks – still pose a grave threat to their survival.

Are elephant populations found elsewhere in South Africa?
A number of nature reserves along the western boundary of the Park accommodate some elephants. The Addo Elephant National Park has a population of about 175 and a few, probably only three, inhabit the Knysna forest between George and Plettenberg Bay. A small number are found at Ndumo in northern Natal, while a number of young elephants have been translocated from the Kruger National Park to Hluhluwe Game Reserve in Natal.

What type of habitat do they prefer?
Elephants have managed to adapt to a wide range of habitats and may be found in savanna, forest and even mountainous areas up to altitudes of more than 3 000 m.

What is their favourite food?
Because of their adaptability to a wide range of habitats, they utilize many different plant species. According to

circumstances, they either browse or graze and there is a pronounced seasonal variation in the composition of their diet. It is said that if sufficient palatable grass is available, they will graze more than browse. Bark of trees, fruit, roots and herbs are also consumed.

How much does an elephant usually eat per day?

Claims by different authors vary between 150 and 300 kg consumed in 24 hours. Close on 18 out of the 24 hours are spent feeding. An estimate of about 200 kg of food per day would seem realistic. The elephant is very extravagant in its feeding habits and often destroys more than it actually consumes.

How much water can an elephant drink?

Research in the Kruger National Park indicates a figure of about 90 litres per day. Large bulls can drink up to 350 litres at a time, averaging about 200 litres per day.

While drinking they squirt copious amounts of water over their bodies to cool themselves.

Do elephants prefer natural waterholes to artificial reservoirs and troughs?

They prefer natural waterholes where they can wallow in the mud or, if the water is deep enough, to swim and play. Dipping each other appears to be a favourite pastime. However, they also readily drink at reservoirs. It is said that cows often suck water from a reservoir and then squirt it into a hollow in the ground for their calves to drink.

At what time of the day do elephants drink?

In summer they usually drink in the early morning or late afternoon, whereas in winter they drink at around midday.

Do elephants dig for water in sandy riverbeds as some other game animals are seen to do?

They can dig holes up to about 1,8 m deep and, after they have had their fill, other animals often make use of these waterholes.

How long can they go without water?

In arid areas they can probably go without water for many days, depending on climatic conditions and the moisture content of the food they eat at that specific time. In the Park they usually visit the waterholes every day. They also tend to drink more water in summer than during the cool winter months.

Can an elephant withdraw water from its stomach?

According to Dr Anthony Hall-Martin (*personal communication*), this happens occasionally.

The water is then squirted over the body to cool it, especially when they are pursued by ardent hunters. This may be a physiological reaction based on extreme stress.

Do elephants follow specific routes to the water?

Elephant footpaths are well known and these huge beasts are very adept at finding the easiest way up a slope or a mountainside. Many an old transport road has been built on an original elephant path.

What are the differences between African and Indian elephants?
The African elephant (*Loxodonta africana*) has a back that is more or less concave and saddle-shaped; enormous ears that, when extended, cover the shoulders; a rounded and sloping forehead; a trunk with two pointed projections at the upper and lower parts of the tip; large and developed tusks in both sexes; and it is bulkier and higher at the shoulder than the Indian species.

The Indian elephant (*Elephas maximus*) has a back that is convex and steeply sloping; small, triangular ears that do not cover the shoulders; prominent bulges on the forehead above the eyes; a trunk with only one upper projection at the tip; small tusks that are usually visible in the male only; and it is obviously smaller than its African counterpart.

What is the mass of an elephant?
Fully grown males normally attain a mass of up to 5 000 kg or slightly more, while cows have a mass of 4 000 to 5 000 kg.

What is the all-out record mass?
A hunter by the name of Fenykovi shot an exceptionally large elephant in Angola on 13 November 1955. Its shoulder height was 4 m and its mass estimated at about 10 900 kg. J. M. Oosterveen shot an elephant with a shoulder height of 4,42 m (Rowland Ward) in Namibia in 1977; the mass was not determined.

What is the normal height of an elephant?
It is about 3 m for a bull and approximately 2,7 m for a cow at the shoulder.

How fast can an elephant run?
It is claimed that they can run about 40 km/h over a short distance.

How is it possible for an elephant to walk so quietly through the bush?
The soles of the feet are covered with thick padding which prevents the elephant from slipping and effectively deadens the sound of twigs trampled underfoot.

It appears difficult to distinguish between bulls and cows. Are there features which could assist one in determining their sex?
The absence of a scrotum in the bull is due to the testicles being situated internally, and the fact that the female genitals are quite often not visible makes it difficult to tell the sexes apart. There are a few features, however, which serve as guidelines. Seen in profile, the cow's head shows a slight angle while that of the bull is rounded. Cows are usually smaller and their tusks are small compared to those of fully grown bulls.

What is the record length for a tusk?
According to Rowland Ward the longest tusk measured was 3,384 m; it belonged to an elephant shot in East Africa. The Kruger National Park record is 2,51 m.

What is the record mass of a tusk?
It is 102,3 kg for a bull and 25,46 kg for a cow. The Park record stands at 63 kg for a bull. Nowadays tusks of more than 40 kg each are rare.

How long before the tusks develop?
In both sexes tusk growth is continuous throughout life. Tusk

growth rates vary considerably in the bulls. The tusks of cows occasionally grow fairly long and slender, while those of bulls continue to thicken as they lengthen.

What is the purpose of the tusks?
The tusks are used for defence, digging up roots and stripping bark from trees.

Is it true that elephants are 'left-' or 'right-handed' in the use of their tusks?
An elephant will often tend to make use of one tusk only, or use one more than the other, and it appears to be mostly the right tusk.

Are the tusks modified canine teeth?
No, they are modified incisors. Instead of the four incisors found in many mammals, the elephant has two tusks, no canines and only three functional molars at a time.

Do they shed their teeth?
Elephants have six sets of four molars in their lifetime. One set is replaced by the next set from the back of the jaw and, as they move forwards to make room for the new set, fragments of the old teeth break off. By the time a new tooth is in position, the last fragment of the previous one has disappeared. Each tooth that comes into wear is longer and wider than the previous one, and this progression helps to establish an elephant's age.

According to Laws (1966) the six molars are fully developed at the following ages: molar one at one year, molar two at two years, molar three at six years, molar four at 15 years, molar five at 28 years and molar six at 47 years. At about 60 years of age only a fragment of the last molar remains in each half of the jaws. At this stage chewing becomes progressively more ineffective and starvation is the animal's fate.

What is the capacity and size of the trunk?
The trunk, which can be up to 2 m long, can weigh 100 kg or more and has a capacity of some 17 litres.

Are elephants really short-sighted?
They cannot see very well, but it would be dangerous to underestimate their visual powers.

Are their other senses well developed?
The senses of hearing and smell are well developed.

It is said that elephants are clever. Is this true?
Intelligence is actually a human virtue, but if we could ascribe this characteristic to animals the elephant would have a high rating.

How big is an elephant's brain?
It is about four times the size of a human brain. Taking the size of the animal into consideration, this means that the human being has proportionally 15 times more brain matter than the elephant.

Does it have a good memory?
The relatively large brains and long lifespan probably implies a good memory.

What is the size of an elephant's heart?
An elephant with body mass 5 000 kg can possess a heart of 25 kg, or 0,5% of its body mass. If this seems small for

such a huge beast, one must remember that an elephant very seldom has to run or exert itself.

How fast does its heart beat?
It is about 50 beats per minute, but under stress can go up to about 90 or 100 beats per minute.

Does an elephant have a tongue?
Yes, and it may have a mass of about 12 kg. Unlike that of a giraffe, it is not protrudable.

What is the average herd size?
Herd sizes can vary from a few animals to a few hundred. In the Park herds usually consist of 10 to 30 animals. Smaller herds may amalgamate to form the large herds that are sometimes reported.

What type of hierarchy exists in an elephant herd?
The social life of elephants is essentially matriarchal and a basic family unit is organized around an adult cow and her offspring of both sexes, or other closely related cows and their offspring. At puberty males leave the family units and join or form small bachelor groups.

Is there no dominant bull in a herd?
Adult bulls join the family units or herds consisting of a number of family units when one or more of the cows is on heat (in oestrus). The strongest bull present at a specific time is therefore also the dominant bull.

Who leads the family unit or herd?
The oldest cow in a unit or a herd usually takes the lead in ordinary herd movements and activities such as

flight or attack. When a family unit is disturbed there is an immediate tendency for members of the unit to bunch around the lead cow. If she stands, or charges, or takes flight, the rest will follow. The members of a bachelor group tend to react individually when danger threatens. If they take flight they often run in different directions with complete disregard for other group members.

Are elephants territorial in habit?
There is no convincing evidence of territorial behaviour, although solitary bulls, bull groups and herds have fairly distinct home ranges.

How big is the home range?
It can vary considerably in different habitat types as well as different climatic conditions. Douglas-Hamilton (1975) found that home ranges in the Manyara Park, Tanzania, varied between 15 and 52 km^2. Leuthold & Sale (1973) established that home ranges in Tsavo West, Kenya, could be about 350 km^2, while in Tsavo East they could be as large as 1 580 km^2. The sizes of home ranges in the Kruger National Park can be approximately 2 500 km^2 in extent.

How stable is the herd composition?
Cow families tend to stay together, but the composition of the rest of the herd may vary considerably from time to time. Large herds often break up into smaller herds and could subsequently amalgamate again.

Are old bulls evicted from the herd?
No, they leave the herd voluntarily but may return later. Young bulls often leave the herd for long periods.

Do bulls often fight?
Mock fights or sparring sessions are observed occasionally, but real fights are not common.

Can a bull kill his opponent in a fight?
It does happen, but only rarely.

Are solitary bulls rogue animals?
Usually not. Only a few become rogue but they are eventually destroyed when they leave the confines of the Kruger National Park.

Why do some elephants become rogue?
All the reasons are probably not known, but animals that have been wounded by hunters or injured in some other way could well turn rogue. Elephants sometimes leave the Kruger National Park to raid greener pastures on farms, where they may then be shot or wounded by man.

Are the elephants in the Park dangerous to human beings?
Any elephant is potentially dangerous. When you stop to observe elephants it is advisable to keep a distance of at least 50 m from them.

How does one know when it is safe to pass an elephant?
Elephants are unpredictable and when one or more is standing next to the road rather wait for them to move away before driving on.

Have elephants actually attacked any vehicles in the Park?
Since 1927, when the first three cars with visitors were allowed into the Park, about ten cars have been damaged by elephants. In most of the cases the motorists were negligent and approached within a few metres of the animals.

Do they often charge cars?
No, not often. Even when an elephant does charge, it is often just a mock charge and therefore not dangerous. However, it is difficult to determine whether a charge will be harmless or serious.

What does one do when surrounded by elephants?
It can happen that, while watching a herd of elephants, they will suddenly start crossing the road in front as well as behind a vehicle. Do not panic and try to drive through the herd. Rather switch off the engine of the vehicle and remain silent until the herd has passed and it is safe to drive on.

Is ear-flapping a sign of danger?
Elephants usually flap their ears to help regulate the body temperature on a hot day. The blood in the large veins and arteries of the ears is cooled by several degrees through this action. This cooled blood plays an important role in the regulation of the body temperature. Ear-flapping could, however, also be a sign of annoyance.

Are elephants aggressive towards other animals?
They do not tolerate other animals at a waterhole and a number of zebras and other game have been killed by them. They lash the unfortunate animal with the trunk, breaking its back. A kudu was once found with its back broken in eight places. This is a rare occurrence, however, as other animals usually give way to elephants at waterholes. It is quite hilarious to see lions fleeing, literally with their tails between their legs, to get out of the way of an approaching elephant.

Have any cases been reported of an elephant attacking any of the large game species, such as rhino?
This occurs very rarely, but in 1964 an elephant and a white rhino got involved in a fight at a waterhole near Shingwedzi. The elephant, although injured, won the encounter; the rhino succumbed to its wounds.

Do elephants migrate?
In the past about 10% of the Park's elephant population moved seasonally between the Park and Mozambique. These migrations came to an end after the erection of the elephant-proof fence. Elephants sometimes break through the fence on the southern and western boundaries to raid farm crops.

They do move from one area to another within the Kruger National Park, depending on the availability of food and water.

How far can they walk daily?
During winter when food is scarce they walk about 7 km per day and 4 km per night. They walk less in summer when food and water are more plentiful. If they had to search for water or food, they could probably cover up to 50 km in one night. Their walking speed is somewhere between 4 and 8 km/h.

At what age do elephants reach sexual maturity?
It seems to vary in different parts of Africa, ranging from about 10 to 15 years of age. Cows breed at an earlier age than bulls.

How do elephants mate?
In the same way as cattle and most other animals.

Does the cow dig a hole to facilitate mating?
No, their anatomy is developed for normal copulation.

Do they mate in water?
They are very fond of playing in water and these movements often resemble the mating act. Mating normally takes place on land.

How long is the gestation period?
On average some 22 months. There is no evidence that the gestation period differs for male and female offspring.

What is the calving interval?
About one calf every four years, but there are indications that reproduction is slowed down during prolonged droughts and times of stress due to famine.

How many calves can a cow produce?
Elephant cows breed well into old age and could produce 10 or more calves in a lifetime.

Can a cow produce twins?
The birth of twins was reported in the Park during the early 1960s but it is a rare occurrence.

Does the cow make a bed of grass for the calf to fall on when it is born?
No, the cow gives birth standing upright and the calf does not fall far due to the low position of the cow's birth canal.

What is the size and mass of a newborn calf?
The mass is about 120 kg and the shoulder height approximately 85 cm. The biggest calf, actually an unborn foetus, that was measured in the Kruger National Park had a mass of 164,4 kg.

How many teats has the mother?
Two, situated between the front legs.

How does the calf suckle?
With its mouth, while the trunk is bent over backwards or to the side. It only gradually learns to use the trunk to drink water, which it does by sucking the water up in the trunk and squirting it into the mouth.

When is the calf weaned?
It is weaned at about two years of age, sometimes older.

Is calf mortality high?
Usually not. Calves are very well protected against predators, and they do not seem to be very susceptible to diseases.
   Droughts, however, can take a toll and calf mortality could be as high as 30% under such conditions.

What is the potential lifespan?
As indicated in the discussion on dentition, the lifespan is about 60 years or slightly longer. It could probably reach 70 years in captivity.

What are elephants' major enemies?
For all practical purposes, elephants have no natural enemies except man in areas where they are still hunted. A small stray calf could well fall prey to predators, but calves and their mothers seldom get separated.

Are elephants prone to diseases?
No epizootics have been reported in the history of the Kruger National

Park and the effect of parasites and diseases in general appears to be negligible. Foot-and-mouth disease has been induced artificially in elephants, but in the wild they seem to be immune to the disease.

Although death due to arteriosclerosis appears to be limited, postmortems have revealed that arteriosclerotic lesions occur more frequently with age, particularly in females. This is particularly interesting because in humans it is usually the males who show the first signs of arteriosclerosis.

Do other mortality factors affect elephants?
Apart from old age, accidents, drought, starvation, fighting, stress due to scarcity of food, hunting and especially poaching – all these factors contribute to elephant mortality.

Are there reported cases where elephants died in large numbers due to drought?
The Tsavo disaster in Kenya is the most spectacular documented case of mass deaths in recent times. During the drought years of 1970 and 1971 an estimated 5 900 elephants died of starvation. Juveniles and lactating cows suffered severely. This disaster and suffering could have been minimized to a great extent if a sound culling policy had existed during the preceding years when water and food were still available in sufficient quantities.

What is the annual increase in numbers?
It can be between 4 and 7,5%, about 300 to 560 per year in the Park.

Why must elephant numbers be controlled?
These animals consume large quantities of water and eat and destroy a great deal of the vegetation, thereby endangering their own survival as well as that of rarer species.

During droughts they often dominate waterholes, preventing other animals from drinking.

Do elephants destroy many trees in the Park?
They do, but the damage appears to be more severe than it really is. Solitary bulls and small bull groups are the main culprits and they often walk along a road pushing trees over and tearing branches down. The amount of damage done along the roads is usually not equalled in the bush.

Why do they push trees over?
One is often left with the impression that they do this with little reason. A big tree is often pushed over for the sake of a few leaves at the top. This habit probably assisted in the formation of savanna veld types, which in turn created favourable conditions for grazing herbivores.

Under conditions of elephant over-population, however, trees can disappear too quickly and with them the habitats and food of a variety of mammalian browsers, as well as birds and reptiles.

What size of tree can be pushed over?
It depends on the root system of the tree and the nature of the soil in which it grows. One often sees trees of about 0,5 m in diameter that have been pushed over.

Does an elephant use a special technique to uproot a tree?
A tree is usually rocked forwards and backwards and if this is not successful the elephant will try from a different position.

It is said that elephants eat mud or soil due to some deficiency in their diet. Is this true?
Elephants dig up termite hills and eat the soil, probably for the sodium content. It has also been established that they show a marked preference for water with a high sodium content. The eating of mud and soil could be regarded as a form of pica. Pica, or the eating of strange objects, is a well known phenomenon among herbivores and is caused by deficiencies in their diet.

At times it is difficult to find elephants. What is the reason?
Most elephants are to be found in the northern part of the Park, where there are fewer tourist roads than in the south. The large herds usually keep away from the roads.

After rain the elephants, like many other game species, disperse to utilize the temporary waterholes which are often some distance from the roads. In winter, when water is scarce, they concentrate more along the rivers and at the permanent waterholes where it is easy for visitors to see them.

It is often heard that tourists blame the culling if they do not see elephants. Is there any truth in this statement?
If the National Parks Board were to suspend all culling procedures, visitors would see more elephant for some time, but the Park may well develop into an elephant reserve, with all the destruction that goes with it. If we accept that the Park cannot accommodate unlimited numbers of elephant, then we also have to accept culling as a managerial action.

How many elephants are culled annually?
This figure varies from season to season.

Elephant populations, like all other animal populations, experience cyclical annual variations in births and early mortalities related to environmental conditions. Hanks (1979) found evidence that droughts can have a very marked influence on the birth rate as well as calf mortality.

In general, the number of elephants culled corresponds to the annual increase in the Park's population. Culling could therefore be in the region of 300 to 560 animals per year.

Is there any selection regarding age or sex when elephants are culled?
No. When culling is done the required number of animals is separated from the herd and destroyed. This separation is achieved easily with a low-flying helicopter. A separated group usually consists of males, females and young in the same percentage as that of the rest of the herd. In this way the normal herd composition is not disrupted. There is only one exception. Bulls with very large tusks, which make up a very small percentage of the population, are spared for breeding purposes and as tourist attractions. Solitary bulls and bull groups are taken into account when the culling figure is calculated.

LION *Panthera leo* (Linnaeus, 1758)

Where can lions be seen in the Park?
Lions may be seen everywhere in the Park, but especially where there are large concentrations of herbivores, such as in the central region and the Crocodile Bridge and Lower Sabie areas. It is essential to travel slowly and carefully scan the vicinity of waterholes in order to spot lions because they blend so well with their background.

What is their distribution in the rest of Africa?
Lion are still fairly common in the savanna areas of Africa, although they are mostly confined to nature reserves. In South Africa they may be found in a number of private game reserves on the western boundary of the Kruger National Park, in the Kalahari Gemsbok National Park and in the Hluhluwe Game Reserve in Natal.

Were lions ever found outside Africa?
At one time lions occurred in Europe and the Middle East. They became extinct in Israel in the thirteenth century, in Pakistan in 1842, in Iraq in 1914, and in Iran in 1941. They were once widespread in India, but the last remaining lions are the small endangered group of less than 200 to be found in the Gir sanctuary in the state of Gujarat.

When is the best time for spotting lions?
During hot weather it is advisable to drive out in the early morning and late afternoon because lions prefer to spend the hot part of the day in shade or dense vegetation. When it is cool in winter they are more often seen throughout the day.

Do lions move around during the day?
Although lions are inactive when not on the hunt, they can nevertheless walk distances of 20 km or more per day if necessary.

Do lions hide during rainy weather?
They tend to hide in thickets where they often sit in a hunched position with their backs turned in the direction from which the rain is coming.

What is the lion's preferred prey species?
Preference ratings have been compiled for lion populations in a number of game reserves, including the Kruger National Park. However, this term is unfortunate, for a kill does not necessarily signify only the predator's preference, but also to some degree the availability and vulnerability of the lions' prey.

Preference ratings differ from one area to another and even in the same area at different times. The rating is calculated by dividing the kill frequency by the relative abundance of the prey. On this basis Pienaar (1969) and Smuts (1975) found that waterbuck appear to be the lion's preferred prey. In proportion to the numbers of waterbuck in the Park, therefore, lions kill more of these animals than any other prey. Should we on the other hand consider the actual numbers of animals killed by lion, we find that wildebeest, zebra and impala actually feature more prominently than waterbuck. When the biomass of animals killed is considered we find yet another picture, with giraffe at the top of the list followed by wildebeest, zebra, buffalo, impala, kudu and only then waterbuck. Nearly 30% of the lion's food consists of giraffe meat.

Lions prey on at least 37 species of large and small mammals as well as ostriches, small crocodiles and tortoises, among others.

Do lions prefer large prey to smaller victims?
They show a definite preference for larger prey. Although large prey such as giraffe and buffalo are more difficult to kill, they provide much more food for the increased effort.

Do lions kill only when they are hungry?
Although lions normally kill only to sustain themselves, they do occasionally kill much more than they can consume. This usually happens when the prey animals are in a weak and emaciated condition and unable to escape or offer resistance. During droughts, when prey animals concentrate in large numbers around the last remaining waterholes, lions, particularly young individuals, sometimes kill several head of prey in a herd.

During the severe drought of 1964 a pride of lions killed five adult and 10 young buffalo from a starving herd in one locality near Punda Maria. In 1970 a pride killed six buffalo from a herd about 22 km from Lower Sabie on the road to Crocodile Bridge.

Is it true that herbivores know whether a lion is hungry or not?
It is highly improbable. Herbivores are not concerned about lions when they are visible and at a safe distance. They only get concerned when they smell or hear a lion without being able to locate it, or when a lion is obviously trying to stalk them.

Do lions eat carrion?
Lions normally kill to eat but when prey is scarce or conditions for hunting unfavourable they do not hesitate to eat putrid meat if it is available. In 1967 a pride of 19 lions, including cubs, fed on a giraffe carcass near Skukuza for 10 days. They took turns to go to the river nearby to drink and virtually never left the carcass unguarded. It was at the end of the rainy season and, because the game was dispersed at the many temporary waterholes, the lions found it difficult to make a kill.

In addition to killing their own prey, lions readily scavenge food from other predators such as leopard, cheetah, wild dogs and hyena.

How often do lions kill?
It depends on the size of their last prey, the size of the pride, and on the availability of suitable prey. They feed about once every three to four days, but they can go without food for more than a week. A pride followed by means of radio transmitters was observed to go without food for 11 days.

How much meat can a lion consume at one sitting?
A lion can probably consume as much as a quarter of its body mass when

starved; some authors estimate even as high as a third. Even a quarter is mind-boggling – a lion with a body mass of, say, 200 kg eating 50 kg food at one sitting!

What is the average daily consumption?
A healthy, fully grown lion in the wild probably needs about 7 kg meat a day, and a lioness about 5 kg.

How many animals are killed by a lion per year?
It depends on the size of the available prey and the size, age and physical condition of the lion. The killing rate of an individual lion in the Kruger National Park is probably less than 15 animals per year.

Estimates by different authors in different areas vary between 10 and 70 animals killed by one adult lion in a given year.

What are the biggest animals attacked by lions?
Normally giraffes will be the largest prey attacked by lions. Cases have, however, been reported of lions successfully attacking weakened hippos on dry land as well as diseased or disabled rhinos.

A healthy, fully grown hippo or rhino is more than a match for a lion, or even for a pride, and are therefore very rarely attacked.

Do lions attack elephants?
Fairly large elephant calves have been attacked occasionally by lions in the Park when no adult elephants were present. However, a fully grown elephant is more than a match for any pride of lions.

Are lions sometimes injured by their prey?
Lions have been killed by sable antelope, kudu, buffalo, giraffe, snakes and even porcupines. When a lion attempts to kill a porcupine, quills may become lodged in its paws or mouth, causing death from infection or starvation.

Can a single lion kill a large animal such as a buffalo or giraffe?
Although solitary lions are occasionally successful in attacking adult giraffes and buffalos, these species are usually hunted by more than one lion at a time.

How do lions kill their prey?
According to many authors lions generally kill by seizing the quarry by the nose with one paw, dragging the head down and biting through the back of the neck. It is also said that the neck of the prey is broken by a sideways and downward pull, or the animal is pulled over in such a way that it breaks its neck with the fall. It is interesting to note that in several hundreds of kills examined by Schaller (1972), he could not find a single case in which the prey's neck had been broken.

The method of killing varies with the type and size of the animal preyed upon. Small animals are usually swatted down and then grabbed with both paws. The killing bite is directed at the back of the neck, throat, head or even the chest.

A lion is generally unable to run as fast as its prey but when it charges unexpectedly, and the prey is still accelerating, it can come up from behind or even run alongside.

Do lions also attack their prey from the front?

Prey is seldom attacked from the front because many species carry effective horns and also because an animal is usually in flight when the lions attack.

Do lions kill their prey quickly?

Small prey probably succumb quickly, but larger prey often die from strangulation, suffocation or loss of blood, processes which can last from a few minutes to as long as 10 minutes.

A buffalo bull can sometimes ward off a lion attack for an hour or more before the lions manage to get hold of a vulnerable part of his body. As one lion attacks the throat, the others usually start to tear the animal apart and it therefore dies from loss of blood rather than strangulation.

Where is one most likely to see a kill?

Most kills are made near a waterhole, especially during droughts.

When do lions hunt?

Although they tend to hunt more during the night when their prey cannot see them so easily, a great deal of hunting also takes place during the cooler part of the day.

Do the females do most of the hunting?

In prides and groups where both sexes are present, females kill proportionately more than the males. However, single males and males from male groups do kill their own prey.

When a large animal is attacked by a pride or group of both sexes, the greater mass and superior strength of the males gives them superiority over the females.

Do lions use a specific strategy when they hunt?

Lions often hunt as a group and, according to various authors, they use a variety of strategies to catch their prey. It is often believed that the males take up a position from where they can induce the intended prey to run in the direction of the hiding females, who stalk upwind to get into position. The males are then supposed to move in a semi-circle to a position where the prey smells their scent and then stampedes downwind in the direction of the waiting females. Schaller (1972) noted the direction of the wind in 300 hunts. Of these 84 were upwind, 85 downwind and in the remaining 131 hunts the wind was blowing from one side or the other.

If one is lucky enough to observe the hunt from start to finish, the above strategy appears to be used. However, many authors doubt the existence of cooperative hunting and assume that each member of the pride goes his own way to catch and kill a victim. Schaller (1972) feels that the actual complexity of communal hunts lies between these two extreme viewpoints. One should be careful not to introduce the reasoning of the human mind into the actions of animals.

Schaller goes on to point out that when several lions spot potential prey they usually fan out and stalk them over a broad front. This fanning action may be well coordinated in that those at the flanks walk rapidly in their chosen direction while those in the centre halt or advance slowly. They are therefore encircling the prey and enhancing their chances of a kill. When the prey animals spot the predators, they tend to scatter and in the process some could well head in the direction of the hidden members of the pride or group.

Do lions normally hunt in groups?
One lion or even the whole pride may attack the intended prey. Single lions, however, account for about half of all the kills.

How far can a lion chase its prey?
In stalking its prey a lion will approach to within about 30 m of its victim before it charges. A lion has little stamina and is exhausted after running a few hundred metres. Nearly 90% of hunts consist of stalks followed by a short run. In the remaining 10% the prey is ambushed.

Do lions often become man-eaters?
In the past lions killed a number of humans in parts of Africa. Although people have been attacked and killed by lions, and even devoured, man-eating has never posed a serious problem in the Kruger National Park. Less than 20 people have been killed and even fewer eaten by lions in the entire history of the Park.
    When a lion kills a human being, everything possible is done to track it down and destroy it.

Does a lion necessarily become a man-eater after only one attack on a human?
Not necessarily so.

What causes a lion to become a man-eater?
If has often been claimed that old or incapacitated lions are the main culprits. This, however, is not always

the case. Many a man-eater has proved to be a healthy animal in its prime.
    Most man-eaters probably started their career after an accidental encounter with a human.

Do lions kill other predators?
They seldom kill other predators for food, but hyenas or jackals that approach to close to lions feeding on a carcass risk the lions' wrath and are sometimes killed. Cheetahs and leopards have been killed by lions from time to time in the Kruger National Park, but they were very seldom consumed.

Could vultures lead lions to a dead animal?
Lions, like hyenas and even wild dogs, are vulture watchers.

Are lions cannibalistic in any way?
Lions are confirmed cannibals and the urge is not necessarily caused by hunger. Although cases of cannibalism have been recorded, they make up only a very small proportion of lion kills.
    Females occasionally kill and eat their own cubs, and males may also kill and eat cubs.

Why do they become cannibalistic?
The reasons are unknown. There have been a number of cases in which lions became cannibalistic after one had been killed in a fight, but this is a rare occurrence.

Does a lion necessarily become a habitual cannibal after one such act?
No, not necessarily, and if it should happen it would be a rare phenomenon.

What are their main physical features?
The body colour varies from an ochre-tinted grey to dark ochre brown on the upper part of the body. The underparts are always lighter in colour. The shoulder height is about 1 m or slightly more, while the mass of a fully grown male could be about 180 to 225 kg. Females could be as much as 40 to 50 kg lighter than the males.

Do all males possess a mane?
Maneless lions are very exceptional, but the sizes of manes differ to an extent. The mane starts to grow when the lion is about 6 months old.

Why do some males have black manes?
The mane usually becomes darker with age, but inherited pigmentation is also important.

What speed can a lion reach when charging?
A lion is deceptively fast over a short distance. Claims of up to 80 km/h have been made but not yet proved. This seems to be high for an animal the size of a lion with its relatively short legs and bulky body.

Can lions climb trees?
Yes, although not very often. They are surprisingly agile in this respect, especially the females. Lions can climb trees far better than humans.

Are all their senses well developed?
Their sense of smell is good, and their senses of hearing and sight are excellent.

Can the females roar?
Males and females roar very similarly, but the male roar is somewhat deeper in tone and louder than that of the female. It is nevertheless difficult to judge the sex of a lion roaring in the distance.

How far can a lion roar be heard?
It could be heard up to 8 km away, but the actual distance depends on the individual roaring as well as on environmental factors such as the denseness of vegetation, wind force and direction, and even the air humidity.

At what age do lions start to roar?
Cubs start to imitate the sounds their parents make at the age of about one month, but a full roar is only accomplished during adulthood.

Do lions have a repertoire of different noises?
Lions are capable of an impressive variety of sounds such as moans, grunts, snarls, growls and roars. Cubs can make miaowing sounds and can also purr. Grunts are used predominantly by lionesses when calling their cubs.

What is the purpose of roaring?
Apart from communicating with other members of the pride which may be spread over a large area, roaring is a way of warning other lions that the area is occupied. Lions roar in different situations. They often appear to roar spontaneously, but they may in fact be replying to a distant call. Lions tend to roar more often during the night than during the day.

Can lions communicate well?
They use an impressive range of facial expressions, body movements and sounds to communicate.

Can lions swim?

Although they do not take to water as readily as tigers or jaguars, they can swim and it is not uncommon for them to cross a river. Tourists once watched two lionesses swimming across the Sabie River to join a male on the other side.

Are lions territorial animals?

In a broad sense we can distinguish between nomadic and resident lions. The former wander widely, often following the movements of migratory game. Resident lions remain in an area for a year or longer, or even for their entire life. Each pride confines itself to a definite area and the main prerequisites for the existence of a pride area are water and sufficient prey throughout the year.

Nomadic lions may become resident, while resident lions may become temporary or even permanent nomads. Young male adults, often become temporary nomads.

Resident lions show a high degree of territory marking but do not defend strict territorial boundaries. They will usually only accept a nomad when it is of the opposite sex. Intruders are driven off, but very often two prides in an area will deliberately avoid each other to prevent a confrontation. It is therefore perhaps more correct to describe a lion's territory as being a home range containing one or more activity zones.

Schaller (1972) calls these home ranges or activity zones pride areas.

Do these home ranges overlap?

Home ranges often overlap, but activity zones or foci of activity seldom do. Direct confrontation is remarkably infrequent and so are actual fights between members of different prides.

What is the size of a pride area or home range?

The actual activity zone is smaller than the home range and both depend on the size of the pride and availability of prey species and water. Home ranges can be as small as perhaps 20 or 30 km^2 or as large as a few hundred km^2. Pride movements are more frequent during the wet season. In winter, when it is dry, they are compelled to concentrate near the permanent watercourses.

How do lions mark their zones?

Urine spraying is a common way of marking, and they also scrape the soil with the paws.

How big is the activity zone?

It again depends on the size of the group or pride and the concentration of game, as well as the population density of lions in the area in general. In winter this area could be a few hundred metres around a waterhole, but after the rains, when the game is spread out, the activity zone could cover many square kilometres.

How large is the average pride?

The size and composition of prides or even groups can change from day to day. A lion pride is not a cohesive unit in the sense that all members are together all the time. The members or even small subgroups of the pride may be widely scattered. Pride sizes can vary from a few individuals to more than thirty. The sex ratio of adults is usually two to one in favour of the females.

Do females become solitary?

Yes, they do, but not as often as males.

Do lions have a social hierarchy?

Due to the loose pride structure one cannot expect a rigid social structure, but both males and females have a dominance hierarchy. Because male members leave and later rejoin the pride, the order of dominance can vary from time to time. Adult males are dominant over all females and young adults. Adult lionesses exhibit a remarkably stable social unit, the composition of which is mainly affected by deaths and the growing up of young adults in the pride.

Is the dominant male the leader of the pride?

There appears to be no consistent leader in a lion pride and either a male or a female can take the lead. Within a short distance several different lions may become the leader. On the other hand, some small nomadic groups tend to have more or less definite leaders.

Is the lack of a constant leader not detrimental to the pride?

A rigid leadership system would probably be of little advantage in a lion pride because it could prohibit the pride from adjusting to various prey conditions. It may even lead to a lack of initiative during hunting.

Are young adults expelled from the pride?

Again, there is no hard and fast rule. One or more of the dominant males may drive off a young male, but young females are usually tolerated provided the pride is not too big for the available prey. When a pride becomes too big, one or more female groups with one or more males may break away to form a new pride which will in turn have to establish its own home range. Female groups may also be taken over by nomadic males. Another interesting phenomenon is that one or more males may associate with two distinct prides of lionesses.

When do young lions become independent?
The majority of young adults become independent at two-and-a-half to three-and-a-half years of age. In general, when the cubs are 17 to 18 months old the mother ceases to lead them to kills or indeed to care for them in any way.

Does a pride of lions accept a stranger?
A pride will readily accept a strange female when she is on heat. A pride of lionesses will also tolerate strange males when the females are in oestrus.

Do males often fight over females or in territorial disputes?
High-intensity fights are not as common as one would imagine. Brief fights over lionesses on heat may occur, but they are uncommon. Males do not dispute the possession of a female. Many of the encounters that do take place consist of a few slaps accompanied by much vocalization and the baring of teeth. Determined biting is rare and fights in which one of the combatants is killed are not common. Lions also have great recuperative powers and even large wounds tend to heal up. Each lion in a group or in a pride usually knows and responds to the fighting potential of every other member. Even when a stranger is driven out of the pride's area, the pursuer usually maintains a certain distance and adjusts his speed to that of the intruder.

Are males more aggressive than females?
Females fight each other probably as much as, if not more than males do. The belief among humans that a lioness is more dangerous than the male could very well be true.

Do males and females sometimes fight each other?
Usually not, because males are dominant over females. However, two or more females will attack a male if he harasses them and they may even put him to flight. A female with cubs may also attack a male and although he could resist her attack he usually refrains.

Do males sometimes intimidate females?
Males often deprive females of a kill. Irrespective of who made the kill, the strongest male usually secures the best for himself. If the prey carcass is small he may take it over entirely, but if the prey is big and he is not too hungry he will allow other members of the pride to feed with him.

Is there a way that one lion or lioness can avoid aggression from another?
Rubbing or 'greeting' serves as a safety measure to avoid fatal fights among powerful males. A lion can avoid aggression from a stronger opponent by rolling over on its back.

Do the females secure food for their cubs?
Apparently not. During the first three to four weeks the cubs subsist on milk,

which is gradually supplemented with meat. As soon as the cubs can walk properly the mother leads them to kills. When a lioness is very hungry, however, she will prevent the cubs from feeding until she has had her fill. Should a cub persist in trying to feed with her, she may even kill it. It is not uncommon for a female to take food from her cubs.

Lionesses attack cubs much more often than they would attack other females. This appears strange when one considers that a lioness will defend her cubs ferociously against other predators or human beings.

What is the gestation period?
The average appears to be 110 days, but it could vary from about 100 up to 114 days.

How often do lionesses produce cubs?
Lions have a high reproductive potential. Females are polyoestrus and are cyclic throughout the year. If a female should lose her litter in some way, she will mate again within a few days to a few weeks. She can then give birth to another litter within four to five months. Under normal circumstances the birth interval is usually more than 18 months and can be as long as 26 months.

What is the size of an average litter?
The number can range from one to six but two or three cubs seems to be the average.

At what age can a lioness have her first litter?
Young females usually become cyclic when they are about three years old. A lioness could therefore give birth to

her first litter at about three-and-a-half to four years of age. Males take a few months longer to reach sexual maturity.

Do lionesses breed throughout their adult life?
Lionesses probably reach the limit of their breeding capability at about 11 to 12 years of age, but it is not impossible that some females could conceive into old age.

What is the normal lifespan of a lion?
It could be up to 20 years or slightly more in captivity. It has been claimed that lions can reach an age of up to 30 years, but this has not been conclusively established. In the wild they probably reach an age of 13 to 15 years.

Is cub mortality high?
Cubs are subjected to a variety of mortality factors, and only about half of those born survive to grow into adulthood.

Of those that die before adulthood, about a quarter are killed by their parents or other predators. Lionesses sometimes abandon their cubs for unknown reasons, and starving cubs too weak to walk are usually left to their fate. If they become separated from their mother they usually either starve to death or fall prey to other predators.

Diseases and parasites take their toll, and bush fires, snakes and ants attacking newborn cubs can account for a number of deaths.

Are cubs born throughout the year?
Cubs can be born at any time of year. Most births in the Park are said to

occur between March and July, whereas those in East Africa occur from November to March. Birth peaks can vary from area to area and from year to year.

How long do cubs suckle?

Usually for about the same length of time as the gestation period, i.e. about three to four months, occasionally longer. Cubs probably do not supplement their milk diet with meat before the age of three to four weeks, when the incisor teeth erupt. Lactation lasts for five to eight months.

Will a lioness allow cubs other than her own to suckle?

Lactating lionesses permit small cubs of any litter to suckle them with no discrimination.

Where are the cubs born?

Prior to giving birth the lioness leaves the pride to find a secluded spot to have her cubs. They are born almost helpless, with their eyes closed for the first seven to 14 days of their lives. The body mass varies between 1 and 2 kg. These tiny creatures can crawl a day after birth but cannot walk well until they are about three weeks old.

Does the lioness conceal her cubs when she goes hunting?

She does and the cubs are so well hidden that the chances of detection by other predators are not high. They even crawl into rock crevices or remain quiet so that they go undetected.

When do the lioness and her cubs join the pride?

Cubs usually remain hidden until they are mobile at four to six weeks old.

Do lions have 'baby-sitters'?

Schaller (1972) found little evidence to support the claim of a number of authors that 'baby-sitters' guard the cubs of a hunting lioness. It is, however, quite normal for any lioness near cubs to function as a guard. The cubs themselves will seek protection from another female in the absence of their own mother.

In this respect a certain incident comes to mind in which four lionesses stalked, ambushed and killed an impala. Within minutes of the kill a lioness emerged from a nearby thicket with six cubs of two different age groups. It appeared as if at least some of these cubs had been left with a 'baby-sitter'. However, there are other possible explanations: the newcomer may have been with the cubs by chance, some of which may have been her own, and when she heard or saw the other lionesses make the kill she decided to investigate, followed by the cubs. It is also possible that she was an old lioness and, instinctively aware of her failing powers to make a kill, deliberately waited for others to kill and then moved in for a share.

Is it true that lions usually mate over a two- to three-day period?

A mating pair usually leaves the pride for one to three days. They often go without food during this period, but they may also join the pride temporarily when a kill is made.

At the beginning of the period intervals between copulations could vary from a minute to about 20 minutes but may become longer at the end of the period. The lion's virility is amazing; Schaller (1972) reports of a mating pair that copulated 157 times in 55 hours, or once every 21 minutes. This male did not eat for three days. It is not known whether lack of appetite or lack of time, or both, were the reasons.

Are mating lions dangerous?
They are aggressive during this period and should be treated with respect.

Does the male initiate copulation?
It has been observed that although either the male or the female can initiate copulation, it is more often the female who does.

Do lions have enemies?
Apart from man and other lions, adult lions do not have natural enemies that would attack them. It has been reported that hyenas and occasionally wild dogs have killed old lions. These predators probably also kill quite a number of cubs hidden by their mother.

Can a crocodile kill a lion?
Large crocodiles can and do kill lions occasionally, but small crocodiles in turn are sometimes killed by lions.

What other mortality factors affect lions?
Lions host a number of endoparasites such as *Babesia*, a blood parasite that causes anaemia in cubs, tapeworms such as *Taenia gonyamai*, and trypanosomes. Mange, caused by a mite, *Sarcoptes scabiei*, also accounts for some deaths. Lion and cheetah have been immobilized and treated for this disease when necessary.

Most lions die from diseases, starvation, old age or as a result of violent attacks from their own species. Although parasites could kill them, healthy animals are usually capable of living with quite a heavy infestation. After all, parasites would become extinct if they killed off all their hosts by overtaxing them.

Are there more than one subspecies of lion?
Some taxonomists regard the extinct Cape lion, the Kalahari lion and the Kruger National Park lions as three different subspecies. As many as 21 subspecies have been described. Meester, Rautenbach, Dippenaar and Baker (1986), however, regard all lions as members of one species.

The Cape lion apparently had a larger mane than lions from the Transvaal and the Kalahari, while those from the latter area tend to be lighter in colour than their counterparts in the Kruger National Park. It is a well-known fact that animals of the same species or subspecies can develop more fur when translocated to a colder climate, while their colour could become lighter when they move to drier and hotter areas. One should therefore be careful not to use these changed features to describe a new subspecies.

The Kalahari lion usually has a larger mane than the Kruger National Park lion. This may be ascribed to the fact that the manes of the Kruger lions are combed out, as it were, by the bushes and thickets through which they move.

LEOPARD *Panthera pardus* (Linnaeus, 1758)

What is the distribution?
These most adaptable predators are distributed over several continents, including a very wide variety of habitats. Their range includes Africa, Arabia and countries of the Middle East, India, Malaysia, China and even Soviet Russia. In South Africa leopard occur in many areas, although on account of their secretive habits and solitary disposition, they can exist in an area for years without being detected. Thirteen subspecies are described by Meester & Setzer (1971). The Kruger National Park population belongs to the subspecies *P. p. melanotica* (Gunther, 1885).

Where can we see leopards in the Park?
Leopards may be seen throughout the Park, especially along rivers, in thickets, on rocky outcrops, or just lying on a branch of a tree.

Why are leopards so seldom seen?
Leopards are predominantly nocturnal in habit and very covert by nature. This, coupled with their excellent camouflage and the type of habitat they prefer, makes them quite difficult to see.

What type of habitat do they prefer?
Within their range of distribution leopards occur in equatorial forest, savanna, steppes, semi-desert regions, swampland and mountainous areas from sea level to altitudes of more than 4 000 m on Mount Kenya and Mount Kilimanjaro.
  Where available, thickets are preferred in the habitat.

What do they eat?
Their prey ranges from rats to fully grown wildebeest, and includes virtually all small and medium-sized mammals, birds and even reptiles and fish. It is interesting to note that leopards often kill porcupines and occasionally also jackals and cheetahs. Baboons probably rank high on their preference list. Outside game sanctuaries, domestic dogs and cats are often killed by leopards.

How do they hunt?
They may either lie in ambush or stalk their prey and then pounce on it. Leopards are most efficient hunters.

How do they locate their prey?
It is said that leopards rely on sight and hearing to locate their prey. Their sense of smell is also well developed.

Why do they hang their prey on trees?
Leopards do this to safeguard it from other predators such as lions, wild dogs and hyenas. These predators have been known to drive a leopard off its kill in order to obtain the food.

Do they return to prey left in a tree?
It is common for leopards to return to their prey, especially if they are not disturbed.

Do they eat carrion?
Although they usually kill their own prey, they will readily eat carrion. A leopard is known to have died of anthrax after feeding on the remains of an antelope that succumbed to this disease.

How much does a leopard eat per day?
According to Turnbull-Kemp (1967) a leopard can eat approximately 8 to 17 kg of meat in 12 hours. Normal daily consumption would probably be 1,5 to 2 kg.

How many prey animals are killed by a leopard annually?
A leopard probably needs about 400 kg of meat per year, and as it usually consumes only about a third of a carcass, it has to kill 1 000 to 1 200 kg of prey annually. If it kills only average-sized impala that have a body mass of, say, 50 kg, it will have to kill about 20 to 24 of these antelopes in a given year.

Is it possible to identify a leopard kill?
Experts can easily identify a leopard kill. It starts to feed either on the viscera or on the meat of the thighs or the chest.

It is said that baboons could kill a leopard. Is this true?
A leopard hunting baboons usually stalks up to a troop where it is roosting for the night, grabs a victim and hastily retreats with it. Occasionally, however, hunger drives a leopard to rashly attempting to snatch a baboon from a troop in broad daylight. When that happens a number of big baboon males usually go to the aid of the shrieking victim and attack the leopard, which in turn could be severely injured or literally torn to pieces.

A case has been reported where a leopard attacked a male baboon and was killed by another male baboon which managed to sever the leopard's jugular vein.

How dependent are leopards on water?
Leopards drink regularly when water is available, but their presence in arid regions suggests that they can go without water for long periods – how long is, as yet, not known.

What are the main physical features?
The leopard is one of nature's most beautiful creatures. This graceful and strongly built cat has a comparatively long body with short, powerful legs and a long tail. The basic colour is yellowish-tawny on the head, the upper parts of the body and the limbs, changing to white on the chin, throat, chest, underparts and insides of the limbs. The spots on the upper part of the body look like rosettes, formed by four to six individual spots, while single spots are found on the legs. The eyes are greenish-yellow and have a fierce, baleful expression. The shoulder height of the male is 60 to 80 cm, and its body mass can vary from 60 to 70 kg. A leopard with a mass of 90 kg was shot in the Sabie Sand Game Reserve to the west of the Kruger National Park. The female has a body mass of some 10 to 12 kg less than that of the male.

What is the difference between a leopard and a cheetah?
In contrast to the slenderly built cheetah, the leopard has a more powerful appearance with its bigger head, thick neck and conspicuously muscular body and limbs. The leopard's spots are more in the form of rosettes on the back and flanks, while those of the cheetah are smaller and single. The so-called 'tear mark' of the cheetah, running from the eye to the upper lip, is absent in the leopard.

Are there black panthers in the Park?
The so-called black panther of the East, a melanistic form of the leopard, is far more common in Asia than in Africa, but is not a different species. The gene for melanism – the opposite of albinism – is actually recessive, and to produce a black race extensive inbreeding would be necessary. Seen obliquely, the black specimens still show faint spots and rosettes. None have been observed in the Park.

Are there albino leopards in the Park?
Partial albinos have been recorded in Africa but these cases are very rare.

Do leopards roar?
No, not like a lion. They utter coarse, grunting sounds and can also emit snarls and growls. Cubs miaow.

Is the leopard a solitary animal?
It is solitary by habit, and the only groups of leopards likely to be seen will probably consist of a mother and her cubs. A pair of adults are only found together for a short while during courtship and mating.

Are leopards territorial?
Yes, but territories can overlap to some degree. Border confrontations are usually avoided, but should a leopard wander too far into a neighbouring territory it will probably become involved in a territorial fight.

Do they mark their territories?
Like lion and other predators, they use urine to mark their territories.

Where do they hide during the day?
They spend the major part of the day in thickets, dense undergrowth, among rocks or even in trees. Despite their nocturnal habit, they are occasionally seen during the day. Cheetah, which are less elusive and predominantly diurnal, are seen more often than leopard despite their lower numbers.

Is the leopard a dangerous animal?
In spite of its elusiveness where man is concerned, it is very bold and courageous. Should a leopard consider itself to be in danger or cornered, it will not hesitate to attack viciously. Only a well-placed bullet from a powerful rifle will stop a charging leopard.

Does it readily attack humans?
It is said that this large cat will attack more readily than a lion when met in the bush. Due to its elusiveness and relatively low numbers, however, contact between leopards and humans seldom occurs.

Have any human beings been killed by leopards in the Park?
Mr Glen Leary, father-in-law of former ranger Harold Trollope, was attacked by a leopard near the old Voortrekker road between Pretoriuskop and Malelane in 1935 and was fatally wounded. A number of other attacks have been reported but none was fatal.

Do leopards ever become man-eaters?
Leopards can become man-eaters but the incidence is much lower than with lions and tigers. Males are usually the culprits; Turnbull-Kemp (1967) reports that out of 152 man-eating leopards, only nine were females. No cases of man-eating have been reported in the Kruger National Park.

Are leopards cannibalistic?
Cannibalism among leopards is rare.
Their solitary disposition, which
affords them less opportunity for
confrontation with each other than is
the case with lions, may explain this
phenomenon.

What are their breeding habits?
One to three cubs, rarely more, are
born after a gestation period of about
105 days.

Does the male help to protect the cubs?
No, after mating the male usually
proceeds on his lone wanderings.

Are the cubs hidden after birth?
Cubs are born in a secluded spot in
dense bush, rocky outcrops or
mountainous areas. Like the lioness,
the mother hides her cubs for a
number of weeks before they
accompany her.

When do the cubs become independent?
Young leopards can become
independent at the early age of one
year, but often stay with the mother
until they are almost two years old.
Full maturity is reached at about three
years of age.

What is their potential lifespan?
In captivity it may be as high as
20 years, but in their natural
environment it is considerably less.

*Is the mortality rate among leopard
cubs high?*
Mortality is fairly high. Cubs left alone
by the mother can fall prey to hyena,
wild dogs and occasionally, even lion.
Pythons probably kill some of them,
and disease also takes its toll.

*Are leopards preyed upon by other
predators?*
Poisonous snakes, crocodiles and
pythons can kill leopards. A case was
reported some years ago of a bushpig
boar killing a leopard. Old or disabled
leopards can also fall prey to wild
dogs and hyenas.

When a leopard is attacking a
porcupine it aims for the only
vulnerable spot, the muzzle. If it
miscalculates when striking out with a
paw or rushing in for a kill, it can be
severely injured by the sharp quills.
Lodged deeply in a pad or jaw, these
quills can cause festering wounds
which may fatally disable the animal.

*Does poaching endanger the survival
of leopards?*
It poses a danger to the survival of
leopards in many parts of their range
in southern Africa.

Fortunately these predators are
protected in many parks and game
reserves in South Africa.

*Are leopards very susceptible to
disease?*
Leopards suffer from a number of
illnesses, such as cat flu, pneumonia,
stomach blockages, parasites and
deficiency diseases, but in general
their survival is not endangered by
these mortality factors.

Are they still increasing in numbers?
It appears that leopards have probably
reached the maximum number for the
available habitats. Should they
increase in numbers, some will have to
leave the Park and would then be
exterminated by stock farmers. Their
population is probably at a stable level
at the moment.

CHEETAH *Acinonyx jubatus* (Schreber, 1776)

What is the distribution?
Cheetah were once found in arid regions from India westward through Iran to Arabia and over most of Africa, except in the driest deserts and dense forests, a distribution similar to that of the lion. It became extinct in India in 1952, but remnant populations may survive in Afghanistan, Iran and possibly in northern Saudi Arabia. South of the Sahara they are found sparsely from Chad and the Sudan through parts of East Africa, Zimbabwe, Angola and Namibia, and in South Africa, where the Vaal River is the southern limit of their distribution. Five subspecies; *A. j. jubatus* (Schreber, 1776) is the local subspecies.

How many are there in the Park?
There could be between 250 and 300; they have never been plentiful in the Kruger National Park.

Where in the Park is one most likely to see cheetah?
They may be found almost everywhere, but mostly in flat, open areas such as the central part of the Park. Surprisingly, they are sometimes also found in dense bush.

What type of habitat do they prefer?
Owing to their way of hunting they prefer fairly open to lightly wooded savanna where visibility is good. They can also survive in semi-deserts, grasslands and fairly thick bush.

What do they eat?
Cheetah prey mainly on the small and medium-sized antelopes such as steenbok, duiker and impala, and also the young of larger antelopes. Warthog, hares, ground birds and even porcupines also feature fairly prominently in their diet. In the Kruger National Park impala make up nearly 70% of cheetah kills.

Do they eat carrion?
They normally hunt their own prey, but occasionally revert to carrion.

Do they kill other predators?
Very seldom, if ever.

What are the main physical features?
This graceful, long-legged cat has a hollow back, relatively small head, a long tail which is rather bushy and white at the tip, and a fairly wiry-haired coat. The spots are small and roundish and spread evenly over the body, in contrast to the leopard's rosettes on the back and flanks.

A conspicuous dark mark or line, known as a 'tear stripe', runs from the front of each eye to the upper lip.

A small mane along the top of the shoulders is sometimes visible, and the ground colour of the coat is tawny above, becoming white along the abdomen.

The eyes are large, yellowish-brown and rather gentle in expression – very different from the leopard's somewhat baleful stare.

The anatomy of the cheetah is adapted for speed. The nasal passages and lungs are large, the heart is large and strong, and the adrenal glands are well developed.

How did the cheetah get its name?
It probably comes from an Indian word 'chita', meaning 'spotted one'.

What is the mass?
Although the shoulder height is usually slightly more than that of the leopard, the cheetah is not as bulky and its body mass is usually 30 to 50 kg.

What is the shoulder height?
It can vary, but is approximately 80 cm.

What kind of sounds do cheetah make?
They snarl, growl and spit like a cat, but they also purr and utter a peculiar whistling sound very similar to the chirping sound of a bird. They cannot roar at all.

It is sometimes claimed that cheetah are not true cats. Is this so?
Cheetahs are true cats. The non-retractile claws of an adult cheetah and its method of hunting led to the popular misconception. Cubs can retract their claws and the loss of this ability in later life is an adaptation for running.

Can cheetah climb trees?
Cheetah sometimes climb trees with a slanted trunk, or jump onto low branches, but their dog-like claws do not allow them to climb trees properly.

How fast can a cheetah run?
According to Eaton (1974) a running cheetah has been timed with a stopwatch and a speed of 114 km/h recorded. Numerous other claims of speeds in excess of 100 km/h have been made, although most of these claims were estimates. One could probably accept that the average cheetah in its prime could reach 80 to 90 km/h or slightly more.

How far can a cheetah run at top speed?
Although the cheetah's anatomy is adapted for speed, it has little stamina. Charges are seldom over a distance greater than 250 to 300 m. Even when the prey is quickly overtaken, the hunter usually appears to be exhausted.

How close does a cheetah approach its prey before it charges?
The distance varies depending on the type of prey; it could be between 60 and 100 m.

What is the success ratio for kills?
Hunting success is related to the distance between the cheetah and its prey when the charge commences, and whether the cheetah or the prey had a flying start.
   When the prey spots the cheetah in good time, killing success could be one out of 10 or even lower, whereas success where the prey was unaware of the cheetah starting its charge could be as high as one kill out of two attempts.

Do more than one cheetah sometimes participate in a hunt?
Hunting in a group is common and the success rate of a group is usually significantly higher than that of a single animal.

When do they hunt?
Mainly during the early morning and late afternoon, and occasionally on brightly moonlit nights.

How is the prey caught?
The cheetah usually knocks the prey off balance by digging the dew claw into its flank and pulling backwards. It may also slap the hindleg, thigh or rump of the prey to bring it down. Once the victim is down the cheetah tries to grab its throat, usually remaining behind the animal and away from the hooves or horns while doing so. Death of the prey is in most cases due to strangulation.

Is it possible to identify a cheetah kill?
Carcasses of animals killed by cheetah can be recognized from the manner in which the jugular veins are severed and the trachea or windpipe is

crushed. Deep claw marks are absent, the rib cartilages are usually chewed up, the heart, liver and kidneys are eaten and the intestines dragged out. Meat on the hindquarters, spine, forequarters and the base of the neck is then consumed. When a single cheetah feeds on a carcass it may not even get further than the hindquarters. The slipshod way in which a carcass is butchered is a general feature of a cheetah kill.

Do cheetah kill their prey quickly?
Cheetah can spend from five to 25 minutes killing their victim. Their relatively small canines, small mouths and claws which cannot effectively

hold a prey animal down, all contribute to their inability to kill quickly.

Do they return to a kill?
Cheetah will seldom, if ever, return to a kill. The kill cannot be secured, and if the cheetah returns he may be confronted by another predator or scavenger.

How many animals does a cheetah kill per year?
The cheetah is often deprived of its prey by other predators, and if this happens before it has eaten its fill it has to kill again. If it kills only animals the size of impala, it could well kill 30 or more per year.

On the other hand, a cheetah very often kills considerably smaller prey and, according to Eaton, could make a kill every two to three days, or about a 150 animals per year.

How much food does it consume per day?
Like most other predators, cheetah could probably eat a large meal at one sitting. Its build, however, suggests that it would not be able to compete with the lion on a comparable basis. Normal consumption would probably be in the region of 1 to 3 kg of meat, depending on how much energy it had to expend on securing its prey.

Are cheetah cannibalistic?
Cannibalism appears to be rare.

Do cheetah drink water regularly?
When water is available they drink regularly, but in the Kalahari and other similar areas they can go without water for considerable lengths of time.

Are cheetah solitary animals?
Cheetahs do not form prides like lions, but small groups of up to about six individuals are frequent. About 50% of cheetahs are solitary.

Are they diurnal in habit?
Their way of hunting limits them largely to a diurnal life.

Are they territorial?
They do not actively defend a territory, but they have preferred home ranges which they mark with urine. Male cheetah, like lion and tiger, are capable of directional urination.

Are cheetah dangerous to man?
They are amongst the most timid of predators. A human being will seldom, if ever, be attacked unless the animal is cornered. As far as wild animals go, it is very trustworthy when tamed.

No report of a cheetah killing a human being could be found in the available literature.

How long is the gestation period?
Approximately 90 to 95 days.

Is there a specific breeding season?
Apparently not.

How long is the birth interval?
About 15 to 18 months.

How many cubs are born?
Between two and six, with an average of about four.

Does the female hide the cubs?
For the first eight weeks the female hides her newborn young effectively.

Are the cubs born with their eyes closed?
The eyes are closed when they are born and they open after some 10 days.

Is cub mortality high?
About half the cubs die within the first few months of life. All the causes are not known, but we do know that small cubs are vulnerable to eagles and mammalian predators such as hyena, leopard and even lion. Diseases such as cat flu and rickets probably also play an important role.

What is the cheetah's lifespan?
It is claimed to be between 15 and 20 years in captivity, but one can assume that it would be much less in nature.

Is it still difficult to breed cheetah in captivity?
With the current knowledge and refined techniques, many problems of the past have been overcome and the success rate is high. Availability of suitable habitats and inadequate conservation measures in certain areas are, however, still limiting factors.

Is it feasible to breed cheetahs in pens and then release them into their natural environment?
This could probably be done but it should first be established whether the Kruger National Park can accommodate much more than the current population, bearing in mind available habitats and competition with other predators.

When was the first successful breeding in captivity achieved?
According to Eaton (1974), it was achieved in the Philadelphia Zoological Gardens in 1956. Unfortunately the mother killed one cub and the other two died within a few days. The first cub raised successfully was claimed to have been born in a private menagerie in Rome in 1966.

South Africa, however, also boasts a success story. Working in conjunction with the National Zoological Gardens in Pretoria, Anne van Dyk's efforts over the last two decades have result in a major and rather special achievement – more than 400 cheetah cubs have been bred on her farm in the Magaliesberg, northwest of Pretoria (van Dyk, 1991).

What are the requirements for successful breeding in captivity?
They need a fairly large area and probably a sex ratio in favour of males. It is said that a female on heat runs away from the courting males, and it is therefore the fastest male which has the best chance of mating.

What is the sex ratio in the wild?
It is about three males to two females.

Do males often fight over females?
Apparently not; as mentioned above, speed is the essential factor in successful courtship. Fights, if they occur, seldom lead to death or severe injury.

Cheetah of both sexes occasionally fight at a kill, but usually a carcass is shared without antagonism.

At what age is a cheetah sexually mature?
It could reach maturity between 14 and 16 months old, but the young usually stay with their mother to the age of about two years.

What are their major enemies?
Hunters and poachers are enemies of cheetah, but these beautiful cats may also be killed by leopard, lion and probably hyena. The effect of injuries is vital for an animal with such a specialized way of hunting; a crippled cheetah has little chance of survival.

How can other predators kill the fleet-footed cheetah?
Leopard and lion do not go out of their way to kill cheetah, but they can stalk and surprise them. Hyena, although they are not very fast animals, have far more stamina and can therefore tire out a cheetah.

Does competition with other predators affect cheetah?
Competition for food with other predators is one of the limiting factors in the survival of cheetah. They can seldom take food from another predator, but are often robbed by lion, leopard, hyena and wild dogs.

Are cheetah still being hunted?
Although protected in nature reserves, they are still hunted when they wander beyond the boundaries of game reserves. They do kill domestic stock in farming areas and therefore come into confrontation with organized agriculture. Their pelts are, like those of leopards, coveted trophies, fetching high prices on illegal markets.

Is it easy to hunt them?
Cheetah are not as covert and cunning as leopards. Their diurnal way of life makes them easy targets for hunters and poachers, causing their rapid disappearance from areas where they are not protected.

What other mortality factors affect cheetahs?
Cheetah are susceptible to a number of diseases such as pneumonia, cat flu, rickets, mange, feline distemper, liver diseases and tuberculosis. Parasites also play a lesser role in their mortality.

Are they in danger of becoming extinct?
Not at this stage, but it would be better if their numbers could be increased.

Is it not possible to boost their numbers in some way?
Some years ago more than 50 of these cats were introduced into the Park, mainly from Namibia. It is also hoped that the programme of veld burning will create suitable habitats in more parts of the Park.

Once the Kruger National Park's carrying capacity for cheetah has been established, breeding them in captivity and then releasing them in the wild could be an option.

Can one keep cheetahs as pets?
They are trustworthy and make excellent pets, but they need a large space to run around in order to keep fit. In this respect they are much more active than lion or leopard. However, the keeping of cheetahs as pets is prohibited in South Africa.

Is the king cheetah a separate species?
The so-called king cheetah is not a separate species, nor even a subspecies, but a mutant form of the cheetah (de Graaff, 1974). It was first reported in Zimbabwe in the previous century.

Reports of this form being seen in the Kruger National Park are received from time to time.

166

SERVAL *Felis serval* (Schreber, 1776)

What is the distribution?
Serval are found from the Cape Province in South Africa northwards through the savanna areas of Africa to the southern boundary of the Sahara. The subspecies *F. s. serval* (Schreber, 1776), is well represented in the Kruger National Park but due to their habits are seldom seen. Five other subspecies have been described.

What kind of habitat do they prefer?
They are usually found in dense vegetation near streams and rivers.

What do they eat?
Birds and rodents feature prominently in their diet, but small antelopes and their young are also preyed upon.

What are the main physical features?
The serval is a large, leggy, tawny-yellowish cat marked with large, rather widely spaced black spots which tend to form bars or a stripy pattern. The underparts are whitish in colour, while the short tail is ringed with black hair. The body colour and spots resemble those of the cheetah to some extent and a serval seen from a distance could be mistaken for a young cheetah. The face is small, but the ears are large and conspicuous.

The shoulder height is about 55 cm and the mass between 14 and 18 kg.

Are they solitary animals?
They are solitary, and when more than one is seen they will either be a mating pair or a mother and young.

Where can they be seen?
They are mainly nocturnal and are very seldom seen as they spend the day hidden in dense bush.

At night they are active and noisy. The characteristic call is a high-pitched 'how! how! how!'.

Are they aggressive?
Servals are quite mild-natured animals and would rarely, if ever, attack a human being.

How do they hunt?
As they hunt at night they usually stalk or ambush their prey. The long legs and slender build suggest that they may run it down.

Are they territorial in habit?
Little is known about them because of their secretive habits, but one may assume that they are territorial.

Why are they so rare outside nature reserves?
Servals have the bad reputation of being notorious poultry thieves on farms and they are therefore usually destroyed on sight. They are also not

as cunning as the leopard or their other felid relative, the caracal.

What are their breeding habits?
Two to four kittens are born in an antbear hole, in large rock crevices or in thickets.

What is the gestation period?
About 68 to 72 days.

What is their lifespan?
Probably about 12 years.

What are their major enemies?
Eagles, pythons, jackal, hyena and other predators could kill young serval kittens.

Although adults are generally not preyed upon by other predators, they may be killed by leopard. Some may succumb in territorial fights.

CARACAL   *Felis caracal*   (Schreber, 1776)

What is the distribution?
Caracal are found in the more open savanna regions of Africa as well as in Arabia, the Near East and India. Although nowhere numerous, they still occur over most of southern Africa, even in areas where most other game has disappeared. The subspecies *F. c. limpopoensis* (Roberts, 1926) occurs in the Park. Six more subspecies occur in its distribution range.

What type of habitat do they prefer?
The caracal occurs in a variety of habitats, from fairly dense bush through open savanna to arid regions with sparse vegetation. Rocky outcrops are often frequented. It is absent from rain forests.

What do caracal eat?
They feed on a variety of small mammals, including rodents, hares, dassies, small antelope and the young of larger antelope. Birds and lizards are also preyed upon. In farming areas they can be destructive to poultry and small stock.

What are the main physical features?
They are fairly big, robustly built cats with rather long limbs, the hindlegs slightly longer than the forelegs. The reddish brown colouring of the pelt and the long tufts of dark hair on the tips of the pointed ears are characteristic of the caracal. Faint spots are sometimes visible on the lighter underparts. The tail is of medium length in contrast to the long tails of the lynxes of the northern hemisphere. The coloration of the eyes is a rich, amber-yellow and very conspicuous.

The shoulder height is about 45 cm and the mass could be up to about 18 kg. Males, with an average mass of 11 kg, are about 1 kg heavier than females.

What sounds do they make?
They appear to be quiet animals
except for the usual cat-like growling,
spitting and hissing.

Are their senses well developed?
Like the other cat species, their senses
are well developed.

Do they climb trees?
Although principally terrestrial
hunters, they can climb well and easily
take to trees when pursued by dogs.

Are they solitary?
A female and her offspring or a
courting couple can sometimes be seen
together, but for the rest they live a
solitary life.

Are they dangerous to man?
Caracals are savage and dangerous
opponents when cornered. They can
put up a terrific fight and are more
than a match for most dogs. When not
disturbed they will seldom, if ever,

attack and would rather try to avoid
conflict. However, if they are
wounded or cornered by a human
being, they can attack fearlessly and
with great determination.

Can they be domesticated?
They can be tamed but it is difficult to
ascertain if they are trustworthy.

How many kittens are born?
Two to three seems to be the normal
litter size but litters of up to five have
also been recorded.

How long is the gestation period?
It is probably about three months and
kittens can be born at any time during
the year.

What are their major enemies?
Kittens fall prey to eagles, pythons,
hyenas and other predators. Adults do
not have many enemies, but in
farming areas they are exterminated
on sight.

AFRICAN WILD CAT *Felis lybica* (Forster, 1780)

What is the distribution?
Although African wild cats are not very numerous in most areas, they occur throughout the savanna areas of Africa. The subspecies *F. l. cafra* (Desmarest, 1822), is well represented in the Kruger National Park. Altogether 10 subspecies are recognized by Meester & Setzer (1971).

What type of habitat do they prefer?
All savanna types of Africa are inhabited, but like most of the other cats of Africa they are not found in the rain forests of central and western Africa. Fairly dense bush and long grass are also often frequented.

What do they eat?
They prey on the young of small antelopes as well as on hares, rodents, birds, small reptiles and even insects.

What are the main physical features?
The African wild cat is similar to, but slightly larger than, an ordinary tabby cat. The upper parts of the body are grey, the lower parts lighter and the body stripes rather indistinct. The upper parts of the legs are marked with fairly distinct bars and the fore parts of the chest and underparts are spotted.

The shoulder height is about 35 cm and the body mass is about 6 kg.

Are these cats nocturnal?
They are nocturnal and shy, and even in areas where they are numerous they are rarely seen during the day.

Are they harmful creatures?
They are not aggressive towards humans but can become poultry thieves. They are said to be difficult to tame and tend to remain fierce and untrustworthy.

Do they make a sound?
The sound made is very much like that of a domestic cat, but deeper in tone and quite harsh. The screeching and caterwauling during mating are similar to such noises made by the domestic cat.

What are their breeding habits?
Two to three kittens are usually born, but litters of up to five have been recorded. The female may give birth at any time of the year. The gestation period is about 56 days and the kittens are born in an antbear hole, a rock crevice or a thicket. Hybridization with domestic cats is common.

What are their major enemies?
Young ones are probably preyed upon by eagles, pythons and some of the smaller predators. Adults could be killed in fights or by other predators.

SPOTTED HYENA *Crocuta crocuta* (Erxleben, 1777)

What is the general distribution?
The spotted hyena is distributed throughout the savanna areas of Africa, but is absent from the rain forests of central Africa. Formerly found over the whole of southern Africa, it is now more or less confined to nature reserves. No subspecies are recognized.

Where can spotted hyena be seen in the Park?
They are to be found all over the Park, with the highest population in the southern and central areas.

What type of habitat do they prefer?
They are found in a variety of habitats, ranging from semi-desert to dense bush, and from sea level to the snowline on high mountains such as Mount Kenya and Mount Kilimanjaro.

It is well known that hyenas are scavengers, but do they ever kill their own prey?
When carrion is freely available they usually make use of it, but if the need arises they do kill their own prey. They are, in fact, more resourceful and formidable predators than their reputation would suggest.

Whether hyenas scavenge or kill their own prey depends very much on the conditions they find themselves in. They are arch opportunists and will not over-exert themselves by hunting their own prey if there is the least chance of obtaining sufficient carrion left by other predators, or where they find it feasible to rob a lesser predator of its kill. Where pure predators and their prey are plentiful, hyenas may live largely as scavengers, but in the absence of other large predators, and therefore a sufficient supply of carrion, they revert to hunting.

Hungry hyenas will take great risks in snatching meat from feeding lions and many of them are mauled or killed in the process.

How do they hunt?
They hunt either singly or in packs, running down their prey in very much the same way as wild dogs. On an average it takes them two or three attempts to make a kill in this way. They also ambush their prey from thick cover near drinking places, and often pounce on animals floundering in the mud of receding waterholes or dams.

How fast can they run?
They are not very fast and probably cannot exceed 50 km/h, but they have tremendous stamina and can maintain their ungainly lope for extremely long distances.

What is the biggest animal killed by hyenas?
Adult wildebeest, zebra, waterbuck and kudu may be pulled down and devoured by packs of hyenas numbering as many as 40 or more. These predators demonstrate an uncanny ability to select vulnerable prey such as sick or disabled animals, and in the Kruger National Park there have been several cases of sick or crippled buffalo having been killed by hyenas.

What other prey would they kill?
Antelopes, as well as aardvark, baboon, guineafowl, snakes, ostrich, tortoise, crabs and fish.

When do they hunt?
As a rule they hunt their larger mammalian prey by moonlight, but hunting can also take place in the early morning or late afternoon.

Do they really have the strongest jaws of the mammalian predators?
It is doubtful whether this has been proved beyond any doubt, but it could well be the case. They possess tremendous power in their jaw muscles and even the thigh bones of buffalo are crushed and eaten.

How much do they eat at a time?
It is said that a hungry hyena could consume meat up to a third of its own body mass. Looking at a gorged hyena, this could well be the case.

Do they attack other predators?
They do not normally prey on other predators but old, weakened lions occasionally fall prey to them and even young healthy cheetahs and leopards could be attacked. In 1937 a ranger based at Letaba saw how three hyenas chased an old lioness up a tree.

Will hyenas attack humans?
As a rule hyenas will run away from humans, but when hungry or cornered they can become extremely dangerous. When driven by hunger they will even enter human dwellings in search of food. They are bolder at night and many a person sleeping out in the open has been attacked. In this respect they could be more dangerous than lions.

Packs of man-eating hyenas have been recorded from various parts of Africa, but it is not a common phenomenon. Man-eating among hyenas may have resulted from them

eating corpses buried in shallow graves, or attacking old people abandoned in the bush by tribe members.

Are they cannibalistic?
Cannibalism does occur, but appears to be rare.

Do hyenas eat strange objects?
They have occasionally chewed up rubber objects such as motorcar tyres and even aircraft tyres.

In the days when they could enter rest camps fairly easy, they would chew up visitors' shoes that had been left outside a hut or tent.

Hyenas have also been seen scooping fish out of pools that were drying up.

Do they store meat?
Hyenas occasionally submerge meat in shallow water, probably for temporary concealment.

What are their main physical features?
They are about the size of a large, powerfully built dog and have a sloping back, broad head with large rounded ears, a thick muscular neck and well-developed forequarters. The body colour varies from buff to grey-brown, or sometimes reddish brown, with a scattering of rounded blackish spots. The coat is wiry and coarse and the tail short. The large, dark eyes have an expressive wistful expression.

Unlike the domestic dog, which has five toes on the front foot, the hyena has only four.

The shoulder height is 80 cm to 1 m and the body mass usually around 40 to 55 kg.

Do the pups resemble their parents?
The pups are nearly black at birth, and it is only after a few months that the pelt becomes lighter and spotted.

Are the hyena's senses well developed?
The large eyes, ears and nostrils indicate well-developed senses.

What sounds do hyenas make?
The hyena's eerie howl is difficult to describe but it is something like a long drawn-out 'oooo-wee', repeated a few times in succession. It is one of the most typical night sounds in the African bush. They also have an astonishing repertoire of wailing, howling, chuckling and laughing sounds. To hear their hysterical cacophony at a kill is an unforgettable experience. Astley Maberly (1967) describes it as follows: 'These are a series of hysterical chattering howls, extraordinarily human in tone, but resembling maniacal rather than normal good-humoured laughter'.

Do they use these sounds for communication?
Their sounds, especially the howls, serve as an effective communication medium.

Do hyenas run in packs?
The basic social unit is the clan, which may consist of 10 to 40 or more individuals of both sexes and all ages. Although clans or packs usually remain stable in composition, members can shift from one clan to another. The clan is very loose, and members are very often scattered singly or in small packs, much as is the case in lion prides. Solitary individuals are common.

Are they territorial in habit?
Territories are marked and, although
not rigidly defended, a neighbouring
clan that trespasses will be met with
aggression. Communal defecating
areas are common and these also serve
to mark the territory.

What is the size of a territory?
It varies from a few to many square
kilometres, depending on the density
of the hyena population and the
available prey, as well as on
competition from other predators.

Do they have a pack leader?
The social roles among hyenas are
distributed fairly equally between
sexes. Both sexes are active in
territorial defence and hunting, with
females tending to take the lead.

Do hyenas have a social hierarchy?
Dominance is determined by size and
strength. Adult females are dominant.

Are they nocturnal in habit?
They are mainly, but not entirely
nocturnal. The day is usually spent in
thick bush, long grass, old aardvark
holes, a den among rocky boulders or
large burrows dug into the soil.
Spotted hyenas can be seen on cool
overcast days or in the early morning
or late afternoon.

Is the hyena really a coward?
The hyena has often been labelled a
coward and although its usual
behaviour supports this belief it can,
when hungry or cornered, put up a
terrific fight. A case is known where
two cornered hyenas killed a fully
grown lioness. A domestic dog is no
match for a determined hyena.

Are they clever animals?
They are cunning animals and could
well be more intelligent than the
domestic dog. Hyenas often watch
vultures and their movements to
locate a carcass.

What are their breeding habits?
Two or three pups are usually born in
an aardvark hole or a burrow dug by
the mother or other hyenas. The pups
are kept underground for about six
weeks after birth, and after the first
few weeks the mother will supplement
their milk diet with meat. The
gestation period is about 110 days.

Spotted hyenas tend to assemble in
groups to mate. Mating often takes
place on moonlit nights amidst a
pandemonium of howling and
laughing.

When are the pups born?
Although there could be birth peaks,
the pups may be born at any time of
the year.

When are hyenas sexually mature?
Sexual maturity is reached at about
three years of age.

What is the lifespan?
It could be up to 20 years.

*Can hyenas change from one sex to the
other?*
The widespread belief that hyenas can
change sex probably arose from the
fact that the external labial swellings of
the female are so large that they
superficially resemble the scrotum of
the male. Although hyenas are
difficult to sex, especially when young,
they are by no means hermaphrodites
and do not change sex.

What are their major enemies?

Hungry hyenas often take incredible risks in an effort to snatch meat from a hungry lion and in the process a number of them are killed or maimed. Pups can fall prey to other predators and even African rock pythons, but man is the only other natural enemy of adult hyenas.

Are they susceptible to diseases?

Although susceptible to diseases and parasites like all other animals, they do not seem to be very vulnerable in this respect and are rarely affected by epizootics. During the severe anthrax epizootic of 1960 to 1961, spotted hyenas fed on anthrax-infested carcasses in large numbers, but failed to contract the disease.

Spotted hyenas do suffer from infestations of the dangerous intramuscular nematode *Trichinella spiralis*, which may cause severe emaciation and paralysis of the host.

Are hyenas related to dogs?

Members of the family Hyaenidae are apparently related to the civets and mongooses, or Viverridae, and they appear to form a link between the dogs and the cats.

Does the hyena feature in witchcraft?

There are many superstitions about the hyena and in tribal medicine the tail, ears, whiskers, lips and genitals are used for certain potions.

BROWN HYENA *Hyaena brunnea* (Thunberg, 1820)

What is the distribution?

Brown hyenas are more or less confined to southern Africa, where they are found in Namibia, parts of Botswana, small areas in Zimbabwe and probably Mozambique. They are still found in the Transvaal, northern Cape Province and occasionally in the Orange Free State, but are mostly confined to nature reserves. No subspecies are recognized.

In the Kruger National Park they may appear anywhere but are extremely rare and seldom seen.

What type of habitat do they prefer?

Dry savanna is preferred, and the highest population densities occur in the drier western parts of the sub-continent, particularly the semi-desert areas of the Kalahari and Namibia.

What do they eat?

They are essentially scavengers and take any carcass or remains of a kill, as well as insects, fruit, birds and eggs. Hyenas that inhabit coastal areas patrol the beach for dead fish and other marine life that has been washed ashore. They seldom kill for themselves, but when they do, they usually take animals smaller than themselves such as springbok lambs.

Are they dependent on water?

Their distribution in arid areas suggests that they are not very dependent on water.

How do they hunt?

They normally hunt in small packs and run down their prey.

What are the main physical features?

Slightly smaller than the spotted hyena, they have a shoulder height of 70 to 80 cm and a body mass of 50 kg or slightly more. The coat is coarse, shaggy and fairly plain, coloured dark brown except on the neck, shoulders and upper part of the back, where the long, lighter hairs form a crest or mane. The limbs are also lighter in colour and are irregularly striped. The face is black, the ears are long and pointed, and the tail is bushy and somewhat truncated. A common feature is that its sloping back appears to be even more sloping and more rounded than the spotted hyena.

Are their senses well developed?

The senses of smell and hearing appear to be well developed.

Do they also have strong teeth and jaws?

In this respect they are very much the same as the spotted hyena.

Is it also difficult to see them?

Owing to their nocturnal habits they are very rarely seen.

Is it difficult to determine their sex?

As opposed to the spotted hyena, the brown hyena's genitals are such that the animals can easily be sexed.

What sound do they make?

The noise they make differs from that of the spotted hyena in that it is more of a series of short 'wah' and 'hi-ha' sounds. Although brown hyenas apparently do not make the typical laughing sound of the spotted species, they are also noisy at a carcass or a kill. As a rule they do not howl.

Do they run in packs?
They are rather solitary animals and spend most of the day lying up in the thick bush, rock crevices, old aardvark holes or other secluded spots.

Brown hyenas, however, frequently form small packs to hunt if the need arises, while they also assemble in fairly large numbers at a carcass in areas where they are still strong in numbers, such as in the Kalahari Gemsbok National Park.

Can they run fast?
It has been reported that they can reach 50 km/h and even more, and they can keep up a fast pace over several kilometres.

Are they territorial in habit?
They are territorial animals and, like the spotted hyena, mark their territory with secretions from the anal glands.

Do they have a social hierarchy?
A temporary hierarchy is established when a number of brown hyenas team up in a pack. They also have a matriarchal system like their spotted relatives.

Are they nocturnal in habit?
Brown hyenas tend to be more nocturnal and elusive than the spotted species, and are rarely seen even where they occur in fair numbers.

Are they dangerous to human beings?
They will seldom attack a human being, but they can be dangerous when cornered.

What are their breeding habits?
Two to four cubs are usually born after a gestation period of three months. They probably breed throughout the year. Sexual maturity is reached at about three years of age.

What is their potential lifespan?
Probably up to 20 years in captivity.

What are their major enemies?
Old age, disease, fights and confrontations with lions are probably the major mortality factors. Young ones can fall prey to a variety of mammalian predators and even reptiles and eagles.

How susceptible are they to diseases?
Little is known about this, but they would probably be susceptible to the same diseases as spotted hyenas.

Why are they so rare?
No satisfactory explanation for this phenomenon could be found in available literature. Generally speaking, however, competition with man, and man's ignorance, are most likely to be responsible for their low numbers.

Are there other hyena species in Africa?
There is a third hyena species, the striped hyena *Hyaena hyaena* (Linnaeus, 1758), which occurs in North Africa, parts of north-east Africa, Asia and India. Three subspecies are described by Meester & Setzer (1971). This species resembles the brown hyena, but the long hairs on the back form a mane from the nape to the rump. The coat is shaggy and decorated with black transverse stripes.

WILD DOG *Lycaon pictus* (Temminck, 1820)

What is the distribution?
The wild dog used to occur throughout the savanna areas of Africa but is now extinct in many parts of its original range. It is virtually impossible to determine its exact current distribution. Fortunately quite a number of game parks still harbour them. Five subspecies are described by Meester & Setzer (1971). The local subspecies is *L. p. pictus*.

Where can one see them in the Park?
They can be seen anywhere in the Park, although there are more of them per unit area in the southern section.

What type of habitat do they prefer?
They inhabit wooded to open savanna areas, but are also found on high mountains and in semi-deserts such as the Kalahari.

What do they eat?
In contrast to lion and leopard, wild dogs prey much more heavily on the females of the antelope population, killing large numbers of parturient females and the newly born young during the calving and lambing seasons of their prey species. Predation by wild dogs may therefore have a more definite limiting influence on the prey population than a comparative toll by lion or leopard.

Wild dogs kill a much narrower spectrum of prey species than lion or leopard, and impala constitute almost 80% of their prey. They also kill other antelopes from the size of steenbok to the cows of wildebeest, kudu and waterbuck. Zebra are not easily taken by wild dogs, and there have been instances of a stallion attacking a pack of dogs that showed an interest in the zebra foals.

Why are wild dogs so cruel when hunting?
Wild dogs lack the strong jaws and teeth and the sharp, powerful claws that are needed to catch and hold down a prey animal, so they kill their prey by tearing it apart. When the dogs close in for the kill, they waste no time in pulling down their prey and killing it. The prey of lion and other cats, on the other hand, often dies a slower death, especially when it is suffocated or mauled as is often the case when buffalo or giraffe are killed.

One should also bear in mind that the dogs' prey is probably in such a state of shock that it feels little pain. If human beings, who are more susceptible to pain than wild animals, can testify that they only felt pain long after a shark attack, then this could also be the case with an animal killed by wild dogs.

How do they hunt?
One or two dogs usually chase the prey while the others trail. At the beginning of the chase the quarry usually runs in a straight line, but when the dogs draw closer and capture becomes imminent it usually starts to zigzag. This action makes it easy for dogs in the rear to 'cut corners' and reach the prey before the leading dogs. A pursued antelope sometimes runs in a wide semi-circle. While some members of the pack

follow the antelope, others will cut across the arc and the quarry will suddenly find itself circled by dogs.

How far do they chase their prey?
Most pursuits end after a short chase but the distances can vary from a few hundred metres to 3 km and more.

Are their senses well developed?
The senses of hearing and smell appear to be well developed.

How successful are they in capturing prey?
This differs from one area to another. In the open country of the Serengeti National Park in Tanzania the success rate could be about 50% when they pursue adult gazelles, but up to 100% when they attack calves, lambs or disabled animals. In denser vegetation their success rate may be considerably lower. The belief that once they select a quarry they will not give up is not entirely substantiated. In fact it has been proved that they usually give up if they do not run down their prey within about 3 km.

When setting out to hunt they often move in single file but soon tend to spread out in a formation more useful for locating resting antelope.

How fast do they run?
The speed during the hunt varies from 50 km/h to as much as 65 km/h. When not hunting they either lie up and rest or trot along at about 8 km/h. In this way they can cover considerable distances in a day.

When do they hunt?
The peak hunting times are early in the morning and late in the afternoon.

What sounds do they make?
The most distinctive call is a bell-like 'hoo-hoo-hoo' sound which is usually uttered when pack members become separated. They can twitter and yip, and they bark when a danger such as a lion is spotted.

Do they tend to attack sick animals?
When attacking large prey they do tend to select old, injured or sick animals.

In the case of small prey, too, this trend is evident to a certain extent.

What is the killing rate of a dog?
In zoological gardens dogs are fed about 1,5 kg of meat per day, but in the wild they need much more – probably two to three times as much to supply sufficient energy for hunting and moving around. Comparatively speaking, a wild dog consumes more food per body mass than a lion. If only impala were preyed upon, a single dog may have to kill about 50 impala per year because only 60% of any prey animal can be consumed. The rest consists of horns, bones, hide and stomach contents.

Can wild dogs go without food for a long time?
This is doubtful for an animal as active as a wild dog. When possible they will probably kill every day.

Do they also eat carrion?
Wild dogs normally prefer fresh meat from their own kills but will scavenge when the need arises. They sometimes take meat from hyena or leopard kills, and cases have been recorded of a pack of wild dogs chasing a lion from its prey.

Do they prey on other predators?
Their normal prey animals do not include other predators, but they will attack old, weakened lions or even leopards and cheetahs in their prime when very hungry.

Are they cannibalistic?
No case of cannibalism has been reported in the Kruger National Park; if it does occur, it must be an extremely rare event.

Are they dependent on water?
They drink regularly where water is available, but their occasional presence in arid regions indicates that they are not completely dependent on regular water supplies.

What are the main physical features?
The wild dog is about the size of a smallish German shepherd dog (or Alsation), without the coat of long hair. The hair on the body is fairly short, with irregular black blotches on a white to sandy-yellow background. No two individual wild dogs have the same colour pattern,

but in most cases the bushy tail has a white terminal tip.

The ears are large, upright and rather rounded, the muzzle is black, and a ruff of long hair adorns the neck. The limbs, although lean, are very muscular. The body mass is 25 to 32 kg and the shoulder height from 55 to 75 cm.

What is the average pack size?
It can vary from one area to another. In the Kruger National Park packs of up to 50 dogs have been recorded, but the average pack sizes are 11 for the southern part, eight in the central area and nine in the northern part of the Park.

What is the sex ratio?
During a period of carnivore control from 1954 to 1960 some 60% of the wild dogs destroyed were males and some 40% were females. A preponderance of males has also been recorded in other parts of Africa.

Is this sex ratio not unfavourable?
It has been speculated that the larger proportion of males is actually of benefit to the pack.

Females with young cannot hunt for the first few weeks after the birth and are fed by other members of the pack. A larger number of males, that are never tied down as the females with young are, therefore helps to secure the survival of the offspring.

Do wild dogs have a social hierarchy?
They do have a social hierarchy, but it is not as rigid as that of many other gregarious animals. The amity that exists between members of the pack is very noticeable, and there is little strife even when the whole pack is crowded around a kill.

There is virtually none of the growling and snapping that characterize feeding lions.

The wild dogs' 'greeting' ritual most probably serves to strengthen social ties. In this procedure two dogs will walk parallel to each other, bodies touching, ears back and lips drawn to expose their teeth while at the same time they nibble and lick each other's mouths. Partners are frequently changed, and the performance is accompanied by twittering and whining sounds.

Do males often fight?
Fights appear to be rare.

Is there a definite pack leader?
There appears to be some kind of dominance, but males and females share most tasks equally, including the hunting and feeding of the pups. While some dogs hunt, others guard the den if there are pups.

Are wild dogs territorial in habit?
When there is a litter of pups a pack will defend the area immediately around their den. The den is abandoned when the pups are old enough to follow the adults.

The wild dogs' habit of roaming over many hundreds of square kilometres precludes a fixed territory. They do, however, have activity zones that shift frequently. The dogs' strong body odour automatically marks any area where they rest or stay for a while.

How long is the gestation period?
About 70 days.

How many pups are born at a time?
Two to eight pups are usually born, but as many as 15 have been noted.

When are they born?
They may be born at any time of year, but in the Park there appears to be a definite peak during the winter months.

Is pup mortality high?
Mortality is very high and few pups usually survive. Very young pups appear susceptible to diseases. When pups accompany the pack for the first time, many of them succumb to the hard life of roaming over large areas.

Apart from pup mortality, the breeding potential of wild dogs is reduced by the unbalanced sex ratio favouring males, and by a large percentage of the females being reproductively inactive.

When are the pups weaned?
Weaning may commence at three weeks, but the normal weaning age is about two months.

Are pups neglected by their parents?
Wild dogs actually care better for their young than many other predators. Both males and females regurgitate food for the pups.

A case has been recorded of five males raising a litter of pups when the mother – the only female in the pack – died a few weeks after giving birth.

At what age are the pups capable of accompanying the adults on their wanderings?
The adults leave the den when the young are about 10 to 12 weeks old, and are followed by the young dogs. Weaklings that cannot keep up with the pack are left to their fate and either starve to death or more often are killed by other predators, particularly hyenas.

What is a wild dog's lifespan?
In captivity it is probably the same as that of a domestic dog, (some 15 years); in the wild it is probably 10 – 12 years.

What are their major enemies?
Wild dogs are not normally preyed upon by other predators, but old or disabled dogs and young ones separated from the pack are easy prey for hyenas.

Are wild dogs susceptible to diseases?
It has been claimed that they are susceptible to canine diseases especially distemper, but this claim has not been substantiated by scientific evidence.

Is the wild dog related to the domestic dog?
Both belong to the family Canidae but not to the same genus. The domestic dog (*Canis familiaris*) and some jackal and wolf species are members of the genus *Canis*, whereas the wild dog belongs to the genus *Lycaon*, of which *pictus* is the only species. Domestic dogs have four toes and a dew claw on the front feet, but only four on the hind feet. The wild dog has four toes on the front and hind feet.

Do wild dogs attack human beings?
When desperately hungry wild dogs may attack a human being, but normally they will try to avoid confrontation.

AARDWOLF *Proteles cristatus* (Sparrman, 1783)

What is the distribution?
Aardwolf are dispersed over the open and savanna veld of southern Africa and parts of East Africa, but are relatively rare. The small population in the Park is sparsely distributed in the Pretoriuskop area, the western border areas and the open grassland of the Lebombo flats.

What habitat do they prefer?
They inhabit open plains, scrubland and lightly wooded savanna, and are seldom found in dense bush.

What does the aardwolf eat?
Termites make up the bulk of its diet, but rodents and birds' eggs are also eaten, and carrion and vegetable matter.

What are the main physical features?
The aardwolf has a superficial resemblance to a small, striped hyena. The colour of its coat is buff-yellowish with vertical stripes along the body. A well-developed mane of buff-coloured long hairs is noticeable along the back. This mane, which can be raised when the aardwolf is excited, makes the animal look bigger and more formidable than it really is. The ears are long, narrow and pointed; the jaws small and weak, the limbs very slender. The tail is fairly long and somewhat bushy.

The shoulder height is 45 to 50 cm and the mass about 10 kg.

Are they solitary animals?
The aardwolf generally lives alone or in pairs, but is also found in small family groups.

Are they nocturnal?
This secretive, shy creature is nocturnal in habit and is very seldom seen during the day. It can live in an area for years without being detected.

Are they territorial?
It is doubtful whether they will defend a territory, but they appear to have a definite home range.

Where do they hide during the day?
During the day they usually hide in an underground burrow. More than one animal may use the same burrow.

What are their breeding habits?
From two to four, but usually three, young are born in an underground burrow.

Is it an endangered animal?
The aardwolf is probably not in immediate danger, but its low numbers make it vulnerable.

BLACK-BACKED JACKAL *Canis mesomelas* (Schreber, 1775)

What is the distribution
The black-backed jackal is the most widely distributed jackal species in southern Africa and also occurs in East Africa. These cunning carnivores are found in areas where almost all other wild animals have long been exterminated, and still hold their own in many sheep-farming areas in spite of intensive efforts to eradicate them. A large number of them occurs in the Kruger National Park and are often seen by visitors. The local subspecies is *C. m. mesomelas* (Schreber, 1775).

What type of habitat do these jackals prefer?
Although they prefer open savanna and light woodland, they are adaptable animals and are also found in arid habitats.

What do they eat?
Jackals are largely scavengers in areas where there are large predators, and will, for example, follow hunting lions until the latter make a kill. They also prey on small and young mammals, birds and reptiles, and even eat insects, birds' eggs and wild fruit.

Are they dependent on water?
They drink regularly when water is available but are not very dependent on a regular supply.

What are the main physical features?
The black back stippled with white is sharply defined from the rufous sides and legs and it is therefore easy to distinguish this species from other jackal and fox species. The ears are long and pointed, the face is greyish in colour, and the underparts are whitish. The tail is bushy and rufous with a black tip. The shoulder height is about 40 cm and the mass 6 to 9 kg.

The jackal is a true 'dog', with five toes on each front foot and four on the back ones. Some authors believe that the jackal and the wolf are the ancestors of the domestic dog.

What sound do they make?
It is difficult to describe the howling of black-backed jackals, but to those familiar with the sound it is one of the most typical noises of the African veld. In the safety of a nature reserve they are noisy animals, but when they are hunted they do not make a sound.

Are they solitary animals?
Jackals can live a solitary life, but are more often found in pairs or small parties. When lions make a kill, up to 30 or more jackals may gather around it, waiting impatiently for the lions to finish and, of course, to leave something for them.

Are they nocturnal?
Although predominantly nocturnal, jackals are often seen during the day, especially in the early morning and late afternoon. They spend the greater part of the day lying under bushes, in rocky outcrops, underground burrows or tall grass.

Do they hunt in packs?
No, they usually hunt alone or in pairs. It is common for one of the pair to try and lure a female antelope from

her newly born young so that the other one can snatch up the lamb.

Are jackals really that clever?
They are cunning animals and despite the concerted efforts of sheep farmers to eradicate them they are still found in most sheep-farming areas.

Are they territorial?
Jackals appear to have home ranges which they mark but do not defend. The fact that large numbers of them gather at a lion kill indicates that they are not strictly territorial in habit.

What are their breeding habits?
Usually about six, but sometimes up to nine pups are born in holes or rock crevices. The gestation period is about two months.

What are their major enemies?
Jackals are mercilessly hunted and poisoned in farming areas. Organized hunts with dogs specially bred for the purpose are carried out regularly and a large number of them are killed annually.

In nature reserves young jackals fall prey to eagles, pythons and mammalian predators. The adults are not particularly preyed upon by larger predators, but they may be killed by lions if they become too bold when the latter are feeding.

SIDE-STRIPED JACKAL *Canis adustus* (Sundevall, 1846)

What is the distribution?
These jackals occur in the savanna areas of Africa. Being more or less a tropical species, they are not found much further south than the Tropic of Capricorn. In South Africa they are confined to the northern parts of the Transvaal and northern Natal. They are found throughout the Park and are represented by the subspecies *C. a. adustus* (Sundevall, 1846).

How many are there in the Park?
They are rare in the Park, but their numbers are not known.

What type of habitat do they prefer?
They avoid open savanna, favouring denser bush.

What do they eat?
They live mainly on small mammals, reptiles, ground birds and their eggs, insects, wild fruit and carrion. In contrast to the black-backed jackal, they are not regarded as stock killers.

Are they dependent on water?
It is not known how dependent they are on water.

What are the main physical features?
The general colour is greyish fawn, darker on the back and lighter on the sides, and without the conspicuous 'saddle' of the black-backed jackal. A whitish line along the flank is usually, but not always, visible. The ears are shorter and less pointed than those of the black-backed species, and the shorter, darker muzzle gives a more wolf-like appearance.

The shoulder height is about 40 cm or slightly more, and the body mass 8 to 10 kg.

Are they solitary?
They tend to be more solitary than the black-backed species and, being more timid and shy, are not often seen by visitors.

Are they nocturnal?
Yes, they are predominantly nocturnal and very seldom seen during the day. They may occasionally be observed at dusk and dawn.

How do they hunt?
They appear to be mainly solitary hunters, although they may also hunt in pairs.

Are they noisy?
They are fairly quiet animals, uttering a barking and howling sound very much like that of the black-backed jackal.

What are their breeding habits?
Usually up to six pups are born in a burrow, after a gestation period of about two months.

What is the lifespan?
Probably 10 to 15 years in captivity, but considerably less in the wild.

What are their major enemies?
The pups have many enemies, including eagles, mammalian predators and pythons; the adults are sometimes killed by lion and hyena at a kill. Nothing is known about their susceptibility to diseases.

BAT-EARED FOX *Otocyon megalotis* (Desmarest, 1822)

What is the distribution?
In southern Africa the bat-eared fox is mostly confined to the dry parts of the Cape Province, the Orange Free State, Transvaal, the southern parts of Zimbabwe, Botswana and Namibia. It also occurs in parts of East Africa. The subspecies in the Park is
O. m. megalotis (Desmarest, 1822).

Until the mid-1960s it was believed to be absent from the Kruger National Park, but then a few animals were seen in the northern part.

How many bat-eared foxes are there in the Park?
They are rare and consequently their numbers are unknown.

What type of habitat do they prefer?
They prefer to exist in savanna and dry, open plains.

Are they dependent on water?
Their presence in arid parts of the country is an indication that they are not dependent on water.

What do they eat?
Although they are mainly insectivorous, they also feed on small rodents, the eggs and chickens of ground birds, lizards, wild fruit, tubers and berries. They have been accused of killing poultry and even young lambs, but this is extremely unlikely as their jaws and teeth are not suited to coping with this type of prey. Bat-eared foxes are beneficial animals, eating large quantities of termites.

What are the main physical features?
The most striking feature of this mammal is the large, oval-shaped, black-tipped ears. The colour of the coat is greyish brown above and paler below, and the bushy tail has a black tip. The rather short legs are also

blackish in colour. The shoulder height is about 30 cm; body mass 4 to 5 kg.

How fast can they run?
It is difficult to determine their speed as they run in a zigzag fashion, changing direction deceptively fast.

Are they solitary?
Sometimes they are solitary, but they are also found in pairs or in small parties. In the Kalahari Gemsbok National Park it is common to see two or more of these animals together.

Are they nocturnal in habit?
Although they are said to be mainly nocturnal, they may be seen during the day, especially in the Kalahari Gemsbok National Park where they like to come out of their burrows in the early morning or late afternoon. The warm part of the day is usually spent lying in a burrow.

What sound do they make?
They can utter a growling noise when agitated, but the normal sound is a rather long drawn-out, slightly melancholic-sounding whine.

What are their natural enemies?
Adult as well as young bat-eared foxes are frequently killed by the larger eagles. They may also fall prey to other predators.

What defence do they have against enemies?
Lacking sharp claws, large teeth or body size, these little creatures prefer to avoid enemies. They crouch down when alarmed, depressing their long ears flat on either side of the head in the hope of escaping detection. If they are flushed out by an enemy, they do not run in a straight line but twist and turn with great agility. The tail is used to maintain balance and to bluff the pursuer by moving it to one side while the body is moved in the opposite direction.

Are they protected animals?
No, and unfortunately some farmers still hunt them in the belief that they kill lambs. People who have seen them feeding on dead lambs without determining the cause of the lambs' death, have reinforced this misconception.

AFRICAN CIVET *Civettictis civetta* (Schreber, 1776)

What is the distribution?
The African civet occurs in the northern coastal areas of Zululand, Mozambique, the eastern and northern Transvaal, northern Botswana, northern Namibia, Angola, Tanzania and other savanna areas of Africa. The subspecies *C. c. australis* (Lundholm, 1955), is found in the Park.

What type of habitat do civets prefer?
Although they inhabit fairly dry areas, they actually prefer warm, bush-covered areas near water.

What do they eat?
They prey on a large variety of small animals as well as carrion and vegetable matter such as wild fruits and berries. They eat the young of small antelopes, as well as rodents,

reptiles, birds and their eggs, and snails, millipedes and other invertebrates. In farming areas they sometimes kill poultry and even domestic cats.

What are the main physical features?
The civet is a rather long-bodied animal with a coarse, wiry coat that has irregular black blotches and stripes on a greyish background. A conspicuous black dorsal crest of hairs runs from the neck to the bushy black-tipped tail. When the civet is angered or alarmed this crest stands erect, making the animal look even more impressive. The legs are short and slender, with non-retractile claws so that the spoor is dog-like, though narrower in form. A black band circles the face and throat. The forehead is

grey, the ears are white-tipped, small and rounded, and the muzzle is rather pointed.

Because the body is usually arched to some extent, with the head carried low, the civet appears to be larger than it actually is. The arched back and dorsal crest of hairs also make it look higher at the back than the front. It is sometimes seen in the lights of a vehicle at night when, alarmed, it often raises the dorsal hairs on end. This, coupled with the arched back and low head, makes it appear strange.

The shoulder height is up to about 40 cm and the head, neck and body may be close to 90 cm long; the mass is about 11 kg.

What sounds do they make?
The normal call, which is rarely uttered, is a series of low-pitched, grating coughs, but they also growl when angered.

What are their habits?
They are solitary, nocturnal; they hide in thickets and tall grass in the day.

Are civets plentiful in the Park?
They are, but owing to their nocturnal way of life they are very seldom seen by visitors.

Are they territorial animals?
They return regularly to chosen middens for their excretions, indicating that although they may not be strictly territorial, they at least have a well-established and recognised home range.

Do they have scent glands?
Their anal glands secrete a strong odour which is used in the manufacture of perfume.

What are their breeding habits?
One to three kittens are born in a secluded spot.

What are their major enemies?
Their nocturnal way of life probably protects them from a wide variety of erstwhile enemies.

Diseases and fights may well be the major mortality factors.

GENETS *Genetta spp.*

What is the distribution?
The genus *Genetta* is represented by a number of species throughout Africa, the range of some extending into Europe and Asia. The remarkable degree of individual variation in genets has led to the description of many species and subspecies, of which the status of a number is uncertain. For example, it is not certain whether the large-spotted genet (*G. tigrina*) and the rusty-spotted genet (*G. rubiginosa*) are different species. If one accepts that *G. tigrina* (Schreber, 1776) and *G. rubiginosa* (Pucheran, 1855) are two separate species, then three species occur in South Africa. The third, and most common species is the small-spotted genet *G. genetta*.

The small-spotted genet occurs mainly in the southern parts of the Kruger National Park, while the rusty-spotted genet inhabits most areas of the Park, with the highest concentration in the south.

What type of habitat do they prefer?
The small-spotted genet prefers the drier, less forested areas, while the rusty-spotted genet more often inhabits dense bush.

What do they eat?
These small carnivores are formidable killers of just about all the smaller vertebrates from hares to birds, lizards and snakes, as well as invertebrates such as insects. Although beneficial in

that they kill a large number of rodents, they are also among the most effective poultry killers. They are wasteful feeders and will often kill more than they can eat, especially when they get into a fowl run.

What are the main physical features?
The genets are long-bodied, cat-like creatures with short legs, narrow, pointed faces, large conical ears and ringed bushy tails. Their greyish bodies are richly marked with dark, reddish brown spots that tend to unite to form longitudinal stripes along the back and shoulders. They are more or less the size of domestic cats, but the shoulder height is less and the body longer. The body length ranges from 40 to 50 cm, while the mass is 2 to 3 kg.

What are their habits?
The habits of the different genet species appear to be very similar. Some are more arboreal than others, but all of them are very agile tree climbers. They are nocturnal animals, spending the day in burrows dug by other animals, in rock crevices or in dense undergrowth. It is exceptional to see them during daylight. They live singly or in pairs and are also territorial in habit. Most of their hunting is done on the ground, but they also climb trees to rob birds' nests or kill roosting or nesting birds.

What are their breeding habits?
Usually two or three, occasionally four kittens are born in a litter, and like many of the smaller carnivores they are born in a burrow or other secluded spot. Gestation is about 2,5 months.

What sounds do they make?
They spit and growl like domestic cats, making noises that sound quite formidable for such small animals.

What are their major enemies?
They may be killed by some of the smaller mammalian and reptilian predators; larger owls kill kittens.

Are they related to the domestic cat?
They are not true cats, although their behaviour and physical features are very much like those of the felids.
Genets are more closely related to the civets than to domestic cats.

SLENDER MONGOOSE   *Galerella sanguinea*   (Rüppell, 1836)

What is the distribution?
The slender mongoose occurs in the Afro-tropical region as far south as the Orange River. The status of the different subspecies is uncertain. This is the species probably most often seen in the Park.

What type of habitat do these mongooses prefer?
Their habitat ranges from desert through savanna to dense bush.

What do they eat?
They feed mainly on rodents, snakes and other reptiles. Birds' eggs, insects and wild fruit are also consumed. In farming areas they can become poultry thieves.

What are their main physical features?
Their general colour is yellowish or reddish brown, with the hairs of the wiry coat giving it a grizzled appearance when seen at close quarters.
  The slender body is 30 to 38 cm long without the tail, which is very long and has a conspicuous black tip. It is often held straight or curled over the back when the mongoose is running. Body mass is about 0,7 kg.

What are their habits?
They are diurnal, and live singly or in pairs.

What are their breeding habits?
Two to four kittens are born in a burrow, a rock crevice or a hollow tree.

What are their major enemies?
They are probably preyed upon by the lesser cats and other small predators.

Which is the most common mongoose species in the Park?
Mongooses are well represented in the Kruger National Park and some species are often seen by visitors. They are the Egyptian mongoose, the slender mongoose, the white-tailed mongoose, the marsh or water mongoose, the banded mongoose, the dwarf mongoose and Selous's mongoose.
  The most common species in the Park are the slender or black-tipped mongoose, the banded mongoose and the dwarf mongoose.

BANDED MONGOOSE *Mungos mungo* (Gmelin, 1788)

What is the distribution?
The banded mongoose occurs in the coastal areas of Natal and the northern half of the Transvaal. They are also found in Namibia, Botswana, Zimbabwe and in Somalia, the Sudan, Guinea, Gambia and Tanzania. The subspecies *M. m. taenianotus* (A Smith, 1834) is found in the Park.

What type of habitat do banded mongooses prefer?
They prefer the more open, dry savanna areas, usually not far from water. They spend the night in burrows or rock crevices.

What do they eat?
Insects probably make up their staple diet, but they also feed on rodents, reptiles, birds and their eggs, amphibians, molluscs, fruit and berries.

What are the main physical features?
This medium-sized, brownish grey mongoose has a coarse coat, conspicuously marked with transverse dark brown stripes alternating with light-coloured bands of about the same width.

The body length is about 40 cm, with a tail that is about 20 cm long, and the body mass is about 1,4 kg. The hairs on the tail decrease to the tip, giving it a tapered appearance.

What are their habits?
They are diurnal and gregarious, running in packs of about 20 individuals and occasionally as many as 50. Members of a pack often follow one another very closely and move like a huge snake winding through the grass or undergrowth. They are fairly noisy and their wide range of sounds include crooning, high-pitched twittering cries, bird-like whistling, and a particular chittering when alarmed. When angered, they growl and utter slight barking sounds.

These active little animals hustle about with much rustling of the grass when they actively search for food among dead leaves or under stones. When alarmed they disappear in a flash, but if one waits patiently they reappear after a few minutes, nervously and warily scanning the surroundings for the source of alarm.

What are their breeding habits?
Two to four kittens are born, usually between October and February. The gestation period is about two months. A female can take care of more than one litter while the other mothers are foraging.

What are their major enemies?
Birds of prey are probably their main enemies, although they may also fall prey to jackals and the lesser felids.

DWARF MONGOOSE *Helogale parvula* (Sundevall, 1846)

What is the distribution?
The dwarf mongoose occurs in many savanna areas of Africa. The local subspecies *H. p. parvula* (Sundevall, 1846) is well represented in the Kruger National Park.

What type of habitat do dwarf mongooses prefer?
They live in dry savanna areas associated with open woodland.

What do they eat?
They feed on insects and other arthropods, as well as small rodents, reptiles, and birds and their eggs.

What are the main physical features?
This stockily built mongoose is the smallest of the African species, with a body mass of about 260 g and a length of 20 to 25 cm excluding the tail, which is about 12 cm long. The colour of the coat is greyish brown to dark brown and the tail has no dark tip.

What are their habits?
These little creatures are diurnal and gregarious, running in parties of about 10 to 20 individuals. It is most interesting to watch a group of them moving about actively looking for food: they clamber in and out of rock crevices and old termitaria, or anthills which are also used as refuges when danger threatens. They appear to be nomadic and are not confined to a specific set of burrows.

Dwarf mongooses are very inquisitive and not timid. When alarmed they scurry back into their burrows or anthills, but after a few minutes of patient waiting they reappear to peep around and eventually proceed with their foraging and rather noisy communicating sounds. Like bigger mongooses, they growl when angered.

What are their breeding habits?
Two to four kittens are born in a burrow, a hollow tree or a rock crevice. The young are born during the summer after a gestation period of about 50 days. Each pack has a dominant pair from which most members of the group are bred. The alpha female is in oestrus for five days and the alpha male copulates with her often during that period, as many as 2 386 times and ejaculating in 10% of these (Rasa, 1985).

STRIPED POLECAT   *Ictonyx striatus*   (Perry, 1810)

What is the distribution?
The striped polecat has a wide distribution in the Afrotropical region. *I. s. striatus* (Perry, 1810) is found throughout the Park.

What type of habitat do striped polecats prefer?
They inhabit a wide variety of areas, including arid and semi-arid environments, open savanna and forests.

What do they eat?
They feed on rodents up to the size of cane rats, hares, snakes and other reptiles, frogs, birds and insects.

What are the main physical features?
Four broad white stripes run from the nape of the neck to the tail, alternating

with narrower black bands. In adults the hair is long and coarse, but the fur of young animals is fairly short. The tail is long and bushy, more or less white with a black tip, while the underparts and short limbs are black. The shoulder height is about 10 cm, the body length 25 to 30 cm, and the mass about 950 g for males and 700 g for females.

What are their habits?
Polecats live singly, in pairs or in small family groups.

Although nocturnal and therefore seldom seen during the day, they are by no means rare. They usually trot along with their backs slightly hunched, but when they are angered or excited the long dorsal hairs become erect and the fluffy tails are raised and curved forwards over the back. They utter a series of high-pitched screams in their anger, at the same time.

What are their breeding habits?
Two to three kittens are born in a burrow or rock crevice after a gestation period of 35 or 36 days.

What are their major enemies?
The medium- and smaller-sized carnivores are probably their main enemies.

As a means of defence a nauseating, musky secretion is ejected forcefully and accurately from their anal glands. It has an extremely unpleasant odour, and a pursuer that receives a direct hit will retain the shocking smell for days afterwards.

CAPE CLAWLESS OTTER *Aonyx capensis* (Schinz, 1821)

What is the distribution?
The Cape clawless otter occurs in most of the savanna areas of Africa south of the Sahara and is well represented in South Africa. The subspecies *A. c. capensis* (Schinz, 1821) occurs in the Kruger National Park.

What type of habitat do these otters prefer?
These water-loving mammals prefer large rivers with quiet pools or slow-flowing streams. They may occasionally be seen far from water.

What do they eat?
Aquatic animals such as crabs, frogs, mussels and fish make up the bulk of their diet, but rodents and other small mammals, terrapins, leguaans, insects, aquatic birds, and even poultry also feature in their diet.

What are the main physical features?
The body mass is about 12 kg and the body length about 90 cm without the tail. The otter is a short-legged creature with no claws on the front feet and only two small nails on the hind feet. Only the toes on the hind feet are webbed. Its general colour is dark brown on the upper parts and paler on the underside, and it has a conspicuous white throat.

What are their habits?
These animals swim well and they may remain submerged for 17 seconds under 'natural' conditions (Rowe-Rowe, 1975).

What are their breeding habits?
One to three pups are born in a burrow or other sheltered places in dense vegetation. The gestation period is about two months.

What are their major enemies?
Crocodiles will kill otters if they get the chance, but the latter's agility often saves them from the huge reptiles' vicious jaws. When on land otters may be attacked by the medium-sized carnivores.

RATEL OR HONEY BADGER *Mellivora capensis* (Schreber, 1776)

What is the distribution?
The ratel is distributed throughout Africa south of the Sahara and are also found in parts of Asia. The local population belongs to the subspecies *M. c. capensis* (Schreber, 1776).

What type of habitat do ratels prefer?
They inhabit just about every type of habitat, ranging from open, dry savanna to dense forest.

What do they eat?
Ratels are omnivores, feeding on small mammals, reptiles, birds' eggs, insects and grubs of all kinds, bulbs, roots, wild fruit and honey. They are fond of honey, and will dig out a hive ruthlessly in spite of being attacked by large numbers of bees. In fact, very few of the stings penetrate the skin. They may also eat carrion.

What are their main physical features?
This stoutly built, tough-looking little beast stands 25 to 30 cm at the shoulder, and attains a mass of up to 12 kg and a body length of 70 to 80 cm, excluding the tail. Its coat is dark grey on the back, with a lateral white stripe on either side extending from the head along the flanks and separating the grey of the back from the black of the face, underparts and limbs. The tail is short, somewhat bushy and usually held upright as the animal moves about. The claws are bear-like and strong, and well adapted for digging out beehives, roots, bulbs and even snakes and other small animals.

Young animals are brown along the back, with no division between it and the darker underparts.

Unlike most other mammals, the ratel is plantigrade, i.e. it walks on the

soles of its feet. Antelopes, for
example, are digitigrade – they walk
on their toes.

What are their habits?
Ratels tend to be nocturnal in habit
and are therefore not often seen
during the day. They live singly or in
pairs and are territorial.

According to popular belief ratels
are aggressive, dangerous animals, but
in fact they are rather shy and retiring.
When cornered by an enemy they are,
however, among the most courageous
animals in the African bush. They are
extremely bold and when disturbed or
cornered will attack an enemy many
times their own size. It is even claimed

that ratels have killed animals as big
as buffalo by severing their genitals,
causing fatal haemorrhage. When
attacked by dogs a ratel can take
incredible mauling without apparent
harm, but will inflict severe and often
fatal wounds with its teeth and claws.
The tough, thick elastic skin plays an
important role in its defence.

What are their breeding habits?
Two to three pups are born in a
burrow or secluded place.

What are their major enemies?
Ratels probably do not have many
enemies. In most cases death is caused
by disease and fighting.

PANGOLIN *Manis temminckii* (Smuts, 1832)

What is the distribution?
Pangolins, or scaly anteaters are widely distributed throughout most of the savanna areas of Africa and also occur in the Kruger National Park.

Meester & Setzer (1971) do not recognize any subspecies.

What type of habitat do pangolins prefer?
They prefer grassland, savanna and lightly wooded areas. In the Kruger National Park they are confined to areas with an abundance of anthills, or termitaria.

When not searching for food they take refuge in burrows or secluded places.

What do they eat?
Pangolins eat ants and termites which they obtain by digging into ant nests and termitaria. They have no teeth and food is easily captured with their long, sticky tongues.

What are their main physical features?
This peculiar, prehistoric-looking mammal is covered with large, brown, overlapping scales and may be considered to be reminiscent of a reptile. The head is small and narrow, the elongated body is about 1 m long, and the mass is about 8 kg. External ears are absent, the eyes are small and the tongue is about 30 cm long.

Pangolins have a curious way of walking in that most of the time they walk on their hindlegs only. The tail is raised and the front legs touch the ground only occasionally. Sometimes they stand up on their hindlegs to look around.

Are they nocturnal in habit?
They are mostly nocturnal, but on rare occasions may be seen during the day.

Are they solitary?
They are solitary, but they may be seen in pairs when mating.

Are they territorial in habit?
Because of their secretive habits it has not been possible to determine whether they are territorial. They do occupy a home range, however, and this covers between 1,3 and 7,9 km^2 (Skinner & Smithers, 1990).

Are their senses well developed?
Their sense of sight appears to be limited, but the senses of smell, hearing and taste seem to be acute.

What are their breeding habits?
A single cub is born after a gestation period of about 140 days. At birth the scales are soft, but they harden within two days. The cub is carried on the mother's tail, and when danger threatens the mother wraps her body around it.

Is the pangolin in danger of extinction?
It is difficult to say, but they are definitely rare and could well be endangered.

What kind of sounds do they make?
The apparently make no sounds.

What are their major enemies?
The pangolin's armour and its habit of rolling up into a tight ball when danger threatens afford excellent protection, and few predators effectively harm it. The availability of food is most probably a limiting factor, and the effect of disease is not clear.

Are the scales its only protection?
When interfered with after it has rolled up, the pangolin may attempt to injure its attacker by scything the tail across its body. The scales can also be moved individually and to catch a finger between them can be a painful experience.

According to Astley Maberly (1967), the pangolin can, as a defensive measure, secrete an extremely unpleasant odour from certain glands. Unsurprisingly, this deters certain predators from attack.

AARDVARK *Orycteropus afer* (Pallas, 1766)

What is the distribution?
Aardvark may be found throughout Africa south of the Sahara, wherever suitable habitats are available. The local population is represented by the subspecies *O. a. afer* (Pallas, 1766).

What type of habitat do aardvark prefer?
They prefer savanna regions, especially sandy areas where there is an abundance of termitaria.

What do they eat?
Their diet consists mainly of termites and ants, but other insects and their larvae, as well as small quantities of vegetable matter, are also consumed. They use their powerful claws to dig out termites which are then caught on the sticky tongue.

What are the main physical features?
Aardvark, literally meaning 'earth-pig', is a unique African mammal. It is as large as a medium-sized pig and has a shoulder height of about 60 cm, a body length of 90 cm to 1,05 m, a tail up to 60 cm long, and a body mass of 60 kg or slightly more. The face is elongated with a long tubular snout and a blunt, pig-like muzzle. The long ears are tubular and pointed. The back is arched and the limbs are short, with four toes on the front and five on the hind foot. The feet are plantigrade. The body is brown and sparsely covered with coarse, reddish brown hairs. Like the pangolin, the aardvark has a long, sticky tongue some 45 cm in length with which it captures its prey. It has no incisors or canines, and the molar teeth are reduced and columnar (de Graaff 1974). The teeth are replaced from the back of the jaw to the front.

Are their senses well developed?
Their sense of smell is acutely developed. Their hearing is also very good, but their sight appears to be poor, particularly in daylight.

What sound do they make?
They are normally silent animals, but they can squeal like pigs when disturbed.

Are they solitary in habit?
They are solitary most of the time, but a mother is accompanied by her offspring for a few months before it becomes independent.

Are they nocturnal in habit?
Aardvark are nocturnal animals, sheltering in burrows during the day. Even in areas where they occur in fair numbers, the only signs of their presence are the large burrows that they excavate. At night they emerge to wander long distances in a zigzag manner in search of food. It is said that they can walk as much as 10 to 15 km in one night. Although aardvark are common in open country where termites abound, their nocturnal habits make them difficult to observe.

Are they territorial?
They probably have a preferred home range, but are not territorial. Although a set of burrows could be used for some time, new burrows are dug from time to time. These burrows are often an extensive set of tunnels and chambers with a number of entrances.

Does it take the aardvark a long time to excavate a burrow?
The digging capacity of this animal is unbelievable. The claws on the front feet are used to dig, while the hind feet are used to remove the loosened soil at considerable speed. Their digging speed and efficiency are amazing, and the aardvark can disappear into the soil within minutes.

How is dust prevented from entering their lungs?
Dense bristles around the nostrils prevents dust from entering the nose.

Are they very strong?
It is said that an aardvark cannot be pulled out of a burrow by a horse once it is halfway or more inside. The senior author had the very rare privilege of watching a 130-kg man well-known for his strength trying to pull an aardvark out of its burrow when it was not more than halfway in. Needless to say, he made no impression on the aardvark!

Are aardvark clumsy?
Their normal gait is slow and their lumbering way of walking creates the impression of clumsiness, but in fact they can run deceptively fast if necessary.

Are aardvark useful animals?
These strange animals play an important, two-fold ecological role: they keep termites in check, and their disused burrows provide shelter and breeding sites for a number of other animal species, including jackals, wild dogs, hyenas, aardwolves, warthogs, mongooses and even birds.

What are their breeding habits?
A single pup is born, usually between May and August, after a gestation period of about seven months. The young aardvark accompanies the mother for many months.

What are their major enemies?
Lion and leopard are their major natural enemies.

Can they defend themselves?
Although their teeth are useless for defence, the aardvark's huge claws are lethal weapons and they are ferocious fighters when cornered.

SOUTH AFRICAN HEDGEHOG *Atelerix frontalis* (A Smith, 1831)

What is the distribution?
The genus *Atelerix* is distributed in the savanna areas of southern Africa. The range of the local subspecies *A. f. frontalis* extends from the eastern parts of the Cape Province through the Orange Free State and western Transvaal into eastern Botswana and western Zimbabwe.

It is rarely seen in the Kruger National Park as this area is to the east of its normal distribution.

What type of habitat do these hedgehogs prefer?
They live in grassland and wooded savanna.

What do they eat?
They are insectivorous animals tending towards omnivory, and consume earthworms, slugs and snails, frogs, fledgling birds, eggs, small mice and wild fruit, berries and other vegetable matter, as well as termites, millipedes, ants and other insects.

What are the main physical features?
The South African hedgehog greatly resembles its European cousin but is slightly smaller. The upper part of the body is covered with short spines that project at all angles. When alarmed it rolls up into a tight ball. The general colour is brown, speckled with white and buff. The spines are white at the base, brown in the middle and white or buff-coloured at the tips. Shades of colours vary considerably in different individuals, and albinism often occurs.

When the hedgehog is walking its legs appear to be abnormally long for the size of its body, which is seldom more than 20 cm long.

Are they nocturnal in habit?
They are predominantly nocturnal and are seldom seen during the day.

Where do they hide during the day?
They spend the day in holes, rock crevices, undergrowth, grass or even piles of debris.

Do they hibernate?
It appears that they do tend to hibernate during the cold and dry months of May to September, and reappear after the first rains, usually during October.

Are they solitary in habit?
Hedgehogs occur singly or in pairs.

Are they related to the porcupine?
Despite also having spines or quills, they are not related to the porcupine. The hedgehog is an insectivore, in contrast with the porcupine which is a rodent.

What are their breeding habits?
Three to six pups are born in a secluded spot during early summer, after a gestation period of about 35 days. The birth weight of each is about 1 g.

What are their major enemies?
Hyenas and eagle owls are said to be among their enemies.

Some people regard their meat as a delicacy, and many of them are killed for this reason.

ROCK DASSIE *Procavia capensis* (Pallas, 1766)

What is the distribution?
Rock dassies, also called rock rabbits or rock hyrax, are distributed in most parts of southern Africa. In the Kruger National Park they are confined to the area between the Olifants and Bububu rivers, with the exception of a small area in the south-western part of the Kruger National Park.

What type of habitat do rock dassies prefer?
As the common name suggests, they prefer rocky hills, koppies or stony outcrops, generally in the drier parts of the country; they are never found in forests. The presence of dassies in an area is betrayed by the urine stains on the rocks and the piles of droppings in certain places. The crystallized urine is supposed to have medicinal value and is sold as hyracium.

What do they eat?
They are vegetarians and subsist on grass, leaves, fruit, bark and twigs. Although not dependent on water, they will nevertheless travel relatively long distances to obtain some.

What are the main physical features?
Resembling a rabbit in size and to some extent in shape, the dassie has a light to dark brown or greyish brown coat of short, thick hairs. The ears are rounded. It has no tail, and the feet are specially adapted to suit its rocky habitats. A glandular secretion that keeps the feet moist enables the animal to climb almost vertical rock faces. The front feet have four toes each without nails, while the three toes on the back feet have flattened nails.

The shoulder height is about 25 cm, the body length 50 cm and the mass about 3 to 4 kg. The upper incisor teeth are well developed and are separated from the molars by a wide space (diastema).

Are they really related to the elephant?
The teeth and the nails on the toes are similar, but otherwise the two animals are as far apart as their respective sizes.

Are they gregarious or solitary in habit?
Rock dassies are gregarious and live in colonies of 20 to 50 individuals.

According to Dorst & Dandelot (1972), the colony is made up of a number of family units each comprising a single adult male and a number of females and their young.

Are they territorial?

They appear to be territorial.

Why do they like to sun themselves?

Their temperature regulation mechanism seems to be rather poor and they need shelter to protect them from extremes of heat and cold. It is therefore necessary for them to seek the warmth of the sun in the morning, particularly on cool days.

On very cold days they remain snug in their warrens.

Are their senses well developed?

Their senses of sight and hearing are keen and it is difficult to surprise them. When alarmed, they dash into their warrens.

Do they make any sounds?

They are quiet animals; when alarmed they utter shrill whistles and barks.

Are they diurnal in habit?

They are diurnal and forage in the evening and early morning.

What are their breeding habits?

Two or three pups are born after a gestation period of just over seven months. This is regarded as a long time for such a small animal.

What are their major enemies?

Their major enemies include leopards, caracals, pythons, eagles and other birds of prey.

Do they damage crops?

In areas where their enemies have been exterminated they can become so numerous that they are forced to supplement their natural food with cultivated crops.

YELLOW-SPOTTED ROCK DASSIE *Heterohyrax brucei* (Gray, 1868)

What is the distribution?
A number of subspecies of *H. brucei* are distributed throughout most of the African savanna areas. *H. b. ruddi* (Wroughton, 1910) is the subspecies found furthest south and its range extends from the north-eastern parts of South Africa through north-eastern Botswana and Zimbabwe to Mozambique. In the Park it is confined to the area north of the Punda Maria-Pafuri Road and along the eastern boundary as far south as the Malonga spring. Although the rock dassie and the yellow-spotted rock dassie live in the same habitats in many parts of their range, they are usually not found together in the Kruger National Park.

What type of habitat do these dassies prefer?
Like the common rock dassie, they are also confined to rocky outcrops, broken veld and koppies.

What is the difference between the two dassie species?
The yellow-spotted rock dassie looks very much like the ordinary rock dassie but is more brownish in colour with lighter flanks, and has a conspicuous white patch above each eye and a large white to yellowish patch on the back. The body mass is about 4 kg, the shoulder height up to 30 cm and the length 45 cm.

What do they eat?
They are vegetarians and their diet includes fruit, berries, grass, bark and roots.

Do they differ in habits?
Their habits are more or less the same, except that the yellow-spotted rock dassie is an even better climber than its relative and is partly arboreal.

Are they not sometimes called tree dassies?
No, the tree dassie *Dendrohyrax arboreus* (A Smith, 1827) is a different species. It is more arboreal, more nocturnal and less gregarious than the two species described above.

What are the breeding habits of the yellow-spotted rock dassie?
One or two pups are born in late summer or autumn, after a gestation period of about seven months.

What are their major enemies?
They are preyed upon by caracal, leopard, raptorial birds and pythons.

CAPE PORCUPINE *Hystrix africaeaustralis* (Peters, 1852)

What is the distribution?
Porcupines are widely distributed
throughout Africa south of the
equator. The subspecies
H. a. africaeaustralis (Peters, 1852), is
found in the Park.

What type of habitat do they prefer?
Porcupines occur in a wide variety of
habitats, ranging from semi-desert to
high-rainfall areas and from low to
high altitudes. Preference is given to
areas with sufficient shelter in the
form of caves, rock crevices, boulders
or piles of loose rock.

What do they eat?
Vegetable matter, including fruit,
berries, roots, tubers, bulbs and the
bark of trees. They are very
destructive to cultivated crops such as
maize, potatoes, groundnuts, melons
and most other vegetables, and even
garden plants. They often ring-bark
trees, especially when food is scarce,
causing extensive damage. Bones are
also gnawed, and this may indicate
some mineral deficiency.

Is the meat edible?
It is tasty and some Africans regard it
as a delicacy.

What are the main physical features?
The upper part of the body is covered
with long, sharp quills measuring up
to 30 cm in length; the head is
furnished with a crest of long, erect
hairs that curve backwards, while the
underparts of the body are covered
with bristly black hairs. The black and
white banded quills covering the back
and the short tail are strong and very
sharp. The feet are equipped with
strong digging claws. The body length
is 60 to 75 cm and the mass up to 18 kg.

Can porcupines eject their quills?
No, but it is a common belief that
porcupines can 'shoot' their quills at
enemies. The quills are easily
dislodged and may become embedded
in the bodies of attackers, but it is also
normal for them to shed quills from
time to time. The presence of
porcupines in an area is often
indicated by dropped quills.

Are they nocturnal in habit?
Despite the wide distribution and common occurrence in some areas, they are seldom seen due to their nocturnal habits.

Do they make any noise?
Yes, a grunting sound is uttered.

Where do they hide during the day?
Porcupines dig their own burrows but also use aardvark holes as a hide-out in which to spend the day. Rock piles or rock crevices are also used as a shelter.

Are they solitary in habit?
Porcupines occur singly, in pairs or in small parties sharing a communal warren, or den.

To which animal group do porcupines belong?
It is largest of the African rodents.

What are their breeding habits?
One to three young are born after a gestation period of two to three months. The quills are soft at birth but harden after about two weeks.

What are their major enemies?
Although lion and leopard are their major enemies, hyena also account for a number of porcupine kills.

Is it difficult for a predator to kill a porcupine?
It is no easy task and even the lion has to exercise caution. To be successful it has to surprise the porcupine and strike it on the head or muzzle. An alert porcupine arches its back and bends its neck to get more protection from the raised quills.

Can a porcupine actively defend itself?
With the back arched, the head tucked away and peeping backwards beneath its belly, the porcupine turns its back on the attacker and charges – the idea being to drive the sharp quills into the attacker.

When an assailant is struck by these sharp quills, they are usually deeply embedded in its flesh, causing serious wounds which rapidly become septic. When quills are lodged in the throat or mouth of the attacker, the affected area becomes swollen and the animal cannot eat. Death through starvation follows.

According to Astley Maberly (1967), it takes a skilled and experienced predator to attack a porcupine and emerge unscathed.

Many lions have become man-eaters because of injuries caused by porcupine quills. A miscalculated blow that lands on the quill-covered body instead of the head could leave a lion with a paw full of quills. Incapacitated and not able to hunt its normal prey, the lion could then be forced by hunger to attack easier prey such as man.

Are the quills poisonous?
Many people believe this, but it is a fallacy. Sepsis in the wound is simply caused by dirt on the quills.

Do porcupines warn potential attackers?
Special hollow quills often vibrate when the animal moves about, producing a characteristic rattle. It is believed that this is a signal to the porcupine's enemies to leave it alone. When it is annoyed it thumps its feet as well as rattling its quills.

TREE SQUIRREL *Paraxerus cepapi* (A Smith, 1836)

What is the distribution?
According to Roberts (1951) *Paraxerus cepapi* is distributed in the northern half of the Transvaal, northern and eastern Botswana, north-eastern Namibia, Zimbabwe and Mozambique. *P. c. cepapi* (A Smith, 1836) is, however, confined to the Transvaal, southern Botswana and the southern parts of Zimbabwe. It is one of the most common animals in the Park and may be encountered everywhere, although it is more numerous in the mopane tree veld than elsewhere.

What habitat do tree squirrels prefer?
They occur mostly in woodland savannas and dry forests, and can live under diverse ecological conditions.

Nests of dry leaves are constructed in holes in trees.

What do they eat?
They feed on a variety of vegetable matter such as seeds, nuts, fruits, kernels of various kinds, roots and even grass. Insects and birds' eggs are also consumed.

What are the main physical features?
The grizzled, greyish yellow colour and the bushy tail are the most characteristic features. The general colour above is buff, becoming darker on the head and back. The underparts are more or less yellowish. The body mass could be up to 0,5 kg, the body length 15 to 25 cm and the tail another 15 cm long.

Have any albinos been recorded in the Kruger National Park?
A number of albinos have been reported, particularly in the northern part of the Kruger National Park.

Are they solitary or gregarious?
Tree squirrels occur singly, in pairs, or in small, territorial family groups.

Are they diurnal or nocturnal?
They are strictly diurnal and predominantly arboreal, but they also feed on the ground. When alarmed they dash for their hole or climb to the top of the nearest tree, where they hide amongst the foliage.

Do they make any sound?
A high-pitched chattering sound is uttered at intruders, and when alarmed they repeat a loud, chattering 'chuck-chuck-chuck' for long periods, and jerk their tails up and down.

Do they hibernate?
They are active throughout the year but, like other squirrels, will store seeds, nuts, kernels and other food stuffs underground or in tree hollows.

What are their breeding habits?
Two to three young are born at any time of the year, but there is a birth peak in summer. The gestation period is about 55 days.

What are their major enemies?
Birds of prey, genets, wild cats and pythons are their principal enemies.

SPRINGHARE *Pedetes capensis* (Forster, 1778)

What is the distribution?
Springhares, subspecies *P. c. capensis* (Wroughton, 1907), occur in most of the savanna areas of southern and East Africa.

What habitat do springhares prefer?
They are usually confined to areas of sandy soil where they can dig their burrows. These habitats are not plentiful in the Park and springhares are therefore not common there.

What do they eat?
Springhares are vegetarians, feeding mainly on roots, tubers, bulbs and grass. They also raid farm crops.

What are the main physical features?
In action and appearance they show a superficial resemblance to a small kangaroo. The hindlegs are powerful and much longer than the short front legs. The springhare usually progresses in a series of kangaroo-like hops, using only the hindlegs. The body colour is pale rufous-brown above, paler on the flanks and white on the underparts. The bushy tail is about 50 cm long and dark at the tip. The head and body are about 60 cm long, and the body mass is approximately 3,5 kg.

Are their senses well developed?
Their senses of sight, hearing and smell are well developed.

Do they dig their own burrows?
Yes, the forepaws with their strong, curved claws are well adapted for digging. The burrows are often constructed in such a manner that they have an entrance tunnel with the sand piled up outside, and an exit tunnel without a pile of sand.

Are springhares solitary or gregarious?
These social animals live in colonies.

Are they nocturnal in habit?
They are nocturnal but may, exceptionally, be seen during the day. Their large luminous eyes are well adapted for night life and they are not easily blinded by electric lights. When a torch is shone at members of a colony emerging from their burrows one sees their eyes as many small, bobbing 'lights'.

Do they make sounds?
These rodents are normally silent, but can scream loudly when frightened or injured.

How did the springhare get its name?
It is derived from the Afrikaans word 'springhaas', which literally means 'jumping hare'.

What are their breeding habits?
Although the mother has two pairs of teats, she usually gives birth to one young. Twins have been recorded, however. The gestation period is about six weeks and most births occur between November and February.

What are their major enemies?
They are probably preyed upon by most of the larger carnivores that also hunt during the night. These include hyena, jackal, leopard and probably even lion.

SNAKES – GENERAL

Why are so few snakes seen in the Kruger National Park?
Most snakes are shy and elusive and tend to keep away from human activities. They also dislike traffic and motor vehicles. Unlike farms, where cultivated crops attract large numbers of rodents which in turn support snakes, the Park accommodates a greater diversity of habitats and consequently a more evenly spread snake population. Furthermore, the natural enemies of snakes such as hawks, eagles, mongooses and other predators abound in the Park.

What is the most dangerous snake in the park?
The Park harbours Africa's most feared snake, the black mamba *Dendroaspis polylepis polylepis* (Günther, 1864). Its potent neurotoxic venom and the large amount it is capable of injecting makes it a very dangerous snake. There are a number of other dangerous snakes in the Park.

What are the chances of being bitten by a snake in the Park?
The chances are remote. If you are reasonably careful and treat the Park reptiles with respect, there is no reason why you should fear snakebite.

Do snakes come into the rest camps?
Snakes seldom enter rest camps and pose little danger. However, as a precaution one should not venture out at night without footwear and a good flashlight. Stumbling over an obstacle in the dark could be more dangerous than encountering a snake in the camp.

How does one know if a snake is dangerous?
The layman should treat all snakes as potentially dangerous. Snakes that rear and spread a hood, hiss or adopt a flattened defensive attitude prior to striking should be given a wide berth.

Where do snakes bite?
According to Visser & Chapman (1978), 67% of bites are below the ankle, 20% between the knee and ankle, and 8% on the wrist or hand.

How many snake species are there in the Park?
Fifty-one species have been recorded, of which only a few are dangerous. According to Visser & Chapman (1978), the South African subcontinent harbours about 140 different species and subspecies, of which only 55 are technically poisonous. Only 14 are regarded as dangerously poisonous. No more than a dozen of the snake species in the Park are dangerous.

Can a snake suck milk from a cow?
Snakes are physiologically and anatomically unable to suck and there is no truth in this belief.

Do snakes have well-developed senses?
The sense of sight is acute at short range but poor at long distances. They cannot hear but are very sensitive to vibrations; smell is well developed.

Can a snake die from its own venom?
Snakes generally exhibit a certain amount of resistance to their own venom and that of other snakes.

Can a snake hypnotize its prey?
Not in the way we understand
hypnotism, but it appears that a
snake's intended victim is sometimes
paralyzed with fear.

Do snakes have vocal chords?
No. The hissing sound they make is
produced by the expulsion of air
through the throat.

When are snakes most active?
Warm, humid weather is usually ideal
for snakes to move around. Cool
weather inhibits their activities.

How often do they kill prey?
Snakes are rather inactive by nature
and do not use much energy. One
good meal per week in summer, and
less in winter, is usually sufficient.

*Are secretary birds and other enemies
of snakes immune to snake venom?*
It is said that secretary birds,
mongooses and jackals have a higher
resistance to snake venom. These
animals are not completely immune to
snakebite, however.

Do snakes move around in pairs?
Snakes are solitary animals and are
found in pairs only during the
courting and mating season.

Do snakes shed their teeth?
Fangs are continually being shed and
replaced. The shedding and replacing
is synchronized in such a manner that
the snake is never without functional
fangs. Even if it loses its fangs for
some abnormal reason, they are
quickly replaced.

PUFFADDER *Bitis arietans* (Merrem, 1820)

Do puffadders often bite humans?
Puffadders are responsible for more bites than all other snakes combined in the whole of Africa.

Why are so many people bitten by puffadders?
The puffadder is normally very sluggish and reluctant to move away from a basking place, which quite often happens to be a footpath. As a result of this habit and the snake's excellent camouflage it is often trodden on and the victim is bitten before he or she is even aware of the snake's presence.

Are puffadders nocturnal or diurnal in habit?
Like most adder species, they are more active at night than during the day.

Which other adder species are found in the Park?
The horned adder (*Bitis caudalis*) and the snouted night adder (*Causus defilippii*).

Are puffadders widely distributed?
It is the most widely distributed snake species in Africa, occurring in most environments except the Sahara and the rain forest areas. In the Park it is also common and widespread, its range of distribution covering the entire area.

Do the different adder species differ a lot from each other?
They differ in size and colouring, but the effects of their haematoxic venom are very similar.

What are the physical features of the puffadder?
It is a very thickset snake, on average about 90 cm long, although specimens of 1,2 m have been reported from other parts of South Africa. A specimen of about 90 cm may have a circumference of more than 20 cm or a diameter of 7 cm or more. The body colour is yellowish or light brown to olive brown, with more or less regular backward pointing, chevron-shaped dark brown to black bars or bands over the back and the tail. The body could also be dark brown to black, with yellow to orange markings. The tail is much longer in males than in females.

What is the origin of the name?
When disturbed it inflates itself with air, which is let out in loud hisses or puffs as a warning that it is ready to strike.

Can puffadders strike backwards?
It is commonly believed that they can strike backwards, but this is not true. Although they are generally very sluggish, when they strike they do so very quickly, and either forwards or sideways, but never backwards.

Where are the fangs situated?
The long curved fangs are situated in the front of the upper jaw.

Do they hold on to the prey after biting?
Unlike the back-fanged snakes and some of the Elapids, they do not hold on after biting.

What is the nature of their venom?
The venom is haematoxic, destroying blood and other tissues. Intense pain, massive swelling and internal bleeding are the most characteristic symptoms. It also possesses some neurotoxic properties.

Is the venom fast acting?
The venom is slow-acting and a life-endangering effect, such as pronounced shock, is usually not observed until 12 hours or more after the bite. It is therefore advisable to get medical treatment as soon as possible to minimize complications such as the loss of a limb or serious infection.

How much puffadder venom is needed to kill a healthy adult person?
As little as four drops, but the size and fitness of the victim is also very important. The bigger the person, the more blood he has and the more venom is necessary to kill him.

How much venom is discharged?
A large puffadder could probably discharge as much as 15 drops at a time. The amount injected varies with the state of excitement of the snake.

How potent is puffadder venom?
Apart from the Gaboon adder, which is found in the northern parts of Natal, Mozambique and in other African countries, the venom of the puffadder is the most potent of the adder venoms.

Will a puffadder deliberately attack humans?
It only attacks when disturbed.

What are their breeding habits?
Puffadders are ovoviviparous; the eggs develop completely within the body of the female. When laid they contain fully developed young that wriggle free of the egg capsule within minutes. Newly born young measure between 15 and 20 cm. An average of 20 to 40 are produced at a time, usually in late summer or early autumn.

It is said that young puffadders eat their way out of the mother's body. Is this true?
On occasion the young hatch inside the mother and are born alive, but they never eat their way out.

Are newly born puffadders poisonous?
Young puffadders are almost immediately active and venomous after hatching.

What are their major enemies?
Man is their major enemy, but they also fall prey to secretary birds, eagles and other birds of prey, mongooses and small carnivores.

BOOMSLANG *Dispholidus typus* (A Smith, 1829)

What is the distribution?
Boomslang are widely distributed in
Africa south of the Sahara and well
represented throughout the Kruger
National Park.

What type of habitat do they prefer?
They are arboreal and tend to confine
themselves to wooded areas.

What do they eat?
The favourite items of diet include
chameleons and other tree-living
lizards, although small birds, mice and
frogs are also eaten.

What are the main physical features?
Because of its different colour phases
the boomslang is often confused with
either the black or green mamba, or
even some of the harmless
green-coloured snakes. For example, it
can vary from light brown to dark
brown in one phase and to green in
another. Body lengths of up to 1,85 m
have been recorded, but the usual
length is 1,35 to 1,5 m.

Is their venom very potent?
Their venom is highly potent,
containing haemotoxic, or
blood-destroying elements, and to a
lesser extent neurotoxic, or
nerve-destroying elements. The
venom is more dangerous than that of
the cobra or puffadder.

What are the effects of the venom?
Severe headache and drowsiness,

confusion, nausea and vomiting are
the first symptoms. This is followed by
bleeding from the mouth and nose,
subcutaneous bleeding and, finally,
internal haemorrhage, which will be
fatal if not treated promptly. Necrosis
of the kidneys and the liver is a further
complication.

*Do many people die from boomslang
venom?*
Very few, and there are some good
reasons for this. Firstly, the boomslang
is not an aggressive snake. When
cornered it will inflate its neck but will
only attack as a last resort. Secondly, it
is a back-fanged snake with a mouth
so small that it finds it difficult to
inflict a fatal bite on a human being.

Is boomslang anti-venom available?
It is obtainable on request from the
South African Institute for Medical
Research in Johannesburg. However, it
is very seldom needed.

*What are the boomslang's breeding
habits?*
Mating takes place in trees. About 10
to 14 eggs are deposited in holes in
tree trunks, and even in the ground
where suitable conditions of moisture
and warmth exist, and they hatch after
4 months, usually in late spring or
early summer. Newly hatched young
average about 33 cm in length.

What are their major enemies?
Birds of prey.

SOUTHERN VINE SNAKE *Thelotornis capensis* (A Smith, 1849)

What is the distribution?

The subspecies *T. c. capensis* is confined to northern Natal and northern and eastern Transvaal.

In the Kruger National Park it is apparently absent from open grassland regions, such as the Tsende and Babalala flats, but otherwise it is widely distributed in the area.

What habitat does the southern vine snake prefer?

It is very well adapted for an arboreal way of life and is therefore mostly found in trees or shrubs, where it can move with astonishing speed.

What does it eat?

It takes other tree-living reptiles, frogs and toads, and birds and eggs.

What are the main physical features?

The southern vine snake has a cryptic coloration consisting of a mixture of green, brown, grey and even pink which gives it excellent camouflage. It is a slender snake with a body length of about 1,2 m. The pupil of the eye is horizontally oval, but dumb-bell shaped in strong light. The tongue is a conspicuous bright orange with a black tip.

When the snake is at rest the anterior third of its body is often projected into the air and held motionless for long periods. It can also inflate its throat like the boomslang.

Is the venom potent?

This snake's venom is similar to that of its close relative, the boomslang, and therefore very potent.

Is the vine snake aggressive?

It is docile and will seldom attempt to bite human beings, but if molested will strike out and even follow up unsuccessful strikes. Like the boomslang it has a small mouth with fangs situated far back. Very few human fatalities have been recorded.

How does it catch its prey?

It is said that the snake flicks its bright, orange-coloured tongue in and out in order to arouse the curiosity of various prey species. When the prey investigates it often comes close enough for the snake to strike.

What are its breeding habits?

Between 6 and 10 eggs are laid in midsummer. The newly hatched young are about 24 cm long.

EGYPTIAN COBRA *Naja haje* var. *annulifera* (Peters, 1854)

What is the distribution?
The subspecies *N. h. haje* occurs in the northern parts of Natal and the Transvaal, and is found throughout the Park.

What type of habitat does the Egyptian cobra prefer?
It is a terrestrial and savanna species, found in drier regions.

What does it eat?
Like other cobra species it is more or less omnivorous, feeding mainly on birds, eggs, frogs and small mammals. These snakes hunt mostly at night.

What are the main physical features?
The Egyptian cobra is the largest of the cobra species in the Park, attaining a length of 1,2 to 1,8 m, with a recorded maximum of 2,24 m. The body colour varies from yellowish or greyish brown to a very dark brown with broad black bands encircling the body. The males appear to grow to a greater length than females, contrary to the usual situation among snakes. When disturbed it can rear up some 45 to 60 cm and at the same time spread a broad hood which could be more than 12 cm across. It is a fast-moving snake and is said to be very 'intelligent'.

Does it spit like the spitting cobra?
No.

Are these snakes very aggressive?
They are relatively docile.

Is their venom very potent?
The venom, which contains powerful neurotoxins, is very potent indeed and the bite of an adult specimen can take rapid effect and be fatal to a human if not promptly treated.

Are they nocturnal or diurnal?
Although they are probably more active at night, they are not strictly nocturnal and may also be seen in daytime.

What are their major enemies?
Birds of prey, small predators and mongooses.

MOZAMBIQUE SPITTING COBRA *Naja mossambica*

What is the distribution?
The Mozambique spitting cobra is probably the most common cobra of the savanna regions of Africa and occurs throughout the Park .

What type of habitat does it prefer?
It is usually found near water and likes to shelter in hollow tree stumps or in old termite nests.

What do these spitting cobras eat?
They are omnivorous, taking a wide variety of food including birds, eggs, small mammals and reptiles. The wide range of food may explain this snake's abundance and extensive distribution.

What are the main physical features?
The top of the body is olive-brown to dark brown, while the under-surface is pinkish brown with a few irregular and conspicuous black bands or blotches across the throat. The snake usually attains a length of about 1 m, but specimens of 1,5 m and over have been recorded.

How far and how accurately can they 'spit'?
This nervous and highly strung snake is the only true cobra that can 'spit' venom like the rinkals (*Hemachatus haemachatus*), but it is far more active and fast-moving than the latter. It usually rears up before spitting, but can also spit very accurately from ground level without raising its head. Two direct streams of venom are propelled from recurved canals opening at right angles to the surface of the fangs near their tips. The venom is

ejected with remarkable accuracy and can reach the target, usually the eyes of the enemy, over a distance of 2 to 3 m, or even 4 m if the snake is large.

Can they spit more than once?
They can spit several times in succession and the spitting is usually accompanied by a forward lunge and hissing sound. The poison glands appear to replenish the poison rapidly for further use.

Can a victim be blinded by the venom?
The effect of the venom entering the eye is instantaneous and may cause permanent blindness if it is not washed out and the eye treated immediately.

How potent is the venom?
It consists of very potent neurotoxins and is fatal if not treated. The bite causes severe local tissue destruction.

Are spitting cobras very aggressive?
These are very dangerous snakes, and although they will not attack unprovoked, they will attack without hesitation when cornered. They can rear up almost two thirds of their length, spreading a hood at the same time. Many people regard them as the second most dangerous snake in Africa, rivalled only by the black mamba.

Are they nocturnal or diurnal?
They are nocturnal to a great extent and are therefore not often seen.

What are their major enemies?
Birds of prey and the lesser predators.

BLACK MAMBA *Dendroaspis polylepis* (Günther, 1864)

What is the distribution?
In South Africa this snake occurs in Natal and the Lowveld and bushveld of northern and eastern Transvaal, including the whole of the Kruger National Park. It is also found throughout the eastern half of tropical Africa.

What type of habitat does the black mamba prefer?
Unlike the arboreal green mamba (*Dendroaspis angusticeps*), which is confined mostly to the more heavily forested coastal areas, the black mamba shows a greater preference for the low-lying, drier and more open bush country at altitudes not exceeding 900 to 1 200 m.

Its favourite retreats are abandoned termite hills, aardvark and other animal holes, among rocks and boulders or under old tree stumps. It will often share its home with other members of the same species, or even with other species such as the spitting cobra. Although mainly a ground-living snake, it is also at home in trees or shrubs and can move over rough terrain effortlessly and gracefully.

What do these snakes eat?
Their diet consists mainly of warm-blooded prey such as birds, small mammals such as rodents, and the young of the dassie, or rock rabbit.

What are the main physical features?
Despite its name, the black mamba is seldom, if ever, really black. The newly hatched snake is greyish green to greyish olive, but with age it gradually darkens, becoming dark olive, olive-brown, greyish brown or a gunmetal colour on top. The underparts are greyish white, often tinged with yellow or green, and frequently with irregular darker spots or blotches over the posterior half of the belly and under the tail (Pienaar, 1966). The inside of the mouth is black, a characteristic that distinguishes it from most other snakes. The body length is 1,8 to 2,4 m, and in exceptional cases up to 3,6 m. The black mamba's length, slenderness, speed and elongated head are the main distinguishing features.

Do black mambas spread a hood?
When really angered they inflate the throat to a half-hood which is not as pronounced as that of the cobra.

How swiftly can they move?
It has often been claimed that a man cannot outrun a mamba, but this is exaggerated as their maximum speed is probably not more than about 15 km/h. They are very fast in striking, however, and can reach between 1,5 and 1,8 m. When they move the head and forepart of the body is raised well off the ground.

How dangerous are they?
Their size, speed of movement and ability to strike very swiftly and accurately in just about any direction, even when moving fast, make them extremely dangerous. They are very fond of basking in the sun but when disturbed usually make for their lair and if a person happens to be in their way they will not hesitate to attack.

Are they aggressive?
Although they will not seek out human beings for attack, they are unpredictable and can strike suddenly with little or no warning at all. They are especially dangerous during periods of mating.

Do they hold on after biting?
Unlike the cobra, which usually holds on for some time after inflicting a bite, the mamba immediately releases its grip but is then ready for another swift strike.

How potent is their venom?
Mamba venom per unit mass is not as potent as that of the Cape cobra (*Naja nivea*), but is more potent than that of the spitting and Egyptian cobras. However, the amount injected at a single bite and the large reserve of venom make them by far the most dangerous of the African snakes.

What is the nature of their venom?
It is essentially neurotoxic and is rapidly absorbed, causing paralysis of the nerves controlling the cardio-respiratory functions.

Is it true that a victim can die within minutes of having been bitten?
It is true if the venom is delivered intravenously, but collapse and death usually take somewhat longer in a case when the venom enters the body through a muscle.

Are black mambas territorial in habit?
Mambas can wander far afield in search of food or to mate, but they often frequent the same lair for extensive periods of time.

Are their senses well developed?
Mambas have very keen eyesight and their general alertness makes it very difficult to approach these snakes unnoticed.

What are their breeding habits?
About 12 to 14 eggs are laid after mating, which usually takes place in spring or early summer. The newly hatched young may measure anything from 37 to 50 cm, and are capable of killing small prey just after hatching.

What are their major enemies?
Birds of prey and mongooses.

AFRICAN ROCK PYTHON *Python sebae* (Gmelin, 1789)

What is the distribution?
The African rock python occurs in many parts of Africa. It is found in suitable habitats throughout the Park.

What type of habitat do rock pythons prefer?
They like water and usually do not venture far from it, even lying submerged with only their eyes and nostrils above the surface. They are excellent climbers, often found on overhanging branches from which they can drop silently onto an unwary victim passing below.

What do they eat?
Mostly dassies, hares, cane rats, other rodents, antelope up to the size of impala, the young of warthogs and bushpigs, and monkeys and birds.

What are the main physical features?
The body colour is variable but the ground colour on the dorsal side is usually light brown to greyish brown, with dark brown, black-edged and somewhat sinuous crossbars or tranverse blotches. By far the largest snake in Africa, it attains a length of 3,6 to 4,5 m. Exceptional individuals measure up to 6 m or more, and the mass can be as much as 60 kg.

How do they compare in size with the anaconda and reticulated python?
There is still some controversy about the size of these large snakes, but it would appear that the African rock python is exceeded in length and mass by both the South American giant anaconda (*Eunectes murinus*) and the reticulated python (*Python reticulatus*) of India and Asia.

Are pythons nocturnal or diurnal?
Although more nocturnal than diurnal, they are often seen in daytime.

How do they kill their prey?
After gripping the prey with their teeth, they coil around the victim's body and constrict it before swallowing it.

Do they wet their victims by licking before swallowing them?
This is a common belief, but false. Saliva is excreted during the swallowing process, but the movement of the tongue has no salivating function.

Can they disgorge a swallowed victim?
When a python is disturbed in swallowing its prey it invariably disgorges it to escape more easily.

Is the python poisonous?
No, but the two rows of needle-sharp teeth can cause a very painful wound that often becomes septic if not treated.

What is their potential lifespan?
They have lived for more than 25 years in captivity, but the maximum age attained in nature is uncertain.

Do they kill human beings?
Substantiated claims of attacks on humans by pythons are very rare.

Are pythons a protected species?
They are protected by law as they are becoming rare and fulfill a very important function controlling rodents.

What are their breeding habits?
About 30 to 50 eggs are laid, of which many are infertile.
The female, unlike other snakes, guards the eggs until shortly before they hatch.

What are their major enemies?
Ratels, or honey badgers, rank high on the list of their natural enemies. They are sometimes also killed by the larger predators, including lion, leopard and crocodile.

LIZARDS

Are snakes and lizards the only reptiles represented in the Park?

No, the Kruger National Park harbours a large variety of reptiles. In addition to the 50 snake and 50 lizard species, there are two leguaan species, two tortoise species, three terrapin species, six amphisbaenian species, and the Nile crocodile.

Are there any poisonous lizards in the Kruger National Park?

There are no poisonous lizards in Africa, and although many African people regard the chameleon and agama as poisonous, they are harmless creatures.

Are there some extraordinary lizards?

Most of the lizards are relatively small, but the giant plated rock lizard (*Gerrhosaurus validus validus*) is quite conspicuous. These very dark, blackish brown lizards are heavily plated and attain a length of about 68 cm, of which the head and body make up 26 cm and the tail 42 cm. Mostly confined to granitic or other boulder-strewn hills and outcrops, they are very wary and will scramble back to their rocky retreats at the slightest alarm.

There are four different species of *Gerrhosaurus* in the Park. A number of smaller types of lizards, many with striking coloration, are also well represented.

To what extent can the chameleon change colour?

Although it can change its colour considerably, depending on the background, it cannot change into a wide variety of colours. The normal colour is green, ranging from pale, yellowish green to dark green. However, it can also change from a light brown or light grey to a very dark, nearly blackish grey.

Do some lizards resemble snakes?

Legless lizards and skinks occur in the Park, and the large legless skink (*Acontias plumbeus*), with a body length of about 55 cm, is very conspicuous. It usually emerges from its underground retreat after heavy rains. Some of the legless lizards resemble snakes to such an extent that only an expert can identify them. There are also a number of worm lizards that live a subterranean life and look more like earthworms than lizards.

LEGUAANS

Are leguaans well represented in the Kruger National Park?

Two leguaan, or monitor lizard, species are represented in the Park, and are well distributed throughout the area. They are the common rock leguaan (*Varanus exanthematicus albigularis*) and the Nile monitor (*Varanus niloticus niloticus*), also called the water or river leguaan.

What type of habitat do they prefer?

Common rock leguaans inhabit savanna and open bush or forest country, and are often found far from water. Although terrestrial in habit they are expert climbers of trees and rocks. Rock crevices and fissures, as well as hollow trees and holes in the ground, are used as dens.

Nile monitors or water leguaans live in or near permanent water in many parts of Africa.

What size can they attain?

The water leguaan can reach a length of 1,9 to 2,1 m, of which two thirds comprise the tail, while the common rock leguaan attains 1,2 to 1,5 m.

What do they eat?

As can be expected, the diets of the two species differ to some extent. The water leguaan feeds mainly on fish, crabs, mussels, small mammals and birds' eggs. They are also persistent robbers of crocodiles' eggs. Common rock leguaans are not as active as water leguaans and live mainly on small mammals, birds, eggs, other reptiles, invertebrates such as the large *Achatina* snails, and also insects.

What are the main physical features?

These monitors are typical lizards, with short, powerful limbs and long, muscular tails. The common rock leguaan is dark greyish brown, while the other species is greenish to greyish brown. The latter also has a dark reticulation and scattered yellow spots, or interrupted greenish yellow transverse bands on the head, back and limbs. The lower surfaces of the body are yellowish, with more or less grey to dark grey or even black crossbands. Bands are also visible on the tail.

The tongue, which is up to 23 cm long, has sensory functions but is also used for drinking.

Can a leguaan suck milk from a cow?

There is no truth in the claim that they can suck milk from the udder of a cow.

Are they gregarious or solitary?

They are usually solitary and only occur in pairs during periods of courtship and mating.

Are leguaans diurnal or nocturnal?

Both species are mainly diurnal and are often seen during the day.

Are they territorial in habit?

The common rock leguaan is a great wanderer and therefore not territorial. The water leguaan is probably more so.

Do they hibernate?

There are indications that leguaans hibernate during severe winters or extremely cold periods. Cases are known of their having been dug up and eaten by ratels. It is evident that if hibernation occurs, it is very sporadic and not a regular annual occurrence.

What are their breeding habits?
About 30 to 40 eggs are deposited in a hole 15 to 20 cm deep, which the female digs in soft soil. After covering the hole neatly she then leaves the eggs to hatch.

What are their major enemies?
Birds of prey kill quite a number of young leguaans, while ratels and some of the large predators also attack these reptiles.

Can they defend themselves?
When cornered, leguaans adopt a very menacing attitude by arching their necks and hissing loudly. They lash out with their powerful tails and will bite viciously at any object within reach, holding on for minutes on end. As a last resort they will feign death and even allow dogs to savage them badly, in the hope of getting away when left for dead. Not only do they have amazing recuperative powers, but they are such formidable fighters that their attackers often come off second best.

Can leguaans run well?
They are strong, fast runners, usually running in short spurts.

Are they dangerous to human beings?
They will not attack humans without provocation, but when cornered will not hesitate to defend themselves. On farms they raid poultry runs for eggs, but are generally beneficial animals, killing rodents, snails and insects.

NILE CROCODILE *Crocodylus niloticus* (Laurentus, 1768)

What is the distribution?
Some 22 species of crocodile are distributed throughout the tropical and subtropical areas of the world, including Africa, Asia, northern Australia and tropical America. The Nile crocodile occurs widely throughout Africa south of the Sahara and is well represented in the Kruger National Park, especially in the major perennial rivers.

What type of habitat do crocodiles prefer?
They may be found near rivers, streams and lakes spreading from the subtropical to the tropical zones. Movement from rivers to man-made impoundments are common.

How many crocodiles are there in the Kruger National Park?
It is impossible to determine the exact number but there are several hundred.

If dams and rivers dry up, what happens to the crocodiles?
They either move to permanent water or adopt a resting phase until the next rains come.

What do they eat?
A baby crocodile lives on insects and other arthropods, but as it grows bigger, snails, mussels, frogs, fish, water birds and small mammals are included. Catfish, however, form the staple diet of the crocodile.

Is it true that crocodiles do not kill waterbuck?
No, waterbuck are killed by crocodiles.

Are crocodiles cannibalistic?
No. Female crocodiles are very protective towards their young and will not eat them. It could, however, happen that a smaller crocodile is accidentally swallowed by a bigger one in its search for food.

What is the biggest prey animal a crocodile can kill?
Animals as large as giraffe, buffalo bulls and male lions have been killed by very big crocodiles, but these cases are rare. Their mammalian prey usually consists of average-sized antelope.

How often does an average-sized crocodile kill?
In hot weather a large crocodile of 4 m will have a full meal every 2 to 3 weeks. Crocodiles 1,5 m in length eat one meal a week, while baby crocodiles eat every day.

As crocodiles are cold-blooded, they need very little energy to maintain their metabolism and body temperature, and as they are fairly inactive they do not need much food either. During cold or rainy weather crocodiles will eat less than usual.

Do crocodiles show a predilection for domesticated dogs?
It is easy for a crocodile to catch a dog as dogs have, through many years of domestication, lost much of their natural instinct which helps other animals to survive.

There is no firm evidence that crocodiles have any special preference for dog meat.

Do crocodiles store their food for some time before eating it?

The prey is drowned and usually consumed immediately. Crocodiles seldom store food, and half-eaten carcasses that are sometimes found under river banks are usually the leftovers from a crocodile meal. These remains may be eaten by other crocodiles that find them.

Do crocodiles feed in a specific manner?

Crocodiles do not chew their food but swallow it whole. In the case of large prey, chunks are torn off by gripping a portion of flesh with the teeth and jerking the head from side to side or spinning the body around.

Do they eat carrion?

There used to be a belief that crocodiles will deliberately leave a carcass to decay before consuming it. This is not the case. Crocodiles prefer fresh meat and will only eat carrion when nothing else is available.

Can food be swallowed under water?

No. When catching fish or drowning mammals, a valve at the back of the mouth prevents water from entering the lungs or alimentary canal. A crocodile has to take its head out of the water in order to swallow. Fish are swallowed head first.

How do crocodiles kill their prey?

The prey is usually seized by the muzzle or leg, pulled into the water and drowned. It has long been believed that the tail was used to bowl the prey over, but the latest research indicates that this is not true. Prey may also be captured on dry land.

When do crocodiles kill their prey?

They can kill at any time, but they tend to be more active at dusk and during the night.

Do they have stronger digestive juices than other predators?

Yes. Crocodiles do not chew but have strong digestive juices that soon dissolve the food, even bones, horns and hooves.

Do crocodiles attack hippos?

Hippo calves are occasionally killed, but a fully grown hippo is more than a match for a crocodile.

How big can a crocodile grow?

In central Africa, with its tropical climate, Nile crocodiles of up to 6 m have been recorded. In South Africa a large crocodile will probably be 5,5 m in length, with a body mass of about 1 000 kg.

When is a crocodile mature?

A crocodile grows throughout its lifetime, but the growth curve flattens out in later life. Sexual maturity is reached when the reptile attains a body length of about 2,5 m and a mass of 80 to 160 kg.

How many toes do they have?

They have 5 toes on the fore feet and 4 on the hind feet. Those on the hind feet are partially webbed.

What is the body temperature?

Like other poikilothermic, or cold-blooded, animals, its body temperature varies with its surroundings. The maximum body temperature in summer could be 38 °C, and in a very cold winter the body temperature could be as low as 5 ℃. The crocodile then usually goes into a state of stupor until seasonal temperatures rise again.

What is the potential lifespan of a crocodile?
They live for a very long time, probably up to a hundred years or more, although the exact lifespan has not yet been determined.

Why does a crocodile lie with its mouth open?
This is to regulate body temperature and can either cool down or warm up the body. Early on cold mornings or late in the afternoon when the sun is not so warm, crocodiles let the sun shine directly into their mouths. The heat is taken up by the soft membrane in the mouth and dispersed throughout the body by means of the blood circulation to raise the body temperature.

During the heat of the day the mouth is kept open, facing away from the sun. The inside of the mouth is thus shaded from the rays of the sun and the membrane now helps to decrease the body temperature. Moving into or out of the water also helps to regulate body temperature.

Do crocodiles have tongues?
The entire length of the broad, flat tongue is fixed to the bottom of the buccal cavity and gives the impression that a crocodile has no tongue.

What is the use of the tongue?
It plays an important part in swallowing food.

Is the blood circulation the same as in other reptiles?
Instead of the three-chambered heart of other reptiles, crocodiles have four-chambered hearts and therefore have more efficient circulatory systems.

Are crocodiles 'intelligent' animals?
Crocodiles have the best developed brain of all reptiles, yet it is only the size of a man's thumb. Although they lack brain size, crocodiles have keenly developed senses and very strong instincts. They can see, hear and smell well, and their hunting, maternal and survival instincts are exceptionally good. Experiments in captivity have also shown that crocodiles are quick to adapt to new conditions and develop new 'skills' to make the best of their environment, so we can credit them with a fair amount of 'intelligence.'

Are crocodiles well adapted to survive?

They are well adapted and have survived in their present form for more than 60 million years. Their inexhaustible patience when hunting, the ability to move in the water with a high degree of concealment, the eyes and nostrils placed in such a position that they can still breathe and see while practically submerged, is proof of their excellent adaptability.

It is said that all crocodiles have stones in their stomachs. What is the purpose of these stones?

The stones sometimes found in crocodiles' stomachs play no part whatsoever in the digestion of their food or balance in the water. Stones are sometimes swallowed accidentally when crocodiles eat their prey. In areas without stones, crocodiles do not have stones in their stomachs.

What is the general body colour?

The colour varies from yellow, with black irregular markings on the back and sides, to dark grey with black markings. The underparts are cream-coloured.

What is the eye colour?

The eyes are yellow-green with a vertical pupil, very much like the eyes of a cat in the daytime.

What is the difference between a crocodile and an alligator?

The easy way to distinguish between an alligator and a crocodile is to look at the head. The alligator's snout is broad and rounded, whilst that of the crocodile is pointed. Other differences are the very prominent teeth of the crocodile, compared to the smaller and less visible teeth of the alligator, as well as the smaller size of the alligator and its black colour, compared to the crocodile's yellowish to greyish colour and black markings on the back.

Are their senses well developed?

Their senses of hearing, smell and sight are all well developed.

Do crocodiles shed their teeth?

The teeth are shed constantly and are usually swallowed and digested with their food.

Young crocodiles shed their teeth every few months, but old ones probably shed them only every year or so. All 70 to 75 teeth are not shed at once, but shed in stages, leaving the crocodile with enough teeth for normal use.

Can they smell under water?

No, the nostrils are kept closed under water to prevent them from drowning.

Are crocodiles gregarious?

Crocodiles are gregarious and they like being in groups where they have a very definite form of communication with each other. If there is a good supply of food in a certain area the crocodiles tend to congregate in large groups. However, if there is not enough food, the big groups break up into smaller units, or the crocodiles become solitary to ensure survival.

Are crocodiles territorial animals?

Males usually have a small territory in which they live and feed, while females are migratory, moving to the males for mating and then to the breeding areas for nesting.

Do crocodiles hibernate?
In tropical areas such as central Africa they do not hibernate. During severe droughts crocodiles bury themselves in sandbanks or in riverbeds to shield themselves from dehydration and high temperatures. While buried they live on body fat and may do so for many months until the rains come.

Do crocodiles move about?
Females move to the males for mating and then back to the nesting areas. Males stay in one place. When rivers or pools dry up, crocodiles will move to another water source if there is one available.

Can they move over land?
They can indeed, and cases have been known of crocodiles making their way overland for several kilometres to new habitats. Some of the man-made dams in the Park have been occupied by crocodiles that moved overland.

Are crocodiles diurnal or nocturnal?
They are more active at night than during the day.

Do crocodiles make any sound?
They utter a kind of roar during mating and fighting.

Do crocodiles prefer quiet water?
They do not like rough water or swift-flowing streams that force them to lift their heads high to breathe. During floods they often move to the shore.

How long can a crocodile remain submerged?
How long they remain submerged depends on the water temperature. In warm water they can stay under for about 15 minutes at a time. In cold water their heart beat is much slower and their metabolism is low, requiring very little oxygen, so they can remain underwater for a considerably longer period.

Can crocodiles run fast?
No running crocodile has ever been timed accurately, but they are nevertheless deceptively fast for their size and short limbs.
However, crocodiles can run only a short distance at a time.

How do they swim?
When swimming they are propelled by the tail only, and changes in direction are achieved also by the tail. The feet are used for stopping and floating.

Where do crocodiles mate?
Mating takes place in water, and they usually prefer shallow areas.

How do they mate?
While the female is suspended in a horizontal position in the water, the male comes from behind and holds onto her body with his feet while bending his pelvic area underneath hers to accomplish fertilization.

Do they mate at any time of the year?
The crocodile's reproductive cycle starts in May, when it takes the form of physical but non-sexual contact. This stimulates the development of the eggs.
Some three months later, during August, mating takes place, always on the initiative of the female. The eggs are laid early in October.

233

How many eggs are laid?
The size of a clutch can vary from
25 to 90, with a mass of some 100 to
120 g per egg.

Where are the eggs laid?
The female digs a boot-shaped hole
30 cm deep in sand well above the
high-water mark. Having dug the hole
with her hindlegs, she forms them into
a chute and then deposits the
hard-shelled eggs in two layers. The
eggs roll down the chute and settle in
the nest. She then covers the nest with
about 12 cm of sand and presses it
down with her hindlegs.

Do the females guard their nests?
During the incubation period the nest
is protected by the female, particularly
during the night, and she will hunt
nearby in order to keep an eye on the
nesting site. Despite the females'
efforts the nests are often robbed.
Water leguaans, otters, water
mongooses, hyenas, baboons and even
marabou storks are among the culprits.

How long is the incubation period?
It takes 90 days, and the crocodile eggs
are incubated by the heat of the sun on
the sand.

*How do the baby crocodiles get out of
the nest after hatching?*
When the young crocodiles are ready
to hatch they utter a chirping sound
which is a signal to the mother to dig
them out. She does so, using her front
legs. At this stage the hatchlings have
already come out of the eggs by
piercing or slashing the eggshell with
their 'egg tooth', a small sharp horny
projection on the tip of the snout. This
projection, called a caruncle, may

persist for weeks but is eventually
shed. The mother picks up the
hatchlings, as well as the unhatched
eggs, and carries them into the water
in her mouth. She releases the
hatchlings into the water and breaks
the unhatched eggs by making a
chewing movement with her jaws. She
has to make several journeys to get all
the hatchlings into the relative safety
of the water.

How big is a newly hatched crocodile?
It is 25 to 30 cm long and has a mass of
80 to 100 g.

*What happens to the baby crocodiles
when they reach the water?*
The hatchlings stay with their mother
for about 10 days while they become
stronger. She will have chosen a small
stream or shallow pool surrounded by
dense vegetation as their first home for
reasons of both safety and food
supply. Here she protects them against
enemies such as marabou storks and
herons. They live on insects, frogs,
dragonfly larvae and baby catfish.

*What are the crocodile's major
enemies?*
From the time they have attained
1,5 m in length crocodiles have
virtually no natural enemies. Hippo
and elephant are capable of killing
large crocodiles, but this is a very rare
occurrence. Baby crocodiles, on the
other hand, have many enemies and
these include leguaans, eagles, herons,
marabou storks, ground hornbills,
genets, water mongooses, otters,
tigerfish, catfish, terrapins and owls.
Eggs are eaten by leguaans,
mongooses, otters, hyenas, baboons,
warthogs and bushpigs. Probably no

more than one crocodile out of a nest of 50 eggs reaches maturity.

Do crocodiles kill many people?
Crocodiles are extremely dangerous reptiles and many people have been killed by them when they go into, or even too close to, rivers and pools where large crocodiles are present.

Have any human beings been killed by crocodiles in the Park?
Yes, but fortunately only a few. These victims, none of them visitors, were mostly Park employees who met their fate through negligence.

Are crocodiles of any benefit to man?
Crocodiles are among the most important animals in nature. A large portion of their diet consists of barbel or catfish. In rivers where crocodiles are exterminated, barbel increase to such high numbers that they then kill off surface fish such as carp, kurper and others. This in turn affects many varieties of fish-eating birds by depriving them of their food supply. It also allows mosquito larvae to hatch in their millions, as there are no surface fish to eat the larvae and maintain nature's balance, thus resulting in increased health hazards. As well as maintaining the natural balance of nature, crocodiles play an important part in clearing the water from carcass pollution. They are often seen eating dead hippos or other animals in the water. Moreover, by laying large numbers of eggs each year, of which only a few ever survive to maturity, crocodiles are a very important source of food to all predators that live on their eggs or babies.

Do birds clean the crocodile's teeth?
No. A crocodile emerging from the water onto a sandbank often has blood-sucking leeches on its body, and birds sometimes peck these leeches from the crocodile's head and body. This has probably led to the belief that the birds clean the crocodile's teeth.

LITERATURE

Astley Maberly, CT 1967. *The game animals of Southern Africa* Nelson: Cape Town

Braack, LEO 1988. *Kruger National Park* (2nd Edition) Struik / National Parks Board: Cape Town

Dagg, Anne and JB Foster 1976. *The Giraffe* Van Nostrand Reinhold: New York

De Graaff, G 1974. A familiar pattern deviation of the cheetah. *Custos* 3(12): 2 – 28

De Graaff, G 1978. The aardvark: an unusual mammal of the South African veld. *Custos* 8(1): 16 – 21

De Vos, V, GL Van Rooyen and JJ Kloppers 1973. Anthrax immunization of free–ranging roan antelope *Hippotragus equinus* in the Kruger National Park *Koedoe* 16: 11 – 25

Dorst, J and P Dandelot 1972. *A field guide to the larger mammals of Africa* Collins: London

Douglas–Hamilton, I and O Douglas–Hamilton 1975. *Among the elephants* Collins & Harvill: London

Dunham, KM 1985. Ages of black rhinos killed by drought and poaching in Zimbabwe *Pachyderm* 5: 12 – 13

Eaton, RL 1974. *The Cheetah* Van Nostrand Reinhold: New York

Goss, RA 1986. *Maberly's mammals of southern Africa* Delta: Johannesburg

Hanks, J 1979. *A struggle for survival – the elephant problem* Struik: Cape Town

Joubert, SCJ 1970. *A study of the social behaviour of the roan antelope, Hippostraus equinus (Desmarest, 1804) in the Kruger National Park.* M.Sc, University of Pretoria, Pretoria

Joubert, SCJ 1986. The Kruger National Park *Koedoe* 29: 1 – 11

Kruuk, H 1972. *The Spotted Hyaena* University of Chicago Press: Chicago

Laws, RM 1966. Age criteria for the African elephant *Loxodonta africana East African Wildlife Journal* 4: 1 – 37

Leuthold, W and JB Sale 1973. Movements and patterns of habitat utilization of elephant in Tsavo National Park, Kenya. *East African Wildlife Journal* 11: 369 – 384

Mason, DR 1991 *Monitoring of ungulate population structure in the Kruger National Park* Unpublished Report, National Parks Board, Skukuza

Meester, J and HW Setzer 1971. *The Mammals of Africa* Smithsonian Institution Press: Washington DC

Meester, JAJ, IL Rautenbach, NJ Dippenaar and CM Baker 1986. Classification of southern African Mammals *Transvaal Museum Monograph* 5: 1 – 359

Milstein P le S 1989. Historical occurrence of Lichtenstein's hartebeest *Alcelaphus lichtensteinii* in Transvaal and Natal *Aepyceros* 2: 1 – 141

Pienaar, U de V 1969. Predator–prey relationships amongst the larger mammals of the Kruger National Park *Koedoe* 12: 108 – 176

Pienaar, U de V 1990. *Neem uit die Verlede* National Parks Board: Pretoria

Pienaar, U de V, WD Haacke and N Jacobsen 1983.*The reptiles of the Kruger National Park* National Parks Board: Pretoria

Pienaar, U de V, SCJ Joubert, AJ Hall–Martin, G De Graaff and IL Rautenbach 1987. *Field Guide to the Mammals of the Kruger National Park* Struik: Cape Town

Pitman, CRS 1942. *A game warden takes stock* Nisbet: London
Rasa, OAE 1985. *Mongoose Watch* John Murray: London
Roberts, A 1951. *The Mammals of South Africa* Trustees of 'The Mammals of South Africa' Book Fund: Johannesburg
Rowe–Rowe, DT 1975. *Biology of Natal Mustelids*. M.Sc thesis, University of Natal, Durban
Schaller, GB 1972. *The Serengeti Lion* University of Chicago Press: Chicago
Skinner, JD and **RHN Smithers** 1990. *The Mammals of the Southern African Subregion* University of Pretoria
Smithers, RHN 1986. *The Mammals of the Southern African Subregion* University of Pretoria: Pretoria
Smuts, GL 1974. *Growth, reproduction and population characteristics of Burchell's zebra Equus burchellii antiquorum (H Smith, 1841) in the Kruger National Park* D.Sc thesis, University of Pretoria

Smuts, GL 1975. *Predator–prey relationships in the Central District of the Kruger National Park with emphasis on wildebeest and zebra populations* Unpublished Report, National Parks Board, Skukuza
Stuart, C and **T Stuart** 1988. *Field Guide to the Mammals of southern Africa* Struik: Cape Town
Turnbull–Kemp, P 1967. *The Leopard* Howard Timmins: Cape Town
Van Dyk, A 1991. *The Cheetahs of De Wildt* Struik: Cape Town
Visser, J and **DS Chapman** 1978. *Snakes and snakebite. Venomous snakes and management of snakebite in southern Africa* Purnell: Cape Town
Ward, Rowland 1986. *Rowland Ward's African Records of Big Game* Rowland Ward Publications: San Antonio
Wolhuter, H 1948. *Memories of a Game Ranger* Wildlife Protection Society: Johannesburg

INDEX

Aardvark 203 – 204
Aardwolf 184
Accommodation 23, 24 – 26, 35
African buffalo 104 – 106
African civet 190 – 191
African elephant 12, 135 – 144
African rock python 224 – 225
African wild cat 171
Amphibians 36
Animals
  counting 41, 42
  distribution 40
  drinking 39
  encounters 42, 43
  extinct 36
  numbers 12, 13, 41
  rare species 36
  run over 30
  survival 36
Antbear
  see Aardvark
Anteater
  see Pangolin
Antelopes, general 70 – 72
Antelopes 70 – 103
  Blue wildebeest 12, 98 – 99
  Bushbuck 12, 85
  Common duiker 77
  Eland 12, 90 – 91
  Grey rhebok 82
  Impala 12, 83 – 84
  Klipspringer 79
  Kudu 12, 88 – 89
  Lichtenstein's hartebeest 96 – 97
  Livingstone's antelope 73
  Mountain reedbuck 12, 80
  Nyala 12, 86 – 87
  Oribi 12, 78
  Red duiker 76
  Reedbuck 12, 81
  Roan antelope 12, 100 – 101
  Sable 12, 102 – 103
  Sharpe's grysbok 75
  Steenbok 74
  Suni 73
  Tsessebe 12, 94 – 95
  Waterbuck 12, 92 – 93
Anthrax 37
Apes, great 60

Baboon, Chacma 56 – 60
Balule Camp 28
Banks, rest camps 29
Bat-eared fox 188 – 189

Bateleur Bushveld Camp 26, 28
Berg-en-dal Camp 23, 25, 26, 28
Bester, Paul 8
Biltong 49
Black mamba 222 – 223
Black rhinoceros 12, 126 – 130
Black-backed jackal 185 – 186
Blue wildebeest 12, 98 – 99
Boomslang 218
Botanists 36
Boulders Private Camp 24
Breakdown service 29
Breeding, camps 36
Brown hyena 177 – 178
Buffalo, African 104 – 106
Burchell's zebra
  see Zebra
Burning
  programme 50 – 52
  veld 50
Bushbaby 63 – 64
  Lesser bushbaby 64
  Thick-tailed bushbaby 63
Bushbuck 12, 85
Bushman Trail 33
Bushpig 65 – 66

Camping sites 35
Camps 24 – 26, 28
  Balule 28
  Berg-en-dal 23, 25, 26, 28
  Crocodile Bridge 28
  Letaba 24, 26, 28
  Lower Sabie 25, 28
  Olifants 24, 25, 28
  Orpen 26, 28
  Maroela 28
  Pretoriuskop 25, 28
  Punda Maria 28
  Mopani 28
  Satara 25, 28
  Shingwedzi 28
  Skukuza 25, 28
Camps, bushveld 26
  Bateleur 26, 28
  Mbyamiti 26, 28
  Shimuwini 26, 28
  Sirheni 26, 28
  Talamati 26, 28
Camps, private 24
  Boulders 24
  Jock of the Bushveld 24
  Malelane 24, 28
  Nwanetsi 24, 28

Roodewal 24
Cape buffalo 12
Cape clawless otter 198
Cape porcupine 209 – 210
Caracal 169 – 170
Caravan sites 35
Carnivores 145 – 200
Chacma baboon 56 – 60
Cheetah 12, 161 – 166
Civet
  see African civet
Cobra
  Egyptian 220
  Mozambique spitting 221
Collision, vehicle 30
Common duiker 77
Crocodile Bridge Camp 28
Crocodile, Nile 229 – 235
Culling 45 – 49

Dams and boreholes 41
Dassies 206 – 208
  Rock dassie 206
  Yellow-spotted rock dassie 208
Day visitors 23, 27
De Kuiper, Francois 8
Delagoa Bay 8
Dessication 41
Diesel 28
Diseases 37, 38
Doctor 31
Dogs 17
Driving 14, 15, 20, 21
Duiker
  Common 77
  Red 76
Dutch East India Company 8

Ecology 11 – 13
Egyptian cobra 220
Eland 12, 90 – 91
Electricity 29
Elephant, African 12, 135 – 144
Emergency 14
Entertainment 19
Entrance documents 21
Entrance gates 35
Even-toed ungulates 65 – 121
Explosives 17

Fatalities, tourists 30
Feeding animals 15 – 16
Fence 38
Film shows 27, 28

Fines 21
Fishes, species 36
Foot and mouth disease 37

Galago
 see Bushbaby
Game
 areas 39
 distribution 40
 extinct 36
 spotting 39
 viewing 39
 watching 39
Game Rangers
 see Rangers
Gates, Park
 Kruger 28
 Numbi 28
 Crocodile Bridge 28
 Phalaborwa 28
Genets 192 – 193
Giraffe 12, 107 – 116
Grey rhebok 82
Grobler, PJ 9

Hedgehog, Southern African 205
Helping animals 16
Herbivores 12
Hippopotamus 12, 117 – 121
History 8 – 9
Holtzhausen, Isak 9
Honey badger
 see Ratel
Hospital, animal 36
Hours, rest camps 20, 27
Hyena 172 – 178
 Brown 177 – 178
 Spotted 12, 172 – 176
Hyrax, rock
 see Dassie

Impala 12, 83 – 84
Insectivores 205

Jackal 185 – 187
 Black-backed 185 – 186
 Side-striped 187
Jock of the Bushveld Private
 Camp 24

Kirkman, Harry 126
Klipspringer 79
Kruger National Park 8
 altitude 11
 animal, species 12 – 13
 code of conduct, 14 – 21

culling 45 – 49
ecology 11 – 13
entrance gates 28
geology 11
history 8 – 9
map 27
nature conservation 36 – 44
poaching 53 – 54
proclamation 9
rainfall 11
rivers 11
role of fire 50 – 52
size of Park 8
temperature 11
topography 11
vegetation 12
Kruger, President SJP 9
Kudu 12, 88 – 89

Laundry 29
Law-breakers 30
Laws, traffic 18
Leary, Glen 42
Lebombo Mountains 8
Leguaans 227 – 228
Leopard 12, 157 – 160
Lesser bushbaby 64
Letaba Camp 25, 28
Licence, drivers 21
Lichtenstein's hartebeest 96 – 97
Lion 12, 145 – 156
Literature 236 – 237
Littering 17, 18
Livingstone's antelope
 see Suni
Lizards 226
Lower Sabie Camp 24, 26, 28
Lowveld 8
Lynx
 see Caracal

Mabatzi 8
Malelane 11
Malelane Private Camp 24
Mamba
 see Black mamba
Mammals 13, 36
Maps, road 27
 ecologiacl 10
 tourist 22
Maroela Camp 28
Mbyamiti Bushveld Camp 26, 28
Meals, preparing 29
Metsi Metsi Trail 34
Migration 38
Milner, Lord 8

Mining in Park 44
Mongoose 194 – 196
 Banded mongoose 195
 Dwarf mongoose 196
 Slender mongoose 194
Monkey, Samango 62
 Vervet 61 – 62
Mopani Camp 28
Mountain reedbuck 12, 80
Mozambique spitting cobra 221

Napi Trail 34
Nature conservation 36 – 44
Nile crocodile 229 – 235
Noise 18
Nwanetsi Private Camp 24
Nyala 12, 86 – 87
Nyalaland Trail 33

Olifants Camp 24, 25, 28
Olifants Trail 33
Oribi 12, 78
Orpen Camp 26, 28
Otter, Cape Clawless 198

Pafuri 11
Pangolin 201 – 202
Parks, new 44
Payment accepted 29
Petrol 28
Pets in Park 17
Plants, collection of 16
Poaching 53 – 54
Polecat, Striped 197
Porcupine, Cape 209 –210
Post office 29
Potgieter AH 8
Predators 12
Pretoriuskop 11
Pretoriuskop Camp 25, 28
Primates 56 – 64
Puffadder 216 – 217
Punda Maria 11, 42
Punda Maria Camp 28
Python, African rock 224 – 225

Rangers 42 – 44
 attacked 42
 duties 44
 first 8
 number 43
 qualification 43
Ratel 199 – 200
Red duiker 76
Reedbuck 12, 81
Regulations 14 – 21

INDEX

Reptiles 214 – 235
Research 41
Reservations 23
Rest camps 24 – 29
Restaurants 28
Rhinoceros 126 – 134
  Black 126 – 130
  White 131 – 134
Rinderpest 38, 45
Rivers
  Crocodile 8, 15, 41
  Letaba 15, 41
  Levuvhu 13, 15, 41, 43
  Limpopo 8, 13, 15
  Mbayamiti 15
  Mphongolo 15
  Nwanedzi 15
  Nwaswitsontso 15
  Nwatindlopfu 15
  Olifants 8, 15, 41, 43
  Sabie 9, 15, 41, 43
  Shingwedzi 15
  Sisha 15
  Timbavati 15, 41
  Tsende 15
Roads 14, 30, 31
Roan antelope 12, 100 – 101
Rock dassie 206
Rock hyrax 206 – 208
  see also Dassie
Rodents 209 – 213
Roodewal Private Camp 24

Sabi Game Reserve 8, 9
Sable 12, 102 – 103
Samango monkey 62
Satara Camp 25, 28
Scaly anteater
  see Pangolin
Serval 167 – 168
Sharpe's grysbok 75
Shilowa 8
Shimuwini Bushveld Camp
  26, 28
Shingwedzi 11

Shingwedzi Camp 28
Shingwedzi Reserve 8, 9
Shops 28
Side-striped jackal 187
Sirheni Bushveld Camp 26, 28
Skukuza 8
Skukuza Camp 25, 28
Snakes, general 214 – 215
Snakes 214 – 225
  African rock python 224 – 225
  Black mamba 222 – 223
  Boomslang 218
  Cobra 220 – 221
  Mamba, Black 222 – 223
  Mozambique spitting cobra 221
  Puffadder 216 – 217
  Southern vine snake 219
  Tree snake
  see Boomslang
Southern African hedgehog 205
Southern vine snake 219
Speed-limit 15
Sport facilities 35
Spotted hyena 12, 172 – 176
Springhare 213
Squirrel
  see Tree squirrel
Steenbok 74
Stevenson-Hamilton, Col. James
  9, 41, 45
Striped polecat 197
Suni 73
Sweni Trail 33
Swimming pools 32

Talamati Bushveld Camp 26, 28
Tariffs 24
Telephone 28
Theft 29, 30
Thick-tailed bushbaby 63
Tourism 22 – 35
Trails 32 – 35
  booking 34
  Bushman 34
  food 33

footwear 33
Metsi Metsi 34
Napi 34
Nyalaland 33
Olifants 33
Sweni 33
Wolhuter 34
Transport, visitors 27
Travelling
  after hours 20
  times 20
Tree snake
  see Boomslang
Tree squirrel 211 – 212
Trollope, Harold 42
Trophies, game 27
Tsessebe 12, 94 – 95

Uneven-toed ungulates
  122 – 134

Venison 49
Vervet monkey 61 – 62
Vetenarians 36
Volksraad 8
Voortrekkers 8

War, Anglo-Boer 9
Warthog 12, 67 – 69
Waterbuck 12, 92 – 93
Waterholes 41
White rhinoceros 12, 131 – 134
Wild cat see African wild cat
Wild dog 12, 179 – 183
Wilderness trails
  see Trails
Wolhuter Trail 34
Wolhuter, Harry 42
Workshop, motor 29

Yellow-spotted rock dassie 208

Zebra 12, 122 – 125
Zoologists 36
Zorilla see Polecat, Striped